Ricarda Denzer – ganz ohr / all ears

Edition Angewandte – Book series of
the University of Applied Arts Vienna
Edited by Gerald Bast, Rector

Edition Angewandte – Buchreihe der
Universität für angewandte Kunst Wien
Herausgegeben von Gerald Bast, Rektor

edition:'ʌngewʌndtə
Universität für angewandte Kunst Wien
University of Applied Arts Vienna

Ricarda Denzer – ganz ohr / all ears

Audio Trouble, Para-Listening, and Sounding Research

Ricarda Denzer, Christian Höller (Hrsg./Eds.)

DE GRUYTER

Texts
Texte

Works
2013–2023

Arbeiten
2013–2023

Selected Collaborative Projects
2013–2023

Auswahl kollaborativer Projekte
2013–2023

Texts
Texte

Ricarda Denzer,
Christian Höller

Foreword

I listen and make notes, filling notebooks with scribblings as I listen.
Ricarda Denzer

Ricarda Denzer,
Christian Höller

Vorwort

Ich horche und notiere und kritzle beim Hören Notizbücher voll.
Ricarda Denzer

Wie lässt sich einer künstlerischen Arbeit Handlungsmacht verleihen, wenn man/frau *nahe dieser Arbeit*, zumal als Künstler*in oder Lehrende*r, spricht? Wenn nicht „über" das Werk gesprochen wird, sondern „entlang von ihm", also in dessen absehbarer bzw. oft auf Anhieb noch nicht abschätzbarer Nähe. Oder wenn, wie die Filmemacherin und Theoretikerin Trinh T. Minh-ha einmal gesagt hat, das „speaking about" durch ein „speaking nearby" ersetzt wird. Fragen wie diese bilden den Ausgangspunkt des vorliegenden Buches, das dem künstlerischen Werk von Ricarda Denzer der letzten zehn Jahre gewidmet ist und in dem Naheverhältnisse zwischen Werk und dem Schreiben darüber ausgelotet werden.

Seit Beginn ihrer künstlerischen Arbeit befasst sich Ricarda Denzer mit gesprochener Sprache: mit Oral History, mit Aufzeichnungsmethoden von mündlicher Rede, mit performativen (Vortrags-)Formaten, mit der räumlichen und medialen Inszenierung von Gesprächen und Interviews. Stets geht es dabei auch darum, multidirektionale Formen von mündlicher Erzählung im Moment ihrer Entstehung sichtbar zu machen. Oder anders gesagt: Es handelt sich dabei um Formen von kontextualisierter Narration, die die Betrachter*innen und Leser*innen – und nicht zu vergessen: die Hörer*innen – über die jeweiligen Hintergründe des Gesprochenen und Gehörten informieren möchte. Und die, gleichermaßen wichtig, auf den Klang des Raums hinter der zu hörenden Stimme aufmerksam machen will.

Darüber hinaus zielt dieser methodische Zugang auch auf Fragestellungen ganz anderer Art – Aspekte, die weit über Orales und Auditives im engeren Sinne hinausgehen. Wie formt bzw. formiert sich Erzählung, wie Geschichte, und wie kann/können diese Geschichte(n) im Moment ihrer Entstehung festgehalten werden? Welche Form ist dem performativen Akt der Darstellung eines Hier

How can an artistic work be given agency by talking about the work in close proximity to it, particularly as an artist or teacher? When rather than talking "about" the work, we talk "alongside" it, in other words, from a position that could be conceived, or indeed often cannot yet be conceived, as being in its vicinity. Or, as filmmaker and theorist Trinh T. Minh-ha once put it, by replacing "speaking about" by "speaking nearby." Such questions, explored through the intimate relationship between the work and the process of writing about it, form the starting point for this book, which considers Ricarda Denzer's artistic oeuvre over the past ten years.

Ricarda Denzer has addressed spoken language since beginning her artistic practice: through oral history, methods of recording oral speech, performative (lecture) formats, spatial and media staging of conversations and interviews. In the process, her concerns always include visualizing multidirectional forms of oral narration at the moment they arise. She engages with forms of contextualized narration that seek to inform viewers and readers—and, of course, listeners—about the backgrounds of what is said and heard in each case. Equally importantly, these forms draw attention to the sound of the space behind the voice that is heard.

Over and above these concerns, this methodological approach also encompasses questions of a very different nature that extend far beyond what can be defined, strictly speaking, as the oral and auditive realm. How are narratives and history formed or rather how do they assume a shape? How can these (hi)stories be recorded at the very moment of emergence? What form is appropriate to the performative act of portraying the here and now? How can the quality of orality be apprehended in a legible visual form? And is it possible to transform the act of speech or the underlying system of language into an instrument that plays a part in ensuring we do not have to accept the world as it is?

Through the prism of these questions, a situated working practice has emerged over the years, giving rise to an exploration of the properties of sound, the political dimension of listening, and above all the performative phenomenon of the human voice. Problems of hearing in a broader sense—*Audio Trouble*—often form the point of departure for particular works, though Denzer's probing of these has always aimed to transform such "troubles" into something constructive, even polyvalent and contextually revealing. In the past decade, Denzer has tackled all these issues in diverse media and in projects of varying scale that often span several exhibitions. The essays in this publication likewise tune in with acute attention to these concerns—*all ears*.

Her earlier artistic research piece *Public Poetic Minutes* (Academy of Fine Arts Vienna, 2012) was already an examination

und Jetzt angemessen? Wie kann die Qualität der Mündlichkeit in eine lesbare, visuelle Form gefasst werden? Und lässt sich der Akt des Sprechens bzw. das zugrunde liegende System der Sprache in ein Instrument verwandeln, das helfen soll, die Welt nicht so hinnehmen zu müssen, wie sie ist?

Entlang dieser Fragestellungen ist über die Jahre eine situierte Arbeitspraxis entstanden, die zu einer Untersuchung der Eigenschaften von Klang, der politischen Dimension des Zuhörens und vor allem auch des performativen Phänomens der menschlichen Stimme geführt hat. Probleme des Hörens in einem erweiterten Sinne – *Audio Trouble* – bilden häufig den Ausgangspunkt einzelner Arbeiten, wobei die Untersuchungen stets darauf angelegt sind, besagte „Troubles“ in etwas Konstruktives, ja Polyvalentes und kontextuell Aufschlussreiches zu verwandeln. All diese Aspekte hat Denzer die letzte Dekade über in oft ausstellungsübergreifenden Projekten mit unterschiedlicher Gewichtung und vielgestaltigem Medieneinsatz ausgeführt. Mit ebensolcher Hellhörigkeit – *all ears* – werden sie nun im vorliegenden Buch bzw. in den einzelnen Beiträgen aufgegriffen.

Bereits die künstlerische Forschungsarbeit *Public Poetic Minutes* (Akademie der bildenden Künste Wien, 2012) verstand sich als ein Projekt zur Erkundung von Zeichensystemen im Kontext der räumlichen Interaktion von Stimmen. Die Stimme wurde in diesem Zusammenhang als ein präsenter und handelnder Körper betrachtet, der sich im Raum bewegt. Zugleich ist sie auch in unseren Köpfen präsent, im Akt des Denkens, oder, anders gesagt, als oftmals unbewusster auditiver Prozess innerhalb unserer kognitiven Wahrnehmung. Audiovisuelle Formen der mündlichen Rede waren bei diesem Projekt ebenso Thema wie die Flüchtigkeit und Unzugänglichkeit der Stimme im Raum. Ähnlich wie wenn man mit einer Kamera einen Ausschnitt wählt, können die Ränder des Gehörten genauso wichtig werden wie der eigentliche Brennpunkt. In dieser Hinsicht kann auch die Stimme Teil eines Bildes sein, selbst wenn ihre Quelle nicht festgehalten wird, sie nicht im Bild ist, was wiederum auf die Position der Betrachter*innen und deren Rezeptionsleistung verweist.

Die im Anschluss an dieses Projekt immer weiter ausformulierte Praxis des Horchens durchläuft im vorliegenden Buch ihren eigenen Prozess der Formfindung. Die daran Beteiligten, allen voran die Grafikdesignerin Hannah Sakai, die das passende gestalterische Konzept entwickelt hat, sowie die hier vertretenen Autor*innen sind aktiv in diese Formfindung involviert. Gemeinsam tragen sie zu einer kollektiven Form der Analyse bei – sowohl textlich als auch räumlich-visuell bzw. in vielfältigen Übersetzungsschritten von Oralem und Gehörtem in das überwiegend zweidimensionale Buchformat. Dies tangiert auch den generellen Stellenwert des sich – gleichsam auditiv öffnenden – Kunstspektrums: Indem ein

of semiotic systems in terms of voices' spatial interactions. In this context the voice was understood as a body that is present, acts, and moves within a space. At the same time it is also present in our minds, in the act of thinking—or, in other words, as an often unconscious auditive process that forms part of our cognitive perception. The project looked at audiovisual forms of speech along with the ephemerality and unreliability of the voice within a space. Akin to the way in which a particular framing is selected using a camera, the periphery of what is heard can be as important as the actual focal point. In this respect the voice can also form part of an image, even if its source is not recorded and is outside the frame, pointing in this respect to the viewers' position and their processes of reception.

Throughout this publication, the practice of listening, which has been articulated repeatedly subsequent to this project, undergoes its own distinctive process of settling upon a certain form. Everyone involved in the book, first and foremost graphic designer Hanna Sakai, who developed a fitting visual concept, as well as the team of authors, played an active part in that process. Together they undertake a collective form of analysis—both textually and spatially/visually, as well as in various stages of translating the oral and aural into the essentially two-dimensional book format. This also touches on the general significance of the art spectrum, opening up aurally, as it were: by following a practice-oriented approach to artistic research in relation to *situated listening*, it becomes possible to experience art production and teaching in proximity to that production as specific *sonic acts* that are directed to experimental practice and designs that draw on these.

Perceived as continual processes, hearing and listening represent physical, performative acts or creative participation in the world that fosters critical and care-driven agency, while seeking to enable alternative narrative modes. In relation to the audiovisual or installation settings discussed in this book, this also entails directing attention to a particular experience, encounter, or place. In order to do justice to these site-specific encounters, Ricarda Denzer realized the performative photo work *Listening to Objects* together with Hannah Sakai, the performer Nazanin Mehraein, and the photographer Michael Giefing. It reflects a stance of openness to change that is apparent throughout this book, or, as one essay puts it, a process in which "something that is not simply already in existence—whether separate or merged—enters into relationship, *becomes* relationship." *Para-Listening*, as one might call this reciprocal process between hearing and who or what is heard, therefore asserts a constitutive element of tension, a "being-with," encompassing myriad cross-references and defying any presumed subject–object difference.

handlungsorientierter Ansatz von künstlerischer Forschung in Bezug auf *situiertes Zuhören* verfolgt wird, werden Kunstproduktion und die in der Nähe dazu angesiedelte Lehre als spezifisch *klangliche Akte* erfahrbar, ausgerichtet auf eine experimentelle Praxis und daran angelehnte Designs.

Als kontinuierlicher Prozess wahrgenommen, stellen Horchen und Zuhören physische, performative Handlungen dar, eine kreative Teilhabe an der Welt, die eine kritische und fürsorgliche Handlungsfähigkeit befördern und alternative Erzählweisen ermöglichen soll. Bezogen auf die audiovisuellen bzw. installativen Settings, die in diesem Buch beleuchtet werden, bedeutet dies auch, die Aufmerksamkeit auf eine bestimmte Erfahrung, eine Begegnung oder einen Ort zu richten. Um diesen ortsspezifischen Begegnungen Rechnung zu tragen, wurde eigens für dieses Buch die performative Fotoarbeit *Listening to Objects* entwickelt, die Ricarda Denzer gemeinsam mit Hannah Sakai, der Performerin Nazanin Mehraein und dem Fotografen Michael Giefing umgesetzt hat. Hier wie in der Gesamtanlage des Bandes spiegelt sich eine gegenüber Veränderungen offene Herangehensweise oder, wie es an einer Stelle heißt, ein „In-Beziehung-Treten, das Beziehung-*Werden* von etwas, das nicht einfach – sei es getrennt voneinander, sei es fusioniert – immer schon da ist". *Para-Listening*, wie man diesen wechselseitigen Prozess zwischen Hören und Gehörtem/n nennen kann, macht insofern ein konstitutives Spannungsmoment geltend, ein vielfältig aufeinander bezogenes „Mit-Sein", das sich über jede vermeintliche Subjekt-Objekt-Differenz hinwegsetzt.

In eine ähnliche Kerbe schlagen die in dem Buch versammelten Textbeiträge: Brandon LaBelle stellt einen Bezug des Werks zum Begriff der „akustische Öffentlichkeit" („sonic publicness") über die bislang noch selten beleuchteten Notizbücher her; diese beschreibt er als akustische Ausdrucksformen, die auf das Ferne und das Nahe – und ihre unauflösliche Verwobenheit – gleichermaßen einstimmen. Christiane Erharter greift bereits im Titel ihres Textes einen wesentlichen Aspekt der von Ricarda Denzer betriebenen künstlerischen Forschungsplattform *Sounding Research* auf: „Berührt zu werden von einer Frage oder Thematik oder von einer Stimme, von etwas Gesprochenem", was sie in der Folge am Beispiel der Geschichte der Riot-Grrrls-Bewegung ausführt. *Sounding Research* in der doppelten Bedeutung von klingender und sondierender Forschung ist auch Thema (und gleichzeitig Form) des hier enthaltenen Gesprächs mit Fouad Asfour, Christina Goestl, Seth Weiner (& Sadie Seagal), Karen Werner und Hui Ye. Dieses geht den Beiträgen einer 2022 organisierten „Listening Session" nach, bei dem eine Reihe von „Audio Papers" präsentiert wurden.

Jaimini Patel schließlich greift den Gedanken auf, wonach sich auch die Lehre als eine Praxis der Kunst betrachten lässt, die in Form von Begegnungen bzw. zuhörendem Denken

The essays in this publication take a similar line. Brandon LaBelle connects the work to the concept of "sonic publicness" via Denzer's notebooks, which to date have rarely been discussed. He describes the notebooks as forms of acoustic expression that are equally attuned to far and near—and to their indissoluble interweaving. The title of Christiane Erharter's text—"to be touched by a question or issue or by a voice, by something spoken"—takes up an essential aspect of Ricarda Denzer's artistic research platform *Sounding Research* that Erharter goes on to explore with reference to the Riot Grrrls movement. *Sounding Research* in the double meaning of being sonorous and sounding the depths also constitutes the theme (and form) of the conversation between Fouad Asfour, Christina Goestl, Seth Weiner, Karen Werner, and Hui Ye. Their discussion examines the contributions to a listening session, organized in 2022, at which a series of "audio papers" were presented.

Finally, Jaimini Patel addresses the idea that teaching can be seen as an artistic practice that occurs in the form of encounters or listening thought. Her text cites "collaborative enquiries, thinking aloud together, generating cascading questions, embracing silence, and taking deep breaths in 'temporary resting places,'" referencing her longstanding dialogue with Denzer. Fouad Asfour's piece is also grounded in many years of exchanges. "My ear is an acoustic universe," his experimental audio paper, deftly articulates the cooperation between the two researchers that cuts through all manner of semantic hurdles. Christa Benzer has compiled a detailed inventory of the works that probes the highly varied interconnections and resonances between the various projects.

Attempting to represent an artistic practice that takes listening as its central concern by deploying the written/visual/haptic form, in other words, the book format, may seem paradoxical. *Ricarda Denzer – ganz ohr / all ears* consciously takes up the gauntlet of this challenge—drawing on means devised specially for this publication. The aim is to render listening comprehensible as a creative process of interpreting the world, including and in particular in the medium of the book. What emerges here is a form of "becoming the world" in which listeners and the listened-to are entangled in equal measure and above all *together*. Resonating polyphonically, it seeks to render perceptible not only how we think (through listening) or listen (while thinking) but also how we relate to the world around (and within) us.

stattfindet. „Kollaborative Fragestellungen, ein gemeinsames lautes Nachdenken, das Erzeugen kaskadenförmiger Fragen, das Annehmen von Stille und ein tiefes Luftholen an ‚temporären Rastorten'", heißt es bei Patel, deren Text auf ihren langjährigen Austausch mit der Künstlerin rekurriert. Von einer solchen, über viele Jahre währenden Wechselseitigkeit zeugt auch der Beitrag von Fouad Asfour, dessen experimentelles Audio Paper „My ear is an acoustic universe" die Kooperation der beiden, über alle möglichen semantischen Hürden hinweg, kongenial zur Sprache bringt. Für den Werkteil hat Christa Benzer ein eingehendes Verzeichnis zusammengestellt, das unterschiedlichste Querverbindungen und Resonanzen zwischen den vielen Einzelprojekten sondiert.

Es mag paradox anmuten, eine Kunstpraxis, die sich zentral dem Hören widmet, schriftlich/bildlich/haptisch, sprich in Buchform, darstellen zu wollen. *Ricarda Denzer – ganz ohr / all ears* stellt sich bewusst – und mit eigens dafür ersonnenen Mitteln – dieser Herausforderung. Zuhören soll so, auch und besonders im Medium Buch, als kreativer Prozess der Welterschließung nachvollziehbar werden. Ja mehr noch: Was sich hier abzeichnet, ist eine Form der „Weltwerdung", in die Hörende und Gehörte(s) gleichermaßen und vor allem: *miteinander* verstrickt sind. Nicht nur wie wir (hörend) denken oder (denkend) hören, sondern auch, wie wir uns mit der Welt um (und in) uns in Beziehung setzen, soll auf diese Weise – vielstimmig nachhallend – vernehmbar werden.

Christian Höller

Para-Listening as World Exploration

Christian Höller

Para-Listening als Welterschließung

„I consider my artistic research as a listening-thinking process in exchange with the world." So lautet eine der Kernaussagen in Ricarda Denzers „Audio-Paper" mit dem Titel *Para-Listening. A Bricolage* (2021).[1] Die Bastelei (bricolage) zeigt sich im Fall des inzwischen auch als Video zugänglichen Papers allein schon in der audiovisuellen Konfiguration des Vortrags: Während wir die gesprochenen Sätze, in deutscher Übersetzung, schriftlich auf ein weißes Blatt Papier projiziert sehen, welches die Künstlerin vor ihrem Gesicht hält, hören wir aus dem Off den englischen Wortlaut des Textes, so auch den eingangs zitierten Satz. Lesen, Hören, dazu das visuelle Setting des Videos und, nicht zu vergessen, die aufgrund der speziellen Montage geforderte Konstruktionsleistung der Betrachter*innen – all das sind Grundkomponenten von Denzers Ansatz, ja sie überlagern sich darin in komprimierter Weise.

Dieser Ansatz eines „hörenden Denkens im Austausch mit der Welt" zieht sich vielgestaltig durch ihr Werk der letzten Jahre und hört dabei nicht auf, einer anhaltenden „Suchbewegung" Ausdruck zu verleihen. So führt sie in einer 2023 publizierten Text-Bild-Assemblage aus: „Wenn ich mich hörend auf die Welt einstimme, richte ich meine Aufmerksamkeit auf eine Erfahrung, eine Begegnung oder einen Ort."[2] Was wiederum einer bezugsorientierten Öffnung gleichkommt – „einer Praxis, in der das Zuhören ein kreativer Prozess der Teilhabe an der Welt ist"[3].

Das teilhabende Zuhören, vom dem Denzer hier spricht, nimmt in ihrer Arbeit eine bemerkenswerte Bandbreite ein. Die akustisch abgetasteten Gegenstandsbereiche reichen von den Gezi-Park-Protesten in der Türkei 2013 über eine Ocker- und Eisenmine im englischen Gloucestershire bis hin zu den Klängen (oder Nicht-Klängen), welche die Lockdown-Erfahrungen der Jahre 2020 bis 2022 in die Erinnerung eingeschrieben haben. Dazu kommt ein weites Referenzspektrum ihrer Arbeit, das sich vom Deep-Listening-Ansatz der Musikerin und Komponistin Pauline Oliveros über die Literatur eines James Baldwin oder W. H. Auden bis hin zur „relationalen Poetik" von Édouard Glissant erstreckt.

1 Präsentiert am 14. März 2022 an der Universität für angewandte Kunst Wien im Rahmen der *Sounding Research Listening Session #1*; online unter https://www.soundingresearch.net/audio-paper/ (abgerufen am 5. Juni 2023).

2 Ricarda Denzer, para-listening, in: *springerin* 1/2023, S. 32.

3 Ebd.

One of the key statements in Ricarda Denzer's audio paper *Para-Listening. A Bricolage* (2021)[1] is "I consider my artistic research as a listening-thinking process in exchange with the world." In this paper, now also available as a video, even the audiovisual configuration of the presentation reflects a spirit of bricolage: while the written German translation of the spoken sentences is visible on a white sheet of paper that the artist holds in front of her face, we can hear the English text, including the sentence cited above, in a voiceover. Reading, listening, the visual setting of the video, and, last but not least, the effort of construction that this special montage demands of viewers—all these components are fundamental to Denzer's approach, superimposed in concentrated form in this piece.

This "listening-thinking process in exchange with the world" runs through Denzer's oeuvre in myriad manifestations in recent years, conveying an enduring questing search. As she explains in a text-image assemblage published in 2023: "When I tune into the world through listening, I direct my attention to an experience, an encounter, or a place."[2] This in turn amounts to "a practice in which listening is a creative process of participation in the world."[3]

The participative listening that Denzer mentions here spans a strikingly broad range in her work. The subject-areas that are acoustically scanned extend from the 2013 Gezi Park protests in Turkey to an ocher and iron mine in Gloucestershire, England, as well embracing the sounds (or non-sounds) branded into memory in the lockdowns of 2020–2022. Denzer's work in addition displays a wide gamut of references, ranging from musician and composer Pauline Oliveros' Deep Listening to literature by James Baldwin or W. H. Auden, not to mention Édouard Glissant's "relational poetics." In methodological terms, these correspond to a sensitive approach that remains open to the changes it undergoes—as Denzer's installations impressively demonstrate in ever-shifting variations—and is aware of its spatial (and thus always limited) situatedness. Irrespective of how broad a range of media are conjoined in this "relationship between near and far,"[4] particular attention, both visual and acoustic, is always given to the "liquid," "mobile" act of modification, which weaves listener and listened-to together.

The minimal alteration effected by Denzer's para-listening could have its roots here: the aural exploration of a world that may lie beyond one's own experience (or the threshold of conscious perception) yet nevertheless consists in a dynamic tandem between the individual engaged in reception and the content received that turns a spotlight on their relationality (and thus alterability). A space opens up here, beyond subject-object duality—an acoustically grounded space that is however also

1 Presented on March 14, 2022, at the University of Applied Arts Vienna during the *Sounding Research Listening Session #1*; online at https://www.soundingresearch.net/audio-paper/ (accessed June 5, 2023).

2 Translated from Ricarda Denzer, "para-listening," in *springerin* 1/2023, 32.

3 Ibid.

4 Ibid.

4 Ebd.

5 Jean-Luc Nancy, *Zum Gehör*. Aus dem Französischen von Esther von der Osten, Zürich: Diaphanes 2022, S. 13.

6 Ebd.

7 Ebd., S. 15.

Methodisch entspricht dem – und Denzers installative Settings stellen dies in immer neuen Abwandlungen eindrucksvoll unter Beweis – ein sensitives, auch der eigenen Veränderung gegenüber offenes Herangehen, das sich seiner räumlichen (und damit stets limitierten) Situiertheit bewusst ist. Egal wie weitläufig der mediale Brückenschlag dieser „Nah-Fern-Beziehung"[4] auch ausfallen mag, bleibt ein zentrales Augen- (und Ohren-)merk auf den „flüssigen", sich „bewegenden" Modifikationsakt gerichtet, der Hörende und Gehörte(s) auf diese Weise zusammenspannt.

Hierin könnte die Minimalumschreibung von Denzers Para-Listening liegen: das hörende Erschließen einer Welt, die jenseits der eigenen Erfahrung (oder der Schwelle bewusster Erfahrbarkeit) liegen mag, die aber nichtsdestotrotz stets in einem dynamischen Gespann besteht – zwischen Rezipierenden und Rezipiertem, was zugleich die Relationalität (und somit auch Veränderbarkeit) der beiden zutage treten lässt. Abseits jeder Subjekt-Objekt-Dualität öffnet sich hier ein Raum – ein akustisch verankerter, aber medial auch anderweitig mitkonstituierter Raum –, der nicht von vornherein gegeben ist, sondern sich erst in einem wechselseitigen Prozess erschließt. Para-Listening, sprich: das „Nebenher-Hören", meint demnach das In-Beziehung-Treten, das Beziehung-*Werden* von etwas, das nicht einfach – sei es getrennt voneinander, sei es fusioniert – immer schon da ist. In den Mittelpunkt rückt vielmehr die Herstellung einer „Spannung"[5], die an beiden Polen der Hörbeziehung gleichermaßen zerrt.

Der Klang von Bildern

Der Philosoph Jean-Luc Nancy hat in seiner komplexen, aber lohnenswerten Studie *Zum Gehör* [*Á l'écoute*, 2002] dem Zuhören genau dieses Spannungsmoment attestiert, das dem passiven Hören versagt bleibt. Oder anders formuliert: Er schreibt dem Horchen – im Unterschied zum bloßen Vernehmen – exakte jene Form der Anspannung zu, die nicht einfach im Gehörten präexistent ist, sondern dieses nach allen Richtungen hin überschreitet: „Horchen ist [...] eine Intensivierung und eine Sorge, eine Neugier oder eine Beunruhigung."[6] Derlei Überschreitung markiert sowohl ein „Darüber" als auch ein „Darunter", ja man könnte versucht sein, sie nach Art von Ober- bzw. Untertönen zu deuten, oder, nochmals anders kodiert, als dasjenige, was im Akustischen an konnotativer Materie, aber auch als unterschwelliger Subtext zum Tragen kommt. Wenn Vernehmen bedeutet, den Sinn von etwas zu erfassen, so Nancy, dann meint Zuhören „gespannt sein hin zu einem möglichen Sinn, der folglich nicht unmittelbar zugänglich ist".[7]

Ricarda Denzer vermittelt in ihrem Video *Kapı açık* (2013) einen Eindruck davon, was es heißt, in dieser „gespannten" Hinsicht Bildern *zu lauschen*. Zwar ist der Blick in dem Video aus dem

co-constituted in other ways through media; it is not preexistent but only becomes evident in a reciprocal process. Para-listening, that is, "listening alongside," therefore means that something that is not simply already in existence—whether separate or merged—enters into relationship, *becomes* relationship. The aspect that takes center-stage is much more the production of a "tension"[5] that pulls at both ends of the aural relationship.

The Sound of Images

In his complex but laudable study on *Listening* [*À l'écoute*, 2002], philosopher Jean-Luc Nancy attributes to listening precisely this dimension of tense straining that cannot be attained by passive hearing. To put it another way: he ascribes to listening—as opposed to merely perceiving—a form of tension that does not simply preexist in what is heard but spills out beyond it in all directions: "To listen [...] is an intensification and a concern, a curiosity or an anxiety."[6] This spilling over boundaries occurs both "over" and "under"; it is even tempting to interpret it in terms of overtones and undertones, or—differently coded—as what comes into play in the acoustic realm as connotative matter, but also as subliminal subtext. "If 'to hear' means to understand the sense," Nancy notes, "to listen is to be straining towards a possible meaning, and consequently one that is not immediately accessible."[7]

In her video *Kapı açık* (2013), Ricarda Denzer conveys an impression of what it means to *listen* to images in this "straining" way. The gaze is directed out of the window, or rather it is directed to an open window, half covered by blinds, with the drama of escalating political protest (demonstrations and daily confrontations with the police during the 2013 Gezi Park protests in Istanbul) playing out below the window, behind the blinds. However, for long sections the decisive level is acoustic and articulates the sense of straining tension mentioned above—bouncing back and forth between listened-to and listener. Long before the demonstration appears in the image, introducing a "turnover" in formal terms too (substantial sections of the video are rotated through ninety degrees), the sonic patchwork announces a veritable urban symphony of everyday life. Although the sources of the sounds mostly remain out of sight, myriad acoustic strands produced by machinery, street-life, traffic, the demonstration and political agitation form a rhythmic mesh in which a whole host of diverse affects converge: intensification and anxiety, curiosity and alarm, to name but a few. Increasingly dense superimpositions of voices, drumming, and pot-banging beat out the meter of insurrection as further ingredients in this mix, joined towards the end by attempts at pacification and consolation. At one point, someone offscreen

5 Jean-Luc Nancy, *Listening*, trans. Charlotte Mandell (New York: Fordham University Press, 2007), 5.

6 Ibid.

7 Ibid., 6.

8 Ebd., S. 28.

Fenster gerichtet, oder besser: auf ein mit einer Jalousie verhängtes und ein daneben befindliches offenes Fenster, unter dem bzw. rund um das sich das Drama des damals eskalierenden politischen Protests abspielt. (Es geht um die Demonstrationen und täglichen Konfrontationen mit der Polizei im Zuge der Istanbuler Gezi-Park-Proteste 2013). Die tragende Rolle spielt jedoch über weite Strecken die Tonebene, auf der sich die zuvor umrissene Angespanntheit – vom Gehörten hin zu den Hörenden und wieder zurück – artikuliert. Lange bevor der Demonstrationszug ins Bild rückt und dieses wie in einem formalen „Turnover“ kippt (weite Teile des Videos sind um 90 Grad gedreht), kündet das flickwerkhafte Sound-Tableau von einer veritablen Alltags-, ja Großstadtsymphonie. Zwar sieht man die Lärmmacher die längste Zeit nicht, doch bilden die vielfältig ineinanderfließenden Maschinen-, Straßen-, Auto-, Agitations- und Demonstrationsklänge ihr eigenes rhythmisches Geflecht aus, in dem ein ganzes Sammelsurium an Affekten konvergiert: Intensivierung und Sorge, Neugier und Beunruhigung sind nur einige davon; immer dichtere Stimmüberlagerungen, Trommel- und Topfschlagen als Metren des Aufstands gehören ebenfalls dazu, gegen Ende hin auch Versuche der Beruhigung und des Zuspruchs. „Die Tür ist offen!“ [kapı açık!], ertönt es an einer Stelle auf Türkisch aus dem Off den flüchtenden Demonstrierenden entgegen.

Was die Bilder von *Kapı açık* solcherart evozieren, ist – über ihren manifesten visuellen Gehalt hinaus – eine Rhythmik, oder besser: eine Polyrhythmik des Aufständischen. Über und unter den Bildern, aber auch über und unter den zu hörenden Klängen breitet sich ein Tableau des Widerstrebigen und Sperrigen aus, das sich keiner Vereinheitlichung fügt. Die Gegenwart des Klanglichen, sagt Nancy, „ist niemals einfaches Dasein oder Stand der Dinge, sondern es ist immer zugleich Voran, Durchdringung, Insistenz, Obsession oder Besessenheit“.[8] Das Nebenher-Gehörte (Para-Listening) drängt so, selbst wenn man es auf keinen eindeutig umrissenen Sinn festschreiben kann, ins Zentrum einer Darstellung, die dem Klang von Bildern weit über alle Visualität hinaus Relevanz verleiht.

Bilder zum Sprechen bringen

Dieses Nebenher- und Durch-Hören ist es auch, das – als medienübergreifendes Nachhall- oder Widerhall-Moment verstanden – in vielerlei Aspekten von Denzers Praxis wirksam ist. Allein, wie sie Teile ihres (selten abgeschlossenen) Œuvres von Ausstellung zu Ausstellung, von einer installativen Variante zur nächsten, „nachhallen“ lässt, spricht diesbezüglich Bände. Dabei spielt es eine eher untergeordnete Rolle, von welcher Art Meistersignifikant die jeweilige Schau geleitet ist. Die Themenanker „Echo“, „Fakt und Fiktion“ oder „Storytelling“ mögen diesbezüglich in den letzten Jahren willkommene Ausgangspunkte für ihren beständig auf

cries out “Kapı açık!” [The door is open!] to the fleeing demonstrators. Over and above their manifest visual content, the images of *Kapı açık* evoke a rhythm, or rather polyrhythm, of insurgence. A recalcitrant, unwieldy tableau of resistance unfolds that defies simplification, over and under the images, as well as over and under the sounds. The presence of the sonorous, Nancy comments, “is never a simple being-there or how things stand, but is always at once an advance, penetration, insistence, obsession, or possession.”[8] Even if it is not possible to ascribe a clearly delineated meaning to what is heard alongside (para-listening), it elbows its way into the center of a portrayal that gives the sound of the images a relevance far beyond all visuality.

Making Images Speak

This listening alongside and through—understood as a cross-media resonance or echo—also comes into play in many aspects of Denzer’s practice. Even the way she causes parts of her (rarely definitely concluded) works to “reverberate” from exhibition to exhibition, from one installation to the next, speaks volumes. The type of overall signifier that acts as a lodestone for each exhibition plays a subordinate role here. In this respect, over the last few years the thematic anchors of “echo,” “fact and fiction,” or “storytelling” may have served as welcome starting points for Denzer’s strategy of continual shifts and fresh emphases.[9] The decisive consideration however is that all the ensuing variations, modifications, and readjustments—cutting across all media boundaries—are always guided by the idea of resonance described above, evoking the game of telephone or Chinese whispers[10] that paradoxically consists in simultaneously passing on as little as possible (of the acoustic content) and as much as possible (of the meaning conveyed).

Denzer has demonstrated how media resonance of this kind might be constituted in tangible terms in *Schwebendes* [Hovering] (2015). The predetermined thematic framework was that of the “speech act” (drawing on John L. Austin’s speech-act theory, first presented in 1955),[11] which focuses on the capacity of language not merely to depict but also to create reality. In *Schwebendes*—the title already implies the peculiar nature of an action that cannot be tied to a place—Denzer draws on photographs and short video sequences shot during her stay in Istanbul in 2013. Photographed inside Atatürk Kültür Merkezi, looking out through the grid pattern outlined on the glass facade, the artifacts depicted here stipulate something akin to an outline for action in their own right. The photographs show preparations—making banners or posters, for example—for demonstrations, with scope to surmise only fragments of the “original act.” At the

8 Ibid., 15.

9 See the group exhibition *CrossSections*, Kunsthalle Exnergasse, Vienna (2018), and *Whispering Dialogues*, Galerie 5020, Salzburg (2019), and the solo exhibitions *Erste Fassung (Interpretation)*, Neue Galerie, Innsbruck and *To Tell A Story*, Kunstraum Lakeside, Klagenfurt (2019).

10 See p. 108 in this book (work descriptions).

11 See J. L. Austin, *How To Do Things With Words. The William James Lectures delivered at Harvard University 1955* (Oxford: Clarendon Press, 1962), https://pure.mpg.de/rest/items/item_2271128/component/file_2271430/content/ (accessed June 5, 2023).

Verschiebung und Neuakzentuierung bedachten Ansatz geboten haben.[9] Entscheidend aber ist, dass all die resultierenden Variationen, Modifikationen und Neuanpassungen – über jegliche mediale Grenze hinweg – stets von besagtem Resonanzgedanken geleitet sind, nach Art eines Stille-Post-Spiels[10], dessen Paradoxon darin besteht, zugleich möglichst wenig (die Akustik betreffend) *und* möglichst viel (den vermittelten Sinn betreffend) von Spieler*in zu Spieler*in weiterzubefördern.

Wie derlei medienübergreifender Widerhall konkret verfasst sein mag, hat Denzer 2015 in der Arbeit *Schwebendes* vorgeführt. Der vorgegebene thematische Rahmen war jener der „Sprechhandlung" (zurückgehend auf John L. Austins erstmals 1955 präsentierte Speech Act Theory)[11], die den nicht bloß realitätsabbildenden, sondern auch realitätsschaffenden Aspekt von Sprache in den Fokus nimmt. In *Schwebendes* – der Titel deutet bereits die Eigenart von etwas nicht ortsfest zu Machendem an – greift Denzer auf Fotografien und kurze Videosequenzen zurück, die im Rahmen ihres Istanbul-Aufenthalts 2013 entstanden sind. Aufgenommen im Innenraum des *Atatürk Kültür Merkezi,* mit Blick nach außen durch die gerasterte Glasfassade, geben die hier aufgegriffenen Artefakte selbst eine Art Handlungsraster vor: Zu sehen sind Vorbereitungen – etwa Transparent- bzw. Plakatanfertigung – von Demonstrationen, deren „Originalhandlung" nur bruchstückhaft zu erahnen ist. Gleichzeitig bildet die riesige Glasfassade in den eingestreuten Totalen eine Art Großraster, das die collageartige Wirkung des Ganzen noch verstärkt. Hinzu kommt in *Schwebendes* nun aber entscheidend die inszenierte Handhabe der großformatig ausgedruckten Fotografien durch fünf Jugendliche, was den prozesshaften Nachhall dieser Bilder zwei Jahre später in einem gänzlich anderen Kontext (*off-site* sozusagen) in den Mittelpunkt rückt.

Erneut ist dieses echohafte Abbilden mit einer markant gestrickten Tonspur versehen, ja wird zentral über diese gesteuert. O-Töne der Istanbuler Kundgebungen mischen sich mit Dialogen der Jugendlichen über die Relevanz ihres Tuns, Klaviermusik von Debussy (*Préludes – Buch* 2) geht verquere Verbindungen mit Klängen von rauschendem Wind, metallischem Knarren, schließlich Klatschen und Jubeln ein. „Der Beginn des Sinns, seine Möglichkeit und sein Startschuss [...] findet vielleicht nirgend anders statt als in einem *Klanganstieg*, einer *Attacke*: eine Reibung, [...] ein Knacken, eine Schrillheit, von einer murmelnden denkenden Materie durchhaucht, geöffnet in der Spaltung ihrer Resonanz."[12] Nancys Charakterisierung, was es heißt, „ganz Ohr zu sein", trifft kongenial auf Denzers Parallelinszenierung zu: Zum einen gibt es hier die gleichsam verborgene oder hinter medialen Artefakten verschwindende „Originalhandlung", zum anderen das „resonante" Hantieren bzw., wie man sagen könnte, „In-den-Griff-kriegen-Wollen" dieser weit hergeholten Dokumente durch die fünf Jugendlichen; und

9 Siehe die Gruppenausstellungen *CrossSections*. Kunsthalle Exnergasse Wien, 2018, und *Whispering Dialogues*, Galerie 5020 Salzburg, 2019, sowie die Einzelausstellungen *Erste Fassung (Interpretation)*, Neue Galerie Innsbruck und *To Tell A Story*, Kunstraum Lakeside Klagenfurt, 2019.

10 Vgl. S. 108 in diesem Band, Werkbeschreibungen).

11 Vgl. J. L. Austin, *How To Do Things With Words. The William James Lectures delivered at Harvard University 1955*, Oxford: Clarendon Press 1962, https://pure.mpg.de/rest/items/item_2271128/component/file_2271430/content/ (abgerufen am 5. Juni 2023).

12 Nancy, *Zum Gehör*, S. 44. Die Ausstellung *Speech Acts*, in der *Schwebendes* erstmals präsentiert wurde, fand 2015 im Forum Stadtpark, beim steirischen herbst Graz statt.

same time the huge facade depicted in the interspersed long shots forms a kind of all-embracing grid that further intensifies the collage-like effect of the whole. In addition *Schwebendes* stages five young people handling large-format prints of these photographs, placing center-stage the images' processual resonance in an entirely different context (off-site, so to speak) two years later.

Once again, a striking soundtrack accompanies or even plays a central part in steering this echo-like depiction. Direct sound recordings from the Istanbul demonstrations are mixed with young people talking about the relevance of their actions; piano music by Debussy (*Preludes, Book 2*) establishes off-kilter connections with the sounds of rushing wind, metal creaking, finally applause and cheering. "The beginning of sense, its possibility and its send-off [...] perhaps takes place nowhere but in a sonorous attack: a friction, [...] a crackle, a stridency where a weighty, murmuring matter breathes, opened into the division of its resonance."[12] Nancy's characterization of what it means to be "all ears" is an apt description of Denzer's parallel mise-en-scène. There is, on the one hand, an "original act," in a sense concealed or disappearing behind media artifacts, on the other the "resonant" manner in which these five young people handle these documents from afar or what could be described as their "desire to get to grips with" them. In between lies an irreparable semantic rupture, "a friction, a crackle," that reveals the fundamentally divided nature of any form of resonance. The speech that can be elicited from the Istanbul images may not be eloquent or entirely replete with signification; it nevertheless presents the possibility of deriving a (partial, "frictional") meaning that is decisively transmitted by acoustic qualities.

12 Nancy, *Listening* (see note 5), 27. The exhibition *Speech Acts*, in which *Schwebendes* was first presented, was held at Forum Stadtpark, steirischer herbst Graz in 2015.

The Materiality of Sounds

In his pioneering text on "Listening" (1976), Roland Barthes noted that these acoustic qualities correspond to differently calibrated "acts of listening" (or contradict them in often odd ways). Barthes distinguishes between three types of listening: physiological listening, directed to *indices* in the surrounding world; semiological listening, which *deciphers* these signs; and the seemingly immeasurable breadth of (psycho-)analytical listening, which aims to derive *significance* in the sense of meaning and understanding. Barthes instances various different "acts of listening" involved in this analytical stance, irrespective of whether such acts aim to discern a particular coherence of meaning or address the plane of "phonic modulations"—which he also described as the "grain of the voice." The voice, Barthes writes, "is not the breath but indeed that materiality of the

dazwischen ein nicht zu kittender semantischer Riss, „eine Reibung, ein Knacken", das die elementare Gespaltenheit jeder Form von Resonanz offenbart. Das Sprechen, zu dem die Istanbul-Bilder gebracht werden, mag kein beredtes, restlos sinnerfülltes sein. Dennoch kündigt sich in ihm die Möglichkeit einer (partiellen, „friktionalen") Sinnerschließung an, die entscheidend von akustischen Qualitäten geleitet ist.

Die Materialität von Klängen

Dass diese akustischen Qualitäten mit unterschiedlich kalibrierten „Hörakten" korrespondieren (oder sich diesen auf oft verquere Art widersetzen), hat schon Roland Barthes in seinem bahnbrechenden Text über das „Zuhören" (1976) festgehalten. Barthes unterscheidet zunächst drei Arten des Hörens: das auf *Indizien* der umgebenden Welt gerichtete physiologische Hören; das diese Zeichen *entziffernde* semiologische Hören; und schließlich das auf *Signifikanz* in seiner ganzen, zunächst unermesslichen Bandbreite gerichtete (psycho-)analytische Hören. Was dieses analytische Hören betrifft, macht Barthes verschiedene Arten von „Hörakten" geltend, abhängig davon, ob es um das Erfassen einer bestimmten Sinnkohärenz geht oder um die Ebene der „lautlichen Modulation" – dasjenige, was auch als die „Rauheit der Stimme" bezeichnet wird. „Die Stimme", schreibt Barthes, „ist nicht der Atem, sondern durchaus jene Materialität des Körpers, die der Kehle entsteigt, dem Ort, an dem das Lautmaterial gehärtet und gestanzt wird."[13]

Jean-Luc Nancy wird 25 Jahre später in seiner Theorie des Zuhörens das *Timbre* – das, was gemeinhin als Klangfarbe angesehen, bei ihm aber umfassender als „Klangmaterie"[14] verstanden wird – neben dem *Rhythmus* als zweite maßgebliche Eigenschaft in den Mittelpunkt der Auseinandersetzung rücken. Damit versucht er ein weitläufiges Spektrum an Phänomenen zu bündeln, das Barthes als „Rauheit der Stimme" bezeichnet, aber bereits in dessen erster Formulierung weit über alles Vokale hinausreicht: „Die ‚Rauheit' ist der Körper in der singenden Stimme, in der schreibenden Hand, im ausführenden Körperteil."[15] Ricarda Denzer bringt in dem Video *Summen Trällern Pfeifen* (2015) ihrerseits Körper zum Singen – und zwar genau in der eben zitierten Version einer Körperlichkeit alles Sonoren, oder wie man umgekehrt auch sagen könnte: der Sonorität alles Körperlich-Materiellen. Die Stimmen bzw. deren Rauheit rühren in diesem Fall von einem speziell arrangierten Set verschieden großer (und verschiedenfarbiger) Gläser her. Von oben gefilmt bringt die Künstlerin diese gläsernen – jeweils ganz eigene Timbres verströmenden – Resonanzkörper mit ihren Hand- bzw. Fingerbewegungen zum Schwingen. „Schreibende Hände" bzw. „ausführende Körperteile" werden damit ebenso Bestandteile

13 Roland Barthes, Zuhören, in: Ders., *Der entgegenkommenden und der stumpfe Sinn. Kritische Essays III*. Aus dem Französischen von Dieter Hornig, Frankfurt am Main: Suhrkamp 1990, S. 259.
14 Nancy, *Zum Gehör*, S. 64.
15 Roland Barthes, Die Rauheit der Stimme, in: Ders., *Der entgegenkommenden und der stumpfe Sinn. Kritische Essays III*. Aus dem Französischen von Dieter Hornig, Frankfurt am Main: Suhrkamp 1990, S. 277.

body emerging from the throat, a site where the phonic metal hardens and takes shape."[13]

Twenty-five years later, in his theory of listening, Jean-Luc Nancy turned the spotlight on *timbre*—generally seen as tonal color, but understood by Nancy more broadly as "sonorous matter"[14]—alongside *rhythm* as the second essential quality in this discourse. He attempted in this context to bring together an extensive range of phenomena that Barthes conceived as the "grain of the voice," yet which even in that first formulation went far beyond the vocal sphere. "The 'grain' is the body in the voice as it sings, the hand as it writes, the limb as it performs."[15] In the video *Summen Trällern Pfeifen* [Humming Warbling Whistling] (2015), Ricarda Denzer makes bodies sing in precisely that sense of the physicality of all that is sonorous, which could conversely also be couched as the sonority of all that is physical or material. In this piece, the voices, along with their grain, come from a specially arranged set of variously sized (and differently colored) glasses. Filmed from above, Denzer's hand and finger movements cause these resonating glass bodies to vibrate, each exuding their own distinctive timbre. "The hand as it writes" or "the limb as it performs" consequently become as much a part of the subtly interwoven tonal cascades as the (invisibly) vibrating glass bodies that form the origin of the sound material that "hardens and takes shape," yet at the same time is lovingly modulated.

Humming, warbling, whistling; the series of terms cites various forms of vocal modulation and is generally emblematic of a resolutely *heightened graininess* in everything vocal (above and beyond the narrow motif of the human voice). Mixing the sound of crumpled or rustling paper into the sonic tableau—part of the video shows the glasses being wrapped up—opens up an additional area of connotation: paper that is "eloquent," complete with its own harsh, rough edges. This extends the frequency spectrum explored or rather adds a further contrapuntal frisson to it. Singing glasses and murmuring paper—far beyond any highly charged anthropomorphic connotation, a "directness"[16] of sounds is articulated that cannot merely be traced back to human parameters or those of the human voice. The materiality performed here is rather in a sense grounded in a transcendence of "tonal, phonetic, even of musical power."[17] This in turn substantially blurs the boundary between physicality in the conventional sense—that is, from the point of view of the human physique—and its subsumption into a larger "para-physical" network.

Vocal Ensembles and Polyphony

The function of entirely renewed listening, as Barthes noted in 1976, could also lie in "playing over unknown spaces: listening

13 Roland Barthes, "Listening," in Roland Barthes, *The Responsibility of Forms: Critical Essays on Music, Art, and Representation*, trans. Richard Howard (New York: Hill and Wang, 1985), 255.

14 Nancy, *Listening* (see note 5), 40.

15 Roland Barthes, "The Grain of the Voice," in Roland Barthes, *Image Music Text*, trans. Stephen Heath (London: Fontana Press, 1977), 188.

16 See Salomé Voegelin, "Wer hat Angst vor Klang? Zuhören als Überschreitung und Infragestellung von kultureller Visualität," in *springerin* 1/2023, 41f.

17 Barthes, "Listening" (see note 13), 255.

von feinsinnig ineinander verwobenen Klangkaskaden wie die (unsichtbar) vibrierenden Glaskörper, von denen das „gehärtete und gestanzte" – aber zugleich auch liebevoll modulierte – Lautmaterial seinen Ausgang nimmt.

Summen Trällern Pfeifen, die Begriffsreihe benennt unterschiedliche Formen der Stimmmodulation, steht insgesamt im Zeichen einer dezidierten *Aufrauhung* alles Stimmlichen (über das engere Motiv der menschlichen Stimme hinaus). Indem etwa auch der Klang von zerknülltem bzw. raschelndem Papier dem Soundtableau beigemischt ist – ein Teil des Videos zeigt das Einpacken der verwendeten Gläser –, wird hier noch ein zusätzlicher Konnotationsbereich eröffnet: derjenige von „sprechendem" Papier, mit seinen eigenen Härten und Kanten, wodurch das angeschnittene Frequenzspektrum nochmals erweitert bzw. kontrapunktisch aufgeladen wird. Singende Gläser und murmelndes Papier – abseits aller anthropomorphen Aufladung artikuliert sich hier eine „Direktheit"[16] von Klängen, die sich nicht einfach auf menschliche Paramater, oder jene der menschlichen Stimme, zurückführen lassen. Vielmehr beruht die hier vorgeführte Materialität, wenn man so will, auf einer Überschreitung von „Tonalität, Phonetik oder [musikalischer] Aussage".[17] Was wiederum die Grenze zwischen Körperlichkeit im herkömmlichen Sinn, sprich: von der menschlichen Physis her gedacht, und deren Aufhebung in einem größeren „para-physischen" Verbund nachhaltig verschwimmen lässt.

Stimm-Ensembles und Polyphonie

Die Funktion eines rundum erneuerten Zuhörens könnte, wie Barthes bereits 1976 festhielt, auch darin liegen, „unbekannte Räume abzutasten: Das Zuhören schließt heute nicht nur das Unbewußte, im topischen Sinn des Worts, in sein Feld ein, sondern sozusagen auch dessen weltliche Formen: das Implizite, das Indirekte, das Zusätzliche, das Hinausgezögerte."[18] Interessanterweise konvergiert Barthes' semiologischer Ansatz – dem Reich der Zeichen immer neue, nicht auf Anhieb zugängliche Signifikanz abzugewinnen – mit Pauline Oliveros' etwa zeitgleich, aber in einem völlig anderen Kontext entwickelten Theorie des „Deep Listening". Oliveros macht den Beginn dieser kontinuierlich bis zu ihrem Tod 2016 weiterentwickelten Theorie retrospektiv an ihrem 1971 entstandenen Werk *Sonic Meditations* fest – „pieces based on the structure of human attention".[19] Später hat sie die „lebenslange Praxis" des Deep Listening einmal so umrissen: „Deep Listening involves going below the surface of what is heard, expanding to the whole field of sound while finding focus. This is the way to connect with the acoustic environment, all that inhabits it. And all that there is."[20]

16 Vgl. Salomé Voegelin, Wer hat Angst vor Klang? Zuhören als Überschreitung und Infragestellung von kultureller Visualität, in: *springerin* 1/2023, S. 41f.
17 Barthes, Zuhören, S. 259.
18 Ebd., S. 261f.
19 Pauline Oliveros, Quantum Listening: From Practice to Theory (To Practice Practice), 1999, https://s3.amazonaws.com/arena-attachments/736945/19af465bc3fcf3c8d5249713cd586b28.pdf, S. 3 (abgerufen am 5. Juni 2023). Vgl. auch den Sammelband *Deep Listening. A Composer's Sound Practice*. New York/Lincoln/Shanghai: iUniverse Books 2005.
20 Oliveros, Quantum Listening, S. 5.

includes in its field not only the unconscious in the topical sense of the term, but also, so to speak, its lay forms: the implicit, the indirect, the supplementary, the delayed."[18] There is an intriguing convergence between Barthes' semiological approach—gleaning new and not immediately accessible significance from the realm of signs—and Pauline Oliveros' theory of Deep Listening, which she developed more or less at the same time but in a completely different context. With hindsight, Oliveros identified her theory, which she continued to develop until her death in 2016, as beginning with her 1971 *Sonic Meditations*—"pieces based on the structure of human attention."[19] She later outlined this "lifelong practice" as follows: "Deep Listening involves going below the surface of what is heard, expanding to the whole field of sound while finding focus. This is the way to connect with the acoustic environment, all that inhabits it. And all that there is."[20]

Whereas Barthes and later Nancy orient the act of listening to the implicit and non-manifest, even to a certain otherness within what always remains the same, Oliveros' exploration of the world through Deep Listening goes still further: "Deep Listening is listening in every possible way to everything possible to hear no matter what you are doing,"[21] she writes, affirming a universality of listening, or rather a reciprocal coupling of listener and listened-to that leaves neither side untouched.[22] Just as all sonorous matter—be it vocal or from other sources—only develops its inner diversity and vibratory richness in the act of listening, conversely the "deep" listener experiences a kind of inner diversification through the gradually emerging multiplicity of what they hear.

A prime example of such internal division and extension is found in Denzer's video *Reflections on a Star-Shaped Masque* (2018–22), which at the outset sets forth the multiple meanings of the word "person"—a kind of zero point of the listening subject. Between the semantic poles of "loudly resounding, loudly calling" and "masque or role-play," a wide, deeply cleft field unfurls, filled in this case with a heterogeneous voice montage. While visually we observe, via a helmet-mounted camera, the process of squeezing through narrow mineshafts in the Forest of Dean in England, the polyphonous voiceover marks out a generously proportioned discursive terrain that, in the most positive sense, shoots off at multiple tangents. One thing leads to another on this acoustic plane and is indeed often erratically entangled, with no holds barred when it comes to the diversity of contexts and disciplines. An arc is traced from iconoclasm and storytelling methodology via iron and ocher extraction in English mines to the restoration of iron artifacts and ultimately to the specific object that holds the whole vocal ensemble together as a "silent"

18 Ibid., 258.

19 Pauline Oliveros, "Quantum Listening: From Practice to Theory (To Practice Practice)" (1999), https://s3.amazonaws.com/arena-attachments/736945/19af465bc3fcf3c8d-5249713cd586b28.pdf, 3 (accessed June 5, 2023). See also the anthology *Deep Listening. A Composer's Sound Practice* (New York/Lincoln/Shanghai: iUniverse Books, 2005).

20 Oliveros, "Quantum Listening" (see note 19), 5.

21 Ibid., 1.

22 "Quantum Listening is listening in as many ways as possible simultaneously—changing and being changed by the listening," writes Oliveros. Ibid., 2.

Wo Barthes und später Nancy den Akt des Zuhörens auf das Implizite und Nicht-Manifeste, ja letztlich auf eine gewisse Alterität innerhalb des immer Gleichen ausrichten, geht Oliveros' Welterschließung mittels Deep Listening noch weiter: „Deep Listening is listening in every possible way to everything possible to hear no matter what you are doing"[21], schreibt sie und macht damit eine Universalität des Hörens, oder besser: der wechselseitigen Koppelung von Hörenden und Gehörtem geltend, die keine der beiden Seiten unberührt lässt.[22] So wie jede Klangmaterie – egal ob vokal oder von anderen Schallerzeugern als der menschlichen Stimme herrührend – erst im Akt des Zuhörens ihre innere Diversität, ja einen gewissen Vibrationsreichtum entfaltet, so erfahren umgekehrt auch die „tief" Zuhörenden durch die sukzessive zutage tretende Vielheit des Gehörten eine Art innere Diversifizierung.

Ein Paradebeispiel solch interner Aufspaltung und Erweiterung findet sich in Denzers Video *Reflections on a Star-Shaped Masque* (2018–2022), worin gleich zu Beginn die Mehrfachbedeutung des Wortes „Person" – eine Art Nullpunkt jedes (zu)hörenden Subjekts – dargelegt wird. Zwischen den semantischen Polen von „laut erschallen, laut rufen" und „Masken- bzw. Rollenspiel" spannt sich in der Folge ein weites, zerklüftetes Feld auf, das in diesem Fall von einer heterogenen Stimm-Montage gefüllt wird. Während wir visuell Zeug*innen eines mit Helmkamera gefilmten Sich-Durchzwängens durch enge Minenschächte im englischen Forest of Dean werden, steckt das polyphone Voice-over-Tableau ein großzügig bemessenes, ja im besten Sinne kreuz und quer verlaufendes Diskursterrain ab. Eines ergibt auf dieser akustischen Ebene das andere, ja greift oft sprunghaft ineinander, wobei mit Kontext- und Disziplinvielfalt nicht gegeizt wird: Der Bogen reicht von Betrachtungen zum Thema Ikonoklasmus und der Methodik des Storytelling über Eisen- und Ockerabbau in englischen Minen bis hin zur Restaurierung von Eisenobjekten und zu guter Letzt dem konkreten Gegenstand, der das ganze Stimm-Ensemble als „stummer" Resonanzkörper zusammenhält – die sternförmige Maske, die Denzer in der Istanbuler Hagia Sophia entdeckt hat und nunmehr als schillerndes Prisma für die hier verzahnten Teilerzählungen und Gedankensplitter dient.

Wobei die Klitterung – und dies ist der entscheidende Deep-Listening-Moment hier – erneut zutiefst klanglichen Charakter hat. Mag das Objekt auch ein matt glänzender und damit allerlei darauf Projiziertes reflektierender Körper sein, so ist und bleibt der Akt der Gegenstands*reflexion* ein ansatzweise akustisch verfasster. Dies belegt allein schon die kunstvoll gewirkte Tonspur, in der Metall- und andere Klänge überraschende Fusionen mit den Stimmen (und Stimmlagen) der Sprechenden eingehen. Dazu kommt, dass die präsentierte Vielstimmigkeit von harten Brüchen, Gegenschnitten, mal mehr, mal weniger expressiven Stimmmodulationen

21 Ebd., S. 1.
22 „Quantum Listening is listening in as many ways as possible simultaneously – changing and being changed by the listening", heißt es bei Oliveros. Ebd., S. 2.

resonant body: the star-shaped mask Denzer stumbled across in Hagia Sophia in Istanbul and that now serves as a glistening prism for these interlocking narratives and slivers of thought.

Yet the patchwork is again profoundly sonorous—that being the decisive Deep Listening dimension here. Even if the mask as a polished matt body will reflect anything projected onto it, the way in which it reflects as an object is to some extent conceived acoustically. This is evidenced in the artfully wrought soundtrack, in which metallic and other sounds fuse surprisingly with the speakers' voices (and pitches). What's more, this polyphony displays sharp caesurae, counter-cuts and vocal modulations of varying degrees of expressivity, giving rise to a complexly blended sound tableau. Implicit, indirect, supplementary, and delayed elements, in Barthes' sense, play contrasting roles here, in the spirit of Oliveros' "listening in every possible way to everything possible to hear"—with hearing in this case signifying every form of resonance that can be built up around a single object.

Denzer's para-listening thus again proves to be a form of exploration of the world without a fixed center or Archimedean point; instead there is an incessant questing search: "this space between ... the gap, the void ... the different ways to tell a story."[23] Or, to underscore this once more, *a friction, [...] a crackle, a stridency—where a weighty, murmuring matter breathes*.

23 Ricarda Denzer, "Reflections on a Star-Shaped Masque," video transcript (2022).

gekennzeichnet ist, sodass ein komplex ineinander verschnittenes Sound-Tableau entsteht. Implizites, Indirektes, Zusätzliches und Hinausgezögertes im Sinne Barthes' spielen hier ebenso kontrastreich eine Rolle wie Oliveros' „listening in every possible way to everything possible to hear" dabei Pate steht. Wobei „hearing" jede Form von Resonanzraum meint, der sich um einen einzelnen Gegenstand herum aufbauen lässt.

Und so erweist sich Denzers Para-Listening ein weiteres Mal als eine Art Welterschließung, die kein fixes Zentrum, keinen archimedischen Ankerpunkt kennt. Vielmehr ist da immer eine unablässige Suchbewegung: „this space between ... the gap, the void ... the different ways to tell the story."[23] Oder, um es nochmals zu betonen: *eine Reibung, ein Knacken, eine Schrillheit – von einer murmelnden denkenden Materie durchhaucht*.

23 Ricarda Denzer, Reflections on a Star-Shaped Masque, Video-Transkript, 2022.

Fouad Asfour

“My ear is an acoustic universe”*

* Pauline Oliveros, “The Earthworm Also Sings. A Composer’s Practice of Deep Listening,” *Leonardo Music Journal* 3:1 (1993), 35–38, https://doi.org/10.2307/1513267 (accessed June 30, 2022)

Fouad Asfour

„Mein Ohr ist ein akustisches Universum“ *

(Mitlesetext, 2023)

Von Anfang an befinden wir uns mitten im Text, oder in den Worten der französischen Schriftstellerin Hélène Cixous: „Wir sind bereits in den Fängen des Buchs.“[1] Anfänge sind andauernde Bewegungen, verwoben in kontinuierlichen Themensträngen. Die Gespräche mit Ricarda reichen weit zurück und in die Zukunft, bevor wir einander das erste Mal begegneten. Dieser Text könnte zu jedem Zeitpunkt oder außerhalb der Zeit geschrieben und veröffentlicht worden sein: Es könnte sich um ein Prequel, einen reflektierenden Bericht, ein Präludium oder einen Epilog, eine Dokumentation oder eine fiktive Erzählung eines Zwischenspiels handeln.

Nun möchten wir euch zu einer Busreise einladen. Es ist Nacht. Wir bewegen uns zwischen Städten, zwischen Ländern. Wir sind in Bewegung, reisen über verschiedene Grenzen – ohne anzuhalten, überquert der Bus Flüsse, wechselt von der Landstraße auf die Autobahn und passiert längst vergessene Grenzmarkierungen. Wir sind umgeben von leeren Sitzen, unsichtbaren Zuhörer*innen, Zeitreisenden und Begleiter*innen aus anderen Dimensionen und Gesprächen.

Erinnerst du dich? Erinnerst du dich an das letzte Mal, als du nachts gereist bist? Kannst du hören, wie die Luft am Busfenster vorbeirauscht und die Reifen den Teer abschleifen, der endlos unter dem Bus sich abspult?

[Kannst du den Klang nächtlichen Reisens abrufen?
Dann höre dem für eine Weile zu.]

* Pauline Oliveros, The Earthworm Also Sings. A Composer’s Practice of Deep Listening, in: Leonardo Music Journal 3:1, 1993, S. 35–38, https://doi.org/10.2307/1513267 (abgerufen am 30. Juni 2022).

1 Hélène Cixous and Mireille Calle-Gruber, *Hélène Cixous, Rootprints: Memory and Life Writing*, London: Routledge 1997.

(read-along paper, 2023)

From the outset, we find ourselves in the middle of the text, or in French writer Hélène Cixous’s words: “We are already in the jaws of the book.”[1] Beginnings are ongoing movements, interwoven into continuous threads. The threads of my conversations with Ricarda reach back before we actually met and well into the future. This text could have been written and published at any moment in time, or out of time. It could be a prequel, a reflective report, a prelude or an epilogue, a documentation or a fictional narrative of an interlude.

Right now, we want to invite you to travel with us, on a bus. It is night. We move between cities, between countries. We are in motion, moving across borders of different kind—without stopping, the bus crosses rivers, moves from road to freeway and across long forgotten demarcations. We are surrounded by empty seats, invisible listeners, time-travelers, and companions from other dimensions and conversations.

Do you remember? Do you remember the last time you traveled at night? Listen to the sound of the air passing bus windows, tires grinding down the endless tar that unwinds underneath the bus.

[Can you hear the sound of traveling at night?
Listen to it for a while.]

While we speak about language, about how to do things with words, composing thoughts as we speak, we cross borders of the self, of imagined language-scapes, as the bus cuts across the wetlands of Lower Austria and Burgenland, where *Eriophorum gracile*, the slender cottongrass, or cottonsedge, and other herbaceous flowering plants and grasses follow displaced marshes. How does it sound when you cross a border? Does it feel similar to changing altitude? Would you respond to border crossings by moving your jaw to release trapped air? How wide is a border? Is it a meter, or a centimeter? The thickness of a wall, or of a fence, or of a line on a map?

A border suggests change, of territory, of time—the decisive moment of crossing a border. How does it feel when you enter a place on either side of it, a home, a school, a doctors’ practice, or a grocery store? Do you feel enveloped in a different language? How do fault lines, borders, and cracks span through our lives?

[Close your eyes and feel borders across the surface of your body: your eyelids, where skin is covered by hair, and where clothes meet skin, the lines of waistbands and cuffs.]

1 Hélène Cixous and Mireille Calle-Gruber, *Hélène Cixous, Rootprints: Memory and Life Writing* (London: Routledge, 1997).

Während wir über Sprache reden und darüber, wie man etwas mit Wörtern tun kann und beim Sprechen Gedanken formen, überqueren wir Grenzen des Selbst, Grenzen imaginärer Sprachlandschaften, genauso wie der Bus die Marschlandschaften Niederösterreichs und des Burgenlandes durchquert, dort wo Eriophorum gracile, das schlanke Wollgras, das auch Baumwollsegge genannt wird, und andere krautartige Blütenpflanzen sowie Gräser den immer mehr verdrängten Sümpfen hinterherziehen. Wie hört es sich an, wenn man eine Grenze überschreitet? Ist es ein Gefühl, wie beim Überwinden von Höhenunterschieden? Würdest du nach einem Grenzübertritt eine kräftige Kieferbewegung machen, wie um eingeschlossene Luft rauszulassen? Wie breit ist eine Grenze? Einen Meter oder einen Zentimeter? Nehmen sie die Breite einer Mauer ein, eines Zauns oder einer Linie auf einer Landkarte?

Grenzen markieren Änderungen, von Gebieten oder auch Zeiten – den einschneidenden Moment des Grenzübertritts. Wie fühlt es sich an, wenn man einen Ort auf der anderen Seite betritt, ein Zuhause, eine Schule, eine Arztpraxis oder ein Lebensmittelgeschäft? Findest du dich von einer anderen Sprache umwoben? Wie ziehen sich Bruchlinien, Grenzen und Risse durch unser Leben?

[Schließe deine Augen und fühle, wo Grenzen über die Oberfläche deines Körpers verlaufen: deine Augenlider, wo die Haut von Haaren bedeckt ist und wo Kleidung auf Haut trifft, die Linien des Hosenbundes und der Säume.]

Dieser Mitlesetext lotet die sich überschneidenden Spannungen zwischen Opazität und Relationalität aus[2], indem Prozesse der Brechung und Ablenkung in den Mittelpunkt gerückt werden.[3] Die französische Philosophin Julia Kristeva untersucht Verbindungen zwischen Sprache und materieller Welt entlang von Spuren, die Signifikanten hinterlassen, wo Bedeutung aus „einem unentscheidbaren Prozess zwischen Sinn und Unsinn, zwischen Sprache und Rhythmus“[4] entsteht. Sollen wir davon ausgehen, dass die Ränder dieser Textcollage Leser*innen sowohl anziehen als auch abstoßen und so Kraftfelder von Anziehung und Unterbrechung bilden, an denen Aufmerksamkeit sich bricht? Könnte man also annehmen, dass Opazität Kraftfelder erzeugt, die zwischen der Ermöglichung und Behinderung von Relationalität oszillieren?

Hörbares schallt über Grenzen hinweg, korrodiert sie und wird an deren Lücken gebrochen. In gleicher Weise sickern Emotionen, die der Sprache innewohnen, durch Schallwellen in Gedanken und Sprache ein. Unkontrollierbare Schallwellen breiten sich aus und durchdringen Räume, Medien, Sinne und Sprachen, ähnlich wie wässrige Tinte, die sich über Papier ausbreitet. Versuchen wir nun zu verfolgen, wie Laute in unser Dasein einsickern und aus

2 Édouard Glissant, *Poetics of Relation*, trans. Betsy Wing, Ann Arbor: The University of Michigan Press 1997, S. 189–194.

3 Karen Barad, Diffracting Diffraction: Cutting Together-Apart, in: *Parallax* 20:3, 2014, S. 168–187, DOI:10.1080/13534645.2014.927623 (abgerufen am 30. Juni 2022).

4 Julia Kristeva, *Desire in Language*, trans. Thomas Gora, Alice Jardine, Leon S. Roudiez, New York: Columbia University Press 1980, S. 135.

This audio-collage sounds out the intersecting tensions between opacity and relationality[2] through the process of refraction.[3] French philosopher Julia Kristeva traces linkages between language and the material world along traces left by signifiers, as signification arises in “an undecidable process between sense and nonsense, between language and rhythm.”[4] Could we consider that the edges of this audio-collage draw the readers in and push them back, thus forming force fields of attraction and disconnection across which attention is refracted? Could we assume, then, that opacity creates force fields that oscillate between enabling and obstructing relationality?

Sounds leak across borders, diffract around their gaps and also corrode them. In the same way, emotions that inhabit language leak into thoughts and speech through waves of sound. Ungovernable sounds spread and leak across spaces, media, minds, and tongues similar to watery ink spilled across paper.

Let’s trace how sounds leak in and out of our lives, through the air that surrounds us. They travel across seas, rivers, oceans, connect islands and archipelagos. Sound floating across the waters turns into relation and disconnect—the sounds of refugee boats sinking—how could this liquid air turn into language, turn language into form? Can you feel how silence’s blurry lines dissolve in water with ease, like ink?

[Listen to sounds leaking across familiar and unfamiliar spaces in the following lines. Try not to focus on meaning and understanding, but to follow how letters break in the surf of your tongue around what you have internalized as different “languages.” Observe how these patterns patter across screen or paper as you read along:]

If language refracts ourselves
Do borders obstruct sense?
Does that mean—und heißt das dann
Wenn wir jemand sprechen hören
—when we hear someone speaking
Our emotional selves respond
—und bemerkt Widerstände?
(are our) languages (are)
shaped around obstacles (?)

How do we sound
within wenn in und aus
Sprache Gefühle sickern?

When Gefühle
den Text im Lesen lösen
and refract.

2 Édouard Glissant, *Poetics of Relation*, trans. Betsy Wing (Ann Arbor: The University of Michigan Press, 1997), 189–194.

3 Karen Barad, “Diffracting Diffraction: Cutting Together-Apart,” *Parallax* 20:3 (2014). 168–187, DOI:10.1080/13534645.2014.927623 (accessed June 30, 2022).

4 Julia Kristeva, *Desire in Language*, trans. Thomas Gora, Alice Jardine, Leon S. Roudiez (New York: Columbia University Press, 1980), 135.

ihm herausrinnen, getragen von der uns umgebenden Luft. Töne werden über das Meer getragen, über Flüsse, Ozeane, und sie verbinden Inseln und Archipele. Laute, die auf dem Wasser schweben, können Verbindungen schaffen und trennen – die Stimmen sinkender Flüchtlingsboote – was, wenn verflüssigte Luft sich in Sprache verwandelt und Sprache Form annimmt? Spürst du, wie verschwimmende Konturen der Stille sich mühelos wie Tinte im Wasser auflösen?

[Versuche nun, den Klängen nachzuhorchen, die sich in den folgenden Zeilen zwischen bekannten und unbekannten Räumen ausbreiten. Versuche dabei, nicht unmittelbar deren Bedeutung zu begreifen oder festzulegen, sondern verfolge eher, wie Buchstaben sich in der Brandung deiner Zunge um Unterschiede herum brechen, die du als „Sprachen“ internalisiert hast. Beobachte dann, wie diese Muster anfangen, über den Bildschirm oder das Papier zu trippeln, während du weiterliest:]

Wenn die Sprache das Selbst bricht
Verstellen Grenzen dann den Sinn?
Bedeutet das dann – and does that mean
When we hear someone speaking
– wenn wir jemanden sprechen hören
Antwortet dann unser emotionales Ich
– and notices obstacles?
(sind unsere) Sprachen (sind)
um Hindernisse herum geformt (?)

Wie hören wir uns an
drinnen – when in and from
emotions oozes language?

When emotions
release text while reading
– und ihn dabei brechen.

Was hast du mitbekommen, von dem, was hier besprochen wird? Kannst du mich hören? Kannst du folgen? Und warum, denkst du, rede ich hier darüber, mit dir?

Ich bin aufgewachsen zwischen Klängen verschiedener Sprachen und fühle mich in der spielerischen Praxis von „Translanguaging“ zu Hause, so wie hier veranschaulicht – wenn Sprachen sich wie Wolken bewegen, vermischen, erstarren und sich auflösen. Ich finde, die unkontrollierbaren Elemente, die sich außerhalb des „einsprachigen“ Geistes[5] befinden, können uns weg von starren Vorstellungen des Selbst/Anderen leiten, hin zum Dialog und

5 Vgl. Yasemin Yildiz, *Beyond the Mother Tongue. The Postmonolingual Condition*, New York: Fordham University Press 2012.

What do you take away from what I said so far? Can you hear me? Do you follow? And why, do you think, am I speaking here about this, to you?

Growing up, stretched across the sounds of different languages throughout my childhood, I feel at home in a playful practice of "translanguaging" that is illustrated here—where languages move, intermingle, congeal and disperse like clouds. I believe that ungovernable elements which we find outside of the "one-languaged" mind[5] can take us outside of ideas of self/other, closer to dialogue and exchange, into *being in communication*—being-with-each-other[6] in a moment, a stretch of time, a nightly travel by bus, a moment of silence on the phone.

In this imaginary bus ride I wanted you to join us constantly moving between moments—sounding out the relations between the movements of meaning-making–speaking, movements of remembering and of removing meaning. In these overlaps our ears seem to have become accustomed to—and learnt to listen to—echoes, suspended time, blurred borders, contexts, and selves.

I guess that Ricarda and I started speaking about this at that time, or even before, and that these moments of shared concern about language, meaning-making, sound, and voice took on a life of their own. Both of us have experienced, to a certain degree, migration, and if you would turn inward to listen closely, you would become aware of it too. Perhaps migration isn't quantifiable in simple terms of citizenship, nationality, heritage, or "home"; it lives in and through the varieties of languages, spoken and written, in and across different spaces that we encounter, across borders, countries, and continents.

And we might never know for sure what we spoke about, on the bus, that time. The conversation carries on across time and space. We re-enter these archipelagos of relationality continually. If you listen hard, you might feel a change in the sound. If you listen closely how they leak across the language borders that have settled in your ears, and on your tongue.

[Now, breathe in, breathe out, slowly. Listen to the sounds, inside and outside of your body, for a little while.]

Glissant writes: "Opacities can coexist and converge, weaving fabrics. To understand these one must focus on the texture of the weave and not on the nature of its components."[7] This short experimental read-along paper tries to map embodied selves while un-mapping identities, and asks how selves are formed. It suggests borders as sites of diffraction that extend into the texture of emotions. Sounding out echoes of echoes, of desires, of conformities and refusals, it is an invitation to join Pauline Oliveros in summoning "acoustic universes" in our ears:

5 See Yasemin Yildiz, *Beyond the Mother Tongue. The Postmonolingual Condition* (New York: Fordham University Press, 2012).

6 Trinh T. Minh-ha, *When the Moon Waxes Red: Representation, Gender, and Cultural Politics* (New York: Routledge, 1991), 12.

7 Édouard Glissant, *Poetics of Relation* (see note 3), 190.

Austausch, dem beständigen Dasein in Kommunikation – dem Miteinander-Sein[6] in bestimmten Momenten, einer Weile, einer nächtlichen Busfahrt, einem Moment der Stille am Telefon.

Diese imaginäre Busfahrt war eine Einladung, an der andauernden Bewegung zwischen einzelnen Momenten teilzuhaben – und die Beziehungen zwischen bedeutungsgenerierenden Bewegungen im Sprechen, im Erinnern und der Aufhebung von Bedeutung auszuloten. Es scheint, als hätten sich unsere Ohren an diese Überlagerungen gewöhnt und erlernt, auf Echos, aufgehobene Zeit, verschwommene Grenzen, Kontexte und das Selbst zu achten.

Ich vermute, dass Ricarda und ich damals begonnen haben, über all das zu sprechen, oder möglicherweise bereits zuvor, und dass mit der Zeit das geteilte Anliegen um Sprache, Sinnbildung, Klang und Stimme ein Eigenleben entwickelt hat. Wir haben beide in unterschiedlicher Weise Migration erlebt, und wenn du auf dein Inneres horchst, kannst auch du das wahrnehmen. Vielleicht lässt sich Migration nicht einfach anhand von Staatsbürgerschaft, Nationalität, Herkunft oder „Heimat“ quantifizieren; vielmehr lebt sie in und durch die Vielfalt der gesprochenen und geschriebenen Sprachen in Räumen und über verschiedene Räume, Grenzen, Länder und Kontinente hinweg.

Und vielleicht werden wir nie genau wissen, worüber wir damals im Bus gesprochen haben. Jedenfalls setzen wir unsere Gespräche über Zeit und Raum hinweg fort. Dabei betreten wir stets aufs Neue Archipele der Relationalität. Wenn du genau hinhörst, spürst du möglicherweise eine Veränderung im Klang – wenn du die Ohren spitzt und lauschst, wie Klänge sich über Sprachgrenzen hinweg fortpflanzen und sich in deinen Ohren und auf deiner Zunge niederlassen.

[Nun atme einmal langsam ein und wieder aus: Höre für eine kurze Dauer den Geräuschen innerhalb und außerhalb deines Körpers zu.]

Glissant schreibt: „Opazitäten können koexistieren, sich einander annähern und sich auf diese Weise zu einem neuen Gewebe verflechten.“[7] Um dies zu verstehen, muss man sich auf die Textur des Gewebes konzentrieren und nicht auf die Beschaffenheit seiner Bestandteile.

Dieser kurze experimentelle Mitlesetext hat versucht, das verkörperte Selbst abzubilden und gleichzeitig Identitäten aufzulösen beziehungsweise zu fragen, wie dieses Selbst überhaupt gebildet wird. Grenzen sind meinem Verständnis nach Orte der Brechung, die bis in die Textur von Emotionen hineinreichen. Das Ausloten der Echos von Emotionen und Wünschen, von Anpassung und Verweigerung lädt dazu ein, gemeinsam mit Pauline Oliveros „akustische Universen“ in unseren Ohren aufzuspüren:

6 Trinh T. Minh-ha, *When the Moon Waxes Red: Representation, Gender, and Cultural Politics*, New York: Routledge 1991, S. 12.

7 Édouard Glissant, *Poetics of Relation* (siehe Fußnote 3), S. 190.

My ear is an acoustic universe
sending and receiving
My ear also sounds
Where are the receivers for these tiny,
mysterious signals? Inside? Outside? The cells? [8]

This read-along paper is based on the audio paper "Dividuality Through Opacity," which was presented during Ricarda Denzer's Sounding Research Listening Session #1 on March 14, 2022. Reflecting on collaborations that were initiated by Ricarda over the past 15 years, these exercises are inspired by the American composer Pauline Oliveros, the German author Friedrich Karl Wächter's book *Grandpa Hucke's Participation Cabinet* (1975),[9] the Chicana feminist writer Gloria Anzaldúa's book *Borderlands/ La Frontera: The New Mestiza*, and the labour of love by others who allow languages to scrape against the emotional edges of the norm, including Leila Sebbar, Emine Sevgi Özdamar, Cecilia Vicuna, Theresa Hak Kyung Cha, Gabeba Baderoon, Sharlene Khan, Philiswa Lila, Gabeba Baderoon.

8 Pauline Oliveros, "The Earthworm Also Sings (see note 1).

9 See Winfred Kaminski and Maureen T. Krause, West German Young People's Literature since 1965, *New German Critique* 30 (1983), 181.

Further reading

Baderoon, G. 2011. "This is our speech: voice, body and poetic form in recent South African writing," in *Social Dynamics: A journal of African studies* 37:2, 213–227. DOI:10.1080/02533952.2011.600822.

Hak Kyung Cha, T. 2001. *Dictee*. Los Angeles: University of California Press.

Khan, S. 2017 (2014). *Sharlene Khan. I Make Art.* Exhibition catalogue. Johannesburg: Sharlene Khan.

Lila, P. 2021. Navigating personal memories in my family photo album. *bopa writers' forum*. https://www.creativeknow.org/bopawritersforum/navigating-personal-memories-in-my-family-photo-album-3nhf8 (accessed June 30, 2022)

Özdamar, E. S. 1990. *Mutterzunge*. Cologne: Kiepenheuer & Witsch.

Sebbar, L. 2015 (2010). *L'arabe comme un chant secret/ Arabic as a Secret Song*. Trans. S. Artes. Charlottesville/London: University of Virginia Press.

Vicuña, C. 2012 (2014). *Spit Temple: The Selected Performances of Cecilia Vicuña*. Trans. R. Alcalá. Brooklyn: Ugly Duckling Press.

Mein Ohr ist ein akustisches Universum
Sendend und empfangend
Klingt auch mein Ohr
Wo befinden sich die Empfänger für diese winzigen,
mysteriöse Signale? Innen? Außen? Die Zellen? [8]

Dieser Mitlesetext basiert auf dem Soundbeitrag „Dividuality Through Opacity“, das während Ricarda Denzers „Sounding Research Session #1“ am 14. März 2022 präsentiert wurde. Es setzt die von Ricarda in den letzten 15 Jahren initiierten Kooperationen fort und ist inspiriert von den Übungen der amerikanischen Komponistin Pauline Oliveros sowie von Friedrich Karl Wächters *Opa Hucke's Mitmachkabinett* (1975)[9], dem Buch der feministischen Chicana-Autorin Gloria Anzaldúa *Borderlands / La Frontera: The New Mestiza* und den Autor*innen und Künstler*innen, deren Spracharbeit die affektiven Grenzen der Sprache unablässig auslotet und erweitert, unter anderem von: Leila Sebbar, Emine Sevgi Özdamar, Cecilia Vicuna, Theresa Hak Kyung Cha, Gabeba Baderoon, Sharlene Khan, Philiswa Lila, Gabeba Baderoon.

8 Pauline Oliveros, The Earthworm Also Sings (siehe Fußnote 1).

9 Vgl. Winfred Kaminski und Maureen T. Krause, West German Young People's Literature since 1965, New German Critique 30, 1983, S. 181.

Weiterführende Literatur

Baderoon, G. (2011), „This is our speech“: voice, body and poetic form in recent South African writing, in: *Social Dynamics: A journal of African studies* 37:2, 213–227. DOI: 10.1080/02533952.2011.600822 (abgerufen am 30. Juni 2022).

Hak Kyung Cha, T. (2001), *Dictee*, Los Angeles: University of California Press.

Khan, S. 2017 (2014), *Sharlene Khan. I Make Art.* Exhibition catalogue, Johannesburg: Sharlene Khan.

Lila, P. (2021), Navigating personal memories in my family photo album. *bopa writers' forum.* https://www.creativeknow.org/bopawritersforum/navigating-personal-memories-in-my- family-photo-album-3nhf8 (abgerufen am 30. Juni 2022).

Özdamar, E. S. (1990), *Mutterzunge*, Köln: Kiepenheuer & Witsch.

Sebbar, L. (2015), *L'arabe comme un chant secret/Arabic as a Secret Song*. Trans. S. Artes, Charlottesville/London: University of Virginia Press.

Vicuña, C. (2012), *Spit Temple: The Selected Performances of Cecilia Vicuña*. Trans. R. Alcalá, Brooklyn: Ugly Duckling Press.

Christiane Erharter

"I think about killing. I think about calling"

"What it means to be touched by a question or issue or by a voice, by something spoken."

1 Sanne Krogh Groth and Kristine Samson, *Audio Papers – a manifesto* (2016), https://seismograf.org/fokus/fluid-sounds/audio_paper_manifesto (accessed July 5, 2023).

Christiane Erharter

„I think about killing. I think about calling“

„Was es heißt, berührt zu werden von einer Frage oder Thematik oder von einer Stimme, von etwas Gesprochenem.“

THE AUDIO PAPER MANIFESTO
The audio paper affords performative aesthetics.
The audio paper is idiosyncratic.
The audio paper is situated and partial.
The audio paper renders affects and sensations.
The audio paper is multifocal; it assembles diverse and often heterogeneous voices.
The audio paper has multiple protagonists, narrators and material agencies.
The audio paper brings aesthetics and technologies together in mediation.
The audio paper is a constituent part of larger ecologies.[1]

1 Sanne Krogh Groth und Kristine Samson, Audio Papers – a manifesto, 2016, https://seismograf.org/fokus/fluid-sounds/audio_paper_manifesto (abgerufen am 5.7.2023).

The collaborative three-hour *Listening Session #1*, conceived and organized by Ricarda Denzer, was held at the University of Applied Arts Vienna on March 14, 2022.[2] Fouad Asfour, Ricarda Denzer, Christina Goestl, Seth Weiner/Sadie Siegel, Karen Werner, and Hui Ye made their contributions in the form of audio papers. At that point the Covid-19 pandemic was still determining how and whether public events and meetings could take place. All the participants apart from Fouad Asfour came together in the university auditorium; they all wore FFP2 masks, which they however removed once they were seated on stage, as a video of the event impressively documents.[3] Ricarda Denzer was the first to take the stage and introduced the event in English. Subsequently, parallel to her live performance in the auditorium, she presented her pre-recorded audio paper *Para-Listening:*

> *Your text behaves in a circular way.*
> *The head does not know what the hand is doing.*
> *Your paper becomes unacceptable as research,*
> *dysfunctional – like art, you want to say.*
> *Conditions are not optimal:*
> *Your body turns on itself – every step hurts.*
> *Flashes of nerve, vulnerability as form.*
> *You receive your wages in a roundabout way.*
> *If you are caught, you are on the run.*
> *You lose track of names when you speak.*
> *You make the voids between found objects sound.*
> *You doodle notebooks while listening.*
> *First words and sentence fragments,*
> *then free signs, lines, drawings.*
> *While listening evenly suspended attention*
> *comes up against free association.*
> *Characters empty out.*
> *You start writing in dialect to make yourself at home.*
> *You can neither prove nor disprove it,*
> *you recognize the world as something undecidable to order.*
> *You deal with the staging of the audible.*
> *If my thinking has a voice and this voice has a body:*
> *Then, Wer bist du.........?*[4]

During the panel discussion after the audio papers were presented, various people mentioned that they were delighted to meet in person in a real space and acknowledged the energy that arose from the shared experience. Positive comments were also made about the scope for communication between the papers, as well as among and with the audience, and also about the informal, brief conversations and rapid exchanges of ideas. I remember, for example, interjections in Hessian dialect from the audience,

2 Part of INTRA, a program of inter- and transdisciplinary projects in art and research, 2021/22.

3 *Sounding Research, Listening Session #1*, audio paper presentations and panel talk (2022), die Angewandte YouTube channel, https://www.youtube.com/watch?v=Sd1h_FI71MQ (accessed July 5, 2023).

4 Ricarda Denzer, *Para-Listening #1*, audio paper, https://www.soundingresearch.net/audio-paper (accessed July 4, 2023). The final three words of this quotation translate as “Who are you?”

2 Im Rahmen von INTRA, dem Angewandte-Programm für inter- und transdisziplinäre Projekte in Kunst und Forschung, 2021/22.

3 Sounding Research, Listening Session #1, Audio paper presentations and panel talk, 2022, YouTube-Kanal die Angewandte: https://www.youtube.com/watch?v=Sd1h_FI71MQ (abgerufen am 5.7.2023).

4 Ricarda Denzer, Para-Listening #1, Audio Paper: https://www.soundingresearch.net/audio-paper (abgerufen am 4.7.2023).

Am 14. März 2022 fand an der Universität für angewandte Kunst Wien die von Ricarda Denzer konzipierte und organisierte gemeinschaftliche, rund dreistündige *Listening Session #1* statt.[2] Fouad Asfour, Ricarda Denzer, Christina Goestl, Seth Weiner/Sadie Siegel, Karen Werner und Hui Ye präsentierten ihre Beiträge als Audio Papers, von Fouad Asfour griffig als „Hörpapiere“ ins Deutsche übersetzt. Zu dem Zeitpunkt gab die Covid-19-Pandemie noch den gesetzlichen Rahmen vor, ob und wie öffentliche Veranstaltungen durchgeführt werden und Zusammenkünfte stattfinden konnten. Bis auf Fouad Asfour kamen alle Beteiligten live im Auditorium der Angewandten zusammen. Alle trugen FFP2-Masken, die sie, sobald sie auf der Bühne Platz nahmen, ablegten. Das dokumentiert die Videoaufnahme der Veranstaltung eindrücklich.[3] Ricarda Denzer betrat als Erste die Bühne und führte in englischer Sprache in die Veranstaltung ein. Dann präsentierte sie, simultan zu ihrer Live-Performance im Auditorium, ihr vorab aufgenommenes Audio Paper *Para-Listening*:

> *Your text behaves in a circular way.*
> *The head does not know what the hand is doing.*
> *Your paper becomes unacceptable as research,*
> *dysfunctional – like art, you want to say.*
> *Conditions are not optimal:*
> *Your body turns on itself – every step hurts.*
> *Flashes of nerve, vulnerability as form.*
> *You receive your wages in a roundabout way.*
> *If you are caught, you are on the run.*
> *You lose track of names when you speak.*
> *You make the voids between found objects sound.*
> *You doodle notebooks while listening.*
> *First words and sentence fragments,*
> *then free signs, lines, drawings.*
> *While listening evenly suspended attention*
> *comes up against free association.*
> *Characters empty out.*
> *You start writing in dialect to make yourself at home.*
> *You can neither prove nor disprove it,*
> *you recognize the world as something undecidable to order.*
> *You deal with the staging of the audible.*
> *If my thinking has a voice and this voice has a body:*
> *Then, Wer bist du.........?*[4]

In der Paneldiskussion, die der Präsentation der Audio Papers folgte, wurde die Freude über das Zusammenkommen in einem realen Raum artikuliert und auf die Energie verwiesen, die aus der gemeinschaftlichen Erfahrung resultierte. Positiv vermerkt wurden auch die Möglichkeit der Kommunikation, die zwischen den

with replies from Fouad Asfour in the selfsame dialect, while Ricarda Denzer responded in Palatine dialect. Or perhaps I am mixing things up and the points in dialect cropped up during the discussion with the audience after the first presentation of Ricarda Denzer's audio paper *Para-Listening #1* at the ÖGGF conference in September 2021?[5]

I also associate dialect with Ricarda Denzer's *Die gute Stube* [The Parlor], a sound-and-slide work from 1995, a video version of which was shot in 1999, with images of her visit to places from her early childhood in provincial Germany. Denzer uses this "best room" as a means to initiate conversations with the villagers. The soundtrack includes stories in the Palatine dialect about family relationships and entanglements. Linguistic mechanisms that generate exclusion and inclusion are recurrent motifs in Ricarda Denzer's artistic explorations. She is interested in spoken language, oral history, recorded interviews, fragments of conversation, and the human voice. The dialectal aspect probably also touches me because I associate our friendship with Kufstein, where we both grew up and—although we don't speak the same dialect—found a common language, namely that of artistic expression. When I left high school in 1993 Ricarda Denzer was recommended as a tutor to help me prepare my application to one of Vienna's art universities. She was just finishing a degree at the University of Applied Arts Vienna at the time and that is how we gradually made friends. Our linguistic socializations differ in that Ricarda Denzer already spoke standard German as a child, as she had lived in Germany before moving to Kufstein before she turned ten, whereas I only learnt standard written German when I attended elementary school. Speaking in dialect was seen as uneducated and provincial. My mild inferiority complex about it only dissolved when I was living in Norway, where the various dialects are outright celebrated—also because Nynorsk (lit. "New Norwegian"), which, along with Bokmål (lit. "book tongue"), is recognized as one of two standard written versions of the language, builds on philologist Ivar Andreas Aasen's dialect collection.

This led to a new perspective on my own dialect and changed my way of engaging with it. Nowadays I pay close attention to spoken dialect or dialectal sprinklings, especially on the radio; I also really enjoy listening to people speaking the dialect of the region where I grew up, for example in May 2023 in a feature by radio journalist Sarah Seekircher on Ö1: *Family Drama in Wildschönau – The Story of the Ascher Sisters*.[6]

To begin is impossible because
we were/are always in the middle of it.[7]

5 The interjections actually occurred during the APL Practice (!) Week on September 22, 2021, at the live panel *In_Visibilities in Recent Sound Interventions*, with Ricarda Denzer, Kristina Pia Hofer, and Huda Takriti, in the studio of the Angewandte Performance Lab as part of the Ambivalente Un_Sichtbarkeiten annual conference of the Österreichische Gesellschaft für Geschlechterforschung (ÖGGF, Gender Studies Association Austria).

6 https://oe1.orf.at/programm/20230513/719334/Familiendrama-in-der-Wildschoenau-Teil-I and https://oe1.orf.at/programm/20230518/719591/Familiendrama-in-der-Wildschoenau-Teil-II (accessed July 4, 2023).

7 Fouad Asfour, *Dividuality Through Opacity*, audio paper, https://www.soundingresearch.net/audio-paper (accessed July 4, 2023).

Vorträgen, auch im und mit dem Publikum stattfand, sowie all die nicht formalisierten Momente des kurzen Gesprächs und schnellen Austauschs. Ich erinnere mich zum Beispiel an Zwischenrufe in hessischem Dialekt aus dem Publikum, die Fouad Asfour auf Hessisch und Ricarda Denzer auf Pfälzisch kommentierten. Oder verwechsle ich das und die dialektalen Pointen erfolgten beim Publikumsgespräch nach der erstmaligen Präsentation von Ricarda Denzers Audio Paper „Para-Listening #1“ im Rahmen der ÖGGF-Tagung im September 2021?[5]

Dialektale Aspekte verbinde ich auch mit Ricarda Denzers Kunstwerk *Die gute Stube*, einer Sound-Dia-Arbeit von 1995, die 1999 auch als Videoarbeit umgesetzt wurde und Bilder ihres Besuches an Orten ihrer frühen Kindheit in der deutschen Provinz enthält. Denzer nimmt den repräsentativen Ort der „guten Stube“ zum Anlass, um mit den Dorfbewohner*innen Gespräche zu führen. Auf der Tonspur zu hören sind Erzählungen in pfälzischem Dialekt, in denen es um verwandtschaftliche Beziehungen und Verwicklungen geht. Die Einschlüsse und Ausschlüsse produzierenden Mechanismen von Sprache stellen wiederkehrende Motive in Ricarda Denzers künstlerischer Auseinandersetzung dar. Ihr Interesse gilt dem (Zu)Hören, der gesprochenen Sprache, Oral History, aufgenommenen Interviews und Gesprächsfragmenten sowie der menschlichen Stimme. Darüber hinaus berühren mich Dialektmomente vermutlich auch deshalb, weil ich unsere Freundschaft mit Kufstein verbinde, wo wir beide aufwuchsen und, obwohl wir nicht denselben Dialekt sprechen, zu einer gemeinsamen Sprache, nämlich der des künstlerischen Ausdrucks fanden. Um mich nach der Matura 1993 auf die Aufnahme an eine der Kunstuniversitäten in Wien vorzubereiten, wurde mir Ricarda Denzer als Tutorin empfohlen. Sie schloss damals ihr Studium an der Angewandten ab und so freundeten wir uns nach und nach an. Unsere sprachliche Sozialisation unterscheidet sich insofern, als Ricarda Denzer, die im Volksschulalter von Deutschland nach Kufstein zog, bereits Hochdeutsch sprach. Ich hingegen musste Schrift- bzw. Hochdeutsch erst in der Volksschule erlernen. Im Dialekt zu sprechen, galt als ungebildet und provinziell. Der daraus resultierende milde Minderwertigkeitskomplex löste sich bei mir erst auf, als ich in Norwegen lebte, wo die verschiedenen Dialekte nachgerade zelebriert werden, auch weil die Schriftsprache Nynorsk (Neu-Norwegisch) erst aufbauend auf der Dialektsammlung des Sprachforschers Ivar Andreas Aasen entstand und neben Bokmål (Buchsprache) als zweite offizielle Schriftsprache des Norwegischen gilt.

So ergaben sich eine neue Perspektive auf meinen eigenen Dialekt und ein anderer Umgang damit. Inzwischen schenke ich im Dialekt Gesprochenem oder dialektal gefärbten Einsprengseln, vor allem im Radio, meine volle Aufmerksamkeit und höre mit Freude

5 Tatsächlich erfolgten die Zwischenrufe im Rahmen der APL Practice (!) Week am 22. September 2021 im Studio des Angewandte Performance Labs beim Live-Panel „In_Visibilities in Recent Sound Interventions“ mit Ricarda Denzer, Kristina Pia Hofer und Huda Takriti im Rahmen der Jahrestagung „Ambivalente Un_Sichtbarkeiten“ der Österreichischen Gesellschaft für Geschlechterforschung (ÖGGF).

The collaboration between Fouad Asfour and Ricarda Denzer is also characterized by pleasurable communication and an interest in language and expression. In his audio paper *Dividuality Through Opacity*, Asfour mentions a bus ride they took together and an intense conversation, the content of which he can however no longer remember. He also refers to their shared, though very different, immigrant backgrounds, which made them both more aware of and attentive to what is said and how.[8] I find these moments in the audio papers, when personal stories and experiences are shared, touching and inspiring.

It was feeling so enthusiastic about the *Sounding Research Collective Listening Session #1* that sparked the idea for the audio panel at the 2022 ÖGGF conference at the University of Salzburg: *The Body of the Voice – Sounding Research Collective Listening Session #2*, conceived with Ricarda Denzer and Christina Goestl. In it, we gave a space and body to the interplay between hearing/listening and acoustic paradigms, as well as to the material, media-related, and performative properties of the voice. Our contributions were the only ones presented to the conference as audio papers.

My audio paper, entitled *some people think little girls should be seen and not heard*,[9] examined the constitution of the voice in pop music. The title quotes the iconic debut single "Oh Bondage Up Yours!" (1977), by British punk singer Poly Styrene (born in 1957 as Marianne Joan Elliot, died from breast cancer in 2011) and her band X-Ray Spex. When I was exchanging emails with music sociology professor Rosa Reitsamer about a request to moderate a panel discussion, she wrote: "I am still convinced that 'Oh Bondage Up Yours!' and the 1978 X-Ray Spex single 'Identity' revolutionized the punk world. Poly Styrene's voice was pioneering in many ways, including as an early embodiment of a queer-feminist voice in punk."

This example took me to the furious voices of the Riot Grrrls, with their rage, punk sound and shrieking denunciation of patriarchy that characterized the 1990s. Bands like Bikini Kill—with frontwoman Kathleen Hanna, along with Tobi Vail and Cathy Wilcox—or Sleater-Kinney were crucial to the sound of this movement, which came into being in Olympia, in the west of the United States, and soon spilled over into Europe. Both bands are renowned for their feminist, anti-capitalist lyrics and intense live performances. Both Kathleen Hanna and Corin Tucker strained their voices to the limit, screaming and accusing. Sleater-Kinney from Olympia (Carrie Brownstein, Corin Tucker, Janet Weiss) was named after a road between Portland and Seattle. The band initially existed from 1994 to 2006, reforming in 2014 after taking a break. Drawing on these examples, I could show what the voice reveals about emotional states.

8 See Fouad Asfour, 032ff. in this publication.

9 Tracklist for the audio paper: X-Ray Spex, "Oh Bondage Up Yours!" (1977); Bikini Kill, "Rebel Girl" (1993); Sleater-Kinney, "Call the Doctor" (1996); Le Tigre, "Deceptacon" (1999); MEN, "Who Am I To Feel so Free" (2011); Hercules and Love Affair, "Blind" (2008); Bronski Beat, "Smalltown Boy" (1984); Mavi Phoenix, "Tokyo Drift" (2021).

zu, wenn wie im Mai 2023 in dem auf Ö1 ausgestrahlten, von der Radiojournalistin Sarah Seekircher gestalteten Audiofeature mit dem Titel „Familiendrama in der Wildschönau – Die Geschichte der Ascher-Schwestern“ Dialekt aus der Region, in der ich aufgewachsen bin, gesprochen wird.[6]

To begin is impossible because
we were/are always in the middle of it.[7]

Freudvolle Kommunikation und die Beschäftigung mit Sprache und Ausdruck prägen auch die Zusammenarbeit zwischen Fouad Asfour und Ricarda Denzer. Asfour erwähnt in seinem Audio Paper „Dividuality Through Opacity“ eine gemeinsame Busfahrt und ein intensives Gespräch der beiden, an dessen Inhalt er sich allerdings nicht mehr erinnern kann. Er weist auch auf die, wenngleich höchst unterschiedlichen, Migrationserfahrungen der beiden hin, die zu einer Sensibilisierung bzw. Aufmerksamkeit dafür führten, was und wie gesprochen wird.[8] Es sind exakt diese Momente in den „Hörpapieren“, in denen persönliche Geschichten und Erfahrungen geteilt werden, die mich berühren und auch inspirieren.

Aus der Begeisterung, die mich bei der *Sounding Research Collective Listening Session #1* erfasste, entstand die Idee für das gemeinsam mit Ricarda Denzer und Christina Goestl konzipierte Audio Paper-Panel „Der Körper der Stimme – Sounding Research Listening Session #2“ bei der ÖGGF-Tagung 2022 an der Universität Salzburg. Dabei gaben wir dem Zusammenspiel der Spezifik des (Zu)Hörens und der Paradigmen des Akustischen sowie den materiellen, medialen und performativen Eigenschaften der Stimme einen Raum und Körper. Unsere Beiträge wurden als einzige auf der Tagung als Audio Papers präsentiert.

In meinem auf der Tagung präsentierten Audio Paper mit dem Titel *some people think little girls should be seen and not heard*[9] spürte ich der Verfasstheit der Stimme in der Popmusik nach. Der Titel zitierte die ikonische Debutsingle „Oh Bondage Up Yours!“ (1977) der britischen Punksängerin Poly Styrene (geboren 1957 als Marianne Joan Elliott, 2011 an Brustkrebs verstorben) und ihrer Band X-Ray Spex. In einer E-Mail-Korrespondenz mit der Professorin für Musiksoziologie Rosa Reitsamer anlässlich einer Anfrage für die Panelmoderation schrieb sie: „Ich bin bis heute davon überzeugt, dass ‚Oh Bondage Up Yours!‘ und die 1978 erschienene X-Ray Spex-Single ‚Identity‘ die Punkwelt revolutioniert haben. Die Stimme von Poly Styrene war in vielerlei Hinsicht bahnbrechend, u. a. für die Verkörperung einer frühen queer-feministischen Stimme im Punk.“

Ausgehend von diesem Beispiel, kam ich auf die wütende Verfasstheit der Stimmen von Riot Grrrls zu sprechen, deren Wut, Punksound und Schreigesang, mit denen sie das Patriarchat

6 https://oe1.orf.at/programm/20230513/719334/Familiendrama-in-der-Wildschoenau-Teil-I bzw. https://oe1.orf.at/programm/20230518/719591/Familiendrama-in-der-Wildschoenau-Teil-II (abgerufen am 4.7. 2023).

7 Fouad Asfour, Dividuality Through Opacity, Audio Paper: https://www.soundingresearch.net/audio-paper (abgerufen am 4.7. 2023).

8 Vgl. Fouad Asfour S. 033ff. in dieser Publikation.

9 Tracklist für das Audio Paper: X-Ray Spex, „Oh Bondage Up Yours!“, 1977; Bikini Kill, „Rebel Girl“, 1993; Sleater-Kinney, „Call the Doctor“, 1996; Le Tigre, „Deceptacon“, 1999; MEN, „Who Am I To Feel so Free“, 2011; Hercules and Love Affair, „Blind“, 2008; Bronski Beat, „Smalltown Boy“, 1984; Mavi Phoenix, „Tokyo Drift“, 2021.

After her time with Bikini Kill (until 1997), Kathleen Hanna founded the band Le Tigre in New York in 1998 with filmmaker Sadie Benning and journalist Johanna Fateman. Once Sadie Benning had left Le Tigre, the band was joined by transgender activist JD Samsonin, who later founded MEN with visual artists Every Ocean Hughes (previously Emily Roysdon), Ginger Brooks Takahashi, and others. One passage in the lyrics of the MEN anthem "Who am I to feel so free" proclaims: "Changed our names, used our hands. We found options that were better than a man. Radical surgery prosthetic sex. We built this world and we are asking your best. Group work and gay power: What's the path to choose now?" I used this example to examine what the voice says about the constitution and construction of gender, likewise considering Jimmy Somerville's falsetto singing in the coming-out song "Smalltown Boy" (1984), as well as the iconic disco hit "Bind" (2008), sung by Antony Hegarty (now Anohni) with Hercules & Love Affair, and the Auto-Tune effects in Mavi Phoenix's vocal tracks on the album *Marlon* (2022) in which he addresses his transidentity. With this underpinning, I raised the question, at the end of the audio paper, of how to move from an emotional constitution of the voice to raising the voice in the sense of (political) action.

The title "*I think about killing. I think about calling* / What it means, *to be touched by a question or issue or by a voice, by something spoken*" is made up of two quotes from *Sounding Research Listening Session #1*, one taken from Seth Weiner's audio paper and one excerpted from a statement by Ricarda Denzer during the panel discussion.

anklagten, die 1990er-Jahre prägten. Bands wie Bikini Kill mit Frontfrau Kathleen Hanna sowie den Mitgliedern Tobi Vail und Cathy Wilcox oder Sleater-Kinney waren maßgeblich für den Sound dieser Bewegung verantwortlich. Diese nahm in Olympia, einer Stadt im Westen der USA, ihren Ausgang und schwappte bald auf Europa über. Beide Bands sind für ihre feministischen und kapitalismuskritischen Texte sowie ihre intensiven Live-Auftritte bekannt. Sowohl Kathleen Hanna als auch Corin Tucker strapazierten ihre Stimmen bis zum Anschlag und schrien und klagten an. Sleater-Kinney (Carrie Brownstein, Corin Tucker, Janet Weiss) aus Olympia benannten sich nach einer Straße zwischen Portland und Seattle. Die Band existierte von 1994 bis 2006 und nach einer Pause wieder ab 2014. Entlang dieser Beispiele konnte ich demonstrieren, was die Stimme über die emotionale Verfassung aussagt.

Nach Bikini Kill (bis 1997) gründete Kathleen Hanna 1998 in New York gemeinsam mit Filmemacher*in Sadie Benning und Journalistin Johanna Fateman die Band Le Tigre. Nachdem Sadie Benning Le Tigre verlassen hatte, stieg Transgender-Aktivist*in JD Samsonin in die Band ein und gründete wiederum später MEN u. a. mit den bildenden Künstler*innen Every Ocean Hughes (früher Emily Roysdon) und Ginger Brooks Takahashi. In der Hymne „Who am I to feel so free“ von MEN lautet es im Text u. a.: „Changed our names, used our hands. We found options that were better than a man. Radical surgery prosthetic sex. We built this world and we are asking your best. Group work and gay power: What's the path to choose now?“ Mit diesem Beispiel sowie dem Falsettgesang von Jimmy Somerville in dem Coming-out-Song „Smalltown Boy“ (1984), dem von Antony Hegarty (heute Anohni) mit Hercules & Love Affair eingesungenen ikonischen Discohit „Blind“ (2008) und den Auto-Tune-Effekten bei den Gesangspuren von Mavi Phoenix auf dem Album *Marlon* (2022), auf dem er seine Transidentität verhandelt, thematisierte ich, was die Stimme über die Konstituierung und Konstruktion von Geschlecht aussagt – um am Schluss des Audio Papers die Frage zu stellen, wie wir von einer emotionalen Verfasstheit der Stimme zu einer Erhebung der Stimme im Sinn eines (politischen) Handelns kommen.

Der Titel „I think about killing. I think about calling. Was es heißt, berührt zu werden von einer Frage oder Thematik oder von einer Stimme, von etwas Gesprochenem.“ sind zwei Zitate aus der *Sounding Research, Listening Session #1*, dem Audiopaper von Seth Weiner und einer Aussage von Ricarda bei der Paneldiskussion.

Panel Discussion[1]

Ricarda Denzer in conversation with Fouad Asfour, Christina Goestl, Karen Werner, Seth Weiner (& Sadie Seagal), and Hui Ye, in the Auditorium of the University of Applied Arts Vienna, March 14, 2022

Sounding Research, Collective Listening Session #1

1 This happening concluded a year-long art-based research project by Ricarda Denzer as part of INTRA, a program of inter- and transdisciplinary projects in art and research. Realized with the support of Zentrum Fokus Forschung, University of Applied Arts Vienna, 2021/ 2022.

1 Diese Veranstaltung bildete den Abschluss eines einjährigen Forschungsprojekts von Ricarda Denzer im Rahmen von INTRA, dem Angewandte Programm für Inter- und transdisziplinäre Projekte in Kunst und Forschung, das 2021/2022 mit Unterstützung des Zentrums Fokus Forschung, an der Universität für angewandte Kunst Wien, durchgeführt wurde.

Podiumsdiskussion[1]

Ricarda Denzer im Gespräch mit Fouad Asfour, Christina Goestl, Karen Werner, Seth Weiner (& Sadie Seagal) und Hui Ye, Auditorium der Universität für angewandte Kunst Wien, 14. März 2022

Sounding Research, Collective Listening Session #1

2 Vgl. auch Sanne Groth Krogh, Kristine Samson, "Audio Papers – a manifesto," in Seismograf Peer, Sonderausgabe, Fluid Sounds, August 2016, https://seismograf.org/fokus/fluid-sounds/audio_paper_manifesto.

Ricarda Denzer

Mich interessiert künstlerische Forschung als akustischer Vorgang. Konkret handelt es sich um ein eigenes künstlerisches Format, das sich aus der Bewegung und der Interaktion ergibt, aus dem Austausch mit den unterschiedlichen Kunstdisziplinen, ihrer Verknüpfung, gegenseitiger Abgrenzung und Durchlässigkeit. Das performative Format des Audio Papers[2] spielt dabei eine zentrale Rolle.

Ich möchte mit einer Frage beginnen, die ich eigentlich erst am Ende der Diskussion stellen wollte: Was unterscheidet ein Hörspiel – das Audio Play – von einem Audio Paper?

Hui Ye

Als jemand, die ursprünglich aus der klassischen Musik kommt, löst das Wort „Audio Paper" Erinnerungen an die Materialität des Notenschreibens auf Notenpapier aus.

Jedes Element, das ich für mein Stück verwendet habe, war schon Teil meiner Forschung. Zum Beispiel das gesprochene

Ricarda Denzer

I'm interested in experiencing artistic research as a sonic act. In practice this is a distinct artistic format that arises from movement and interaction, from the exchange with, linking of, demarcation from, and permeability between various artistic disciplines. The performative format of the audio paper[2] is central here.

I'd like to start with a question I had originally intended to put at the end of this discussion: what is the difference between a Hörspiel (audio play) and an audio paper?

Hui Ye

As someone with a background in classical music, the word "audio paper" takes me back to the materiality of writing notes on music paper.

Every component I used for this sound piece was already part of my research. For example this section of the speech by Jane Roberts, who is an American author and spiritual medium. She somehow used her voice to channel this energy personality called Seth, who speaks through her voice: "Now, I am speaking through the auspices of a woman, of whom might have become quite fond." This is one of the essential parts of my research. The vocal identity, even in the spiritual practice of this kind of voice-channeling. Who is the authority of the voice? If I use this digital voice-cloning technique and resynthesize it, is this the computer speaking now or is the voice still from Jane Roberts or Seth? It's about how we transmit this multilayered vocal identity in digital time. I love to just montage the material I get through the research process.

Seth Weiner

For me it basically started with this piece of music I'd been working on, which was really sculptural and got a bit more subdued in this version. What happened was that I wrote the abstract and it turned into a narrative meditation on a sonic landscape in Semmering. Then I took that and asked my son Manès to read it. I did one take with him, and that's what you heard. I thought at least I'll try to have these two layers of time interact with one another. They live in the same space, they occupy similar registers, and they have moments where they infect one another. But sometimes they just ignore each other. I would say that in a Hörspiel sound becomes a sort of narrative-like, propulsion. I didn't really illustrate things though. In my case it was a little more systematic. The content itself isn't systematic though; it comes and goes.

Christina Goestl

I have an obsession with flying fish and diving birds, and for many years I've had an obsession with underwater sound. For the past two years I've been working scientifically, and I wrote an

2 See also Sanne Groth Krogh, Kristine Samson, "Audio Papers – a manifesto," in Seismograf Peer, special issue, Fluid Sounds (August 2016), https://seismograf.org/fokus/fluid-sounds/audio_paper_manifesto

Fragment von Jane Roberts, einer amerikanischen Autorin, die ein spirituelles Medium ist. Sie benutzte ihre Stimme als Channeling für diese Energie, eine Persönlichkeit namens Seth, die durch ihre Stimme spricht: „Jetzt spreche ich unter dem Schutz einer Frau, die ich liebgewonnen habe.“ Damit sind wir bei einem wesentlichen Element meiner Forschung. Die vokale Identität, selbst dann, wenn es sich um diese Art von spirituellem Channeling der Stimme handelt. Wer hat die Macht über die Stimme? Wenn ich die Stimmen digital klone und sie anschließend neu synthetisiere – spricht dann der Computer oder höre ich immer noch die Stimme von Jane Roberts bzw. Seth? Die Frage lautet, wie wir diese vielschichtige stimmliche Identität im digitalen Zeitalter übertragen. Mir macht es Spaß, das im Forschungsprozess gewonnene Material durch Montage zusammenzusetzen.

Seth Weiner

Bei mir hat es mit einem Musikstück begonnen, einer Arbeit, die sehr plastisch war und in dieser Version etwas verhaltener ausgefallen ist. Das kam so: Ich schrieb ein Abstract, das sich in eine erzählerische Meditation über eine Klanglandschaft am Semmering verwandelte. Dann bat ich meinen Sohn Manés, den Text vorzulesen. Ich habe eine Aufzeichnung mit ihm gemacht, und die habt ihr gehört. Ich dachte, ich will es wenigstens versuchen, diese beiden Zeitebenen aufeinander einwirken zu lassen. Sie wohnen am selben Ort, sie besetzen ähnliche Register und sie haben Momente, in denen sie sich gegenseitig inspirieren. Manchmal ignorieren sie sich aber auch. Ich würde sagen, in einem Hörspiel wird Klang zu einer Art Schubkraft, die etwas Erzählerisches hat. Illustriert habe ich dabei eigentlich nichts. In meinem Fall ist es systematischer abgelaufen. Obwohl, der Inhalt an sich ist nicht systematisch; er kommt und geht.

Christina Goestl

Eine meiner großen Leidenschaften sind fliegende Fische und tauchende Vögel, außerdem beschäftige ich mich seit vielen Jahren intensiv mit Unterwasserklängen. In den letzten zwei Jahren habe ich wissenschaftlich gearbeitet und einen Aufsatz geschrieben, der dieses Jahr im von Emma Rees herausgegebenen *The Routledge Companion to Gender, Sexuality and Culture* erscheint. Dieses hardcore-wissenschaftliche Arbeiten hat Spaß gemacht und war eine Herausforderung, aber ich bin Künstlerin. Die wissenschaftliche Arbeit unterliegt ganz bestimmten Regeln. Das heißt, man kann nicht die superverspielte Künstlerin sein, die ich sonst bin. Ich musste mich also fragen, was ich da tue. Als Erstes las ich Bücher über das Geschichtenerzählen. Joanna Frueh hat viel dazu geschrieben, aber auch Amelia Jones und Peggy Phelan; sie sprechen von der Theorie des Geschichtenerzählens oder vom poetischen Geschichtenerzählen. Das hat mich total fasziniert, weil es die Theorie und das Persönliche mit dem Politischen und dem

essay that's going to be published this year in *The Routledge Companion to Gender, Sexuality and Culture*, edited by Emma Rees, but I'm an artist and it's been fun and challenging to do hardcore scientific work. Scientific work has a whole set of rules, and they're pretty strict. So you can't be the super-playful artist, as I am usually. This made me think about what I'm doing here. I started reading about storytelling. There is Joanna Frueh, who wrote a lot about it, and also Amelia Jones and Peggy Phelan, and they call it storytelling theory or poetic storytelling theory. I was totally fascinated by that because it intertwines theory and the personal and the political and the poetic. You signal-point to things that fascinate you, and you don't elaborate every detail but you make a story out of it. So for me, at the moment, an audio paper is a story based on hardcore scientific facts.

Fouad Asfour

I've experimented with performative talks and lecture presentations before, and in live events different elements are at play. Watching the sound waves while recording the audio introduced unexpected moments of playfulness. An otherworldly experience of an infinite loop of simultaneously speaking while listening to myself. Watching the shifting waveform of a sound recording is quite different from experiencing the response of an audience. For me, automatic writing, where I write and rewrite and rewrite, is about experiencing synchronicities. Rather different from the relentless registration of sound as displayed in the timeline running across the screen. You can't just go back and scribble over it.

Writing on paper feels like a re-coding of language, while a voice recording is different, but how? I guess one aspect is that both writing and audio papers will be edited before publishing, such as this conversation, for example. So, the word "play" in "Hörspiel" activates a quite literal sense what a "paper" can be or do. For me it's about form, really. From the beginning the conversations with Ricarda revolved around these questions. How do you notate language? And is writing the notation of sound or is it the voice of what you're thinking in writing? I'm still very excited by the play between these two elements, which I think introduce new performative dimensions in audio papers.

Karen Werner

When I hear the term "audio paper" I have this understanding that it comes from the field of artistic research with one foot in the academy and one foot in the world of art, and there's a funding infrastructure connected to the emergence of this discipline of artistic research, which is the context for sounding research, of course. I feel like I want to jam research and jam what we think knowledge is and what the purpose of research is. When I hear "audio paper" I feel that it might still want to be connected

Poetischen verknüpft. Dabei steuert man Dinge an, die einen faszinieren, arbeitet aber nicht jedes Detail heraus, sondern macht eine Erzählung daraus. Insofern ist ein Audio Paper im Moment für mich eine Geschichte, die sich auf hardcore-wissenschaftliche Fakten stützt.

Fouad Asfour

Ich experimentiere schon länger mit performativen Vorträgen und Vorlesungen, doch bei Live-Events kommen weitere Elemente hinzu. Als ich während der Audio-Aufnahme die Klangwellen beobachtete, taten sich unerwartete Momente für Verspieltheit auf – eine jenseitige Erfahrung eines Endlosloops, in dem ich spreche und mir gleichzeitig selbst zuhöre. Der veränderlichen Wellenform eines Klangs zuzuschauen, ist etwas anderes, als der Resonanz eines Publikums zu lauschen. Mir geht es beim automatischen Schreiben, bei dem ich schreibe und umschreibe und wieder neu schreibe, um die Erfahrung von Gleichzeitigkeiten. Das unterscheidet sich ziemlich vom unablässigen Registrieren von Klängen, die auf der Timeline über den Bildschirm laufen. Man kann nicht einfach zurückgehen und etwas darüber kritzeln.

Auf Papier schreiben ist so, als würde man Sprache neu codieren, wohingegen eine Stimme aufzeichnen etwas anderes ist. Aber inwiefern? Ich vermute, ein Aspekt ist der, dass Geschriebenes und Audio Papers vor der Veröffentlichung lektoriert werden – so wie dieses Gespräch zum Beispiel. Insofern aktiviert das Wort „Spiel“ in Hörspiel einen buchstäblichen Sinn dafür, was ein „Paper“ sein oder tun kann. Mir geht es dabei um die Form. Die Gespräche mit Ricarda haben sich von Anfang an um diese Fragen gedreht. Wie notiert man Sprache? Und ist Schreiben die Notierung von Klang oder ist es – in schriftlicher Form – die Stimme dessen, was man denkt? Ich finde das Spiel zwischen diesen beiden Elementen immer noch sehr spannend, da sie dem Audio Paper meiner Meinung nach neue performative Dimensionen verleihen.

Karen Werner

Wenn ich „Audio Paper“ höre, verstehe ich den Begriff so, dass er zwar aus der künstlerischen Forschung kommt, allerdings mit einem Fuß in der akademischen Welt steht und mit dem anderen in der Welt der Kunst, und dass mit dem Aufkommen dieser künstlerischen Forschungsdisziplin, die natürlich der Kontext für Sounding Research ist, eine Förderinfrastruktur einhergeht. Ich möchte die Forschung jammen, und das, was wir für Wissen halten und was die Forschung bezweckt. Wenn ich „Audio Paper“ höre, denke ich, dass ich vielleicht doch noch mit der akademischen Welt verbunden sein möchte. Ich wollte mein Stück so performativ oder so erzählerisch wie möglich gestalten, um eine Politik des Wissens zu vermitteln. Meiner Meinung nach ist eine Erzählung eine fundierte Form von Wissen. Vielleicht ist sie sogar eine

to the academy in some way. My aim was to make my piece as performative or storytelling-based as possible in order to convey a politics of knowledge. I think story is a profound form of knowledge. It's maybe an indigenous form of knowledge. So there's a politics in how I engage with this concept of an audio paper and academia generally, and putting forward the profound power of art as a way of being and knowing.

One thing that was interesting to me is the relationship between the written word and the audio, the spoken word. It's interesting how we all worked with that. In a way, I think all of our pieces have an element of writing in them, and yet here we are doing audio, which is more the medium of an oral tradition.

Seth Weiner

We've all decided that the audio paper is a sort of sonic piece of writing. I think with the voice and with text you have these references that are much clearer. In my case I thought I'd better do something conceptual that we can talk about and was feeling a little bit of pressure in this academic context. Once Ricarda said we were in the auditorium, I realized that we're in a black-box theater typology. Basically, everyone looks forward, we're on stage, there's a screen behind us. It's more of a visual experience we're being asked to participate in.

In my case using the visual was a way to focus the listening or maybe a way of carving paths through it. I'd call it a sculptural, sonic element or a body that the voice leads you through, around, and vice versa.

Hui Ye

First I also thought I'd make a purely sonic piece. But as I started with this voice-cloning program, I realized it wasn't really possible to do without a text because people want to understand the content. But in your case I really enjoyed it. Especially the design of these different fonts, which signalize your voice and your son's voice.

Fouad Asfour

When I see scribbles on a page, that's a story already. I'm thinking of what Christina said about fables. The American writer Kate Bernheimer says that four elements of traditional fairy tales or fables are flatness, abstraction, intuitive logic, and normalized magic.

And if you think about it, with language you can perform each of those through speaking. How can storytelling be carried by voice? And continued in writing? A slip of the tongue can turn into a story, so can any form of stumble or of stutter and accent, or what is perceived as "grammatical errors" by multilingual speakers, subconsciously subvert and expand languages. For me, reading a text is having the writer's voice in my head. How do you activate these levels in your conceptual practice?

indigene Form von Wissen. Es hat also eine politische Dimension, wie ich mich auf das Konzept Audio Paper und die akademische Welt generell einlasse und die Kraft der Kunst als eine Möglichkeit des Seins und Wissens geltend mache.

Interessant fand ich das Verhältnis zwischen dem geschriebenen und dem gesprochenen Wort, dem Audio. Es ist interessant, wie wir alle damit gearbeitet haben. In gewisser Weise ist in allen unseren Arbeiten ein Element des Schriftlichen enthalten, und dennoch machen wir hier Audio, was eher dem Medium der mündlichen Überlieferung angehört.

Seth Weiner

Wir sind alle zu dem Schluss gelangt, dass das Audio Paper eine Art akustisches Schriftstück ist. Ich finde, mit Stimme und Text hat man viel eindeutigere Referenzpunkte. Ich dachte, ich mache lieber etwas Konzeptuelles, über das wir reden können, außerdem fühlte ich mich in diesem akademischen Kontext auch ein wenig unter Druck. Als Ricarda sagte, wir würden im Auditorium sein, war klar, dass wir uns in einer Blackbox-Typologie wie im Theater befinden würden. Jeder von uns blickt nach vorne, wir sitzen auf der Bühne, hinter uns ist ein Bildschirm. Das, woran teilzunehmen wir gebeten wurden, würde ich eher als visuelle Erfahrung bezeichnen.

Insofern war der Einsatz des Visuellen für mich eine Möglichkeit, das Zuhören zu fokussieren bzw. einen Weg vorzugeben. Ich würde es ein plastisches, klangliches Element nennen, oder einen Körper, durch den die Stimme hindurch und um ihn herumführt, und umgekehrt.

Hui Ye

Zuerst dachte ich auch an ein rein akustisches Stück. Aber als ich mit dem Voice-Cloning-Programm anfing, wurde mir klar, ganz ohne Text lässt sich das nicht machen, denn das Publikum möchte den Inhalt ja verstehen. Aber in deiner Arbeit habe ich es wirklich genossen. Vor allem das Design dieser verschiedenen Fonts, die jeweils deine Stimme und die deines Sohns signalisieren.

Fouad Asfour

Wenn ich auf einer Seite Kritzeleien sehe, ist das bereits eine Geschichte. Und um Christinas Überlegungen weiterzuführen: Die amerikanische Autorin Kate Bernheimer sagt, dass die vier Grundelemente traditioneller Märchen und Fabeln Flachheit, Abstraktion, intuitive Logik und normalisierte Magie sind.

Wenn man darüber nachdenkt, kann man jedes dieser Elemente über das Sprechen performen. Wie wird das Erzählen einer Geschichte von der Stimme getragen? Und wie lässt es sich schriftlich fortsetzen? Ein Versprecher kann zu einer Geschichte werden, ebenso jede Art von Stolpern oder Stottern und von Akzent, oder das, was von Mehrsprachigen als „grammatikalisch falsch“ wahrgenommen wird und Sprache unbewusst untergräbt

Christina Goestl

We've all used writing or text as a medium, but I think there's also another layer. It's the acoustic layer, which has an element of the live event. My piece is a recording, but I envisioned you, the place, the space, the effect of the hall in the auditorium.

And this is something that starts very early, in the writing. I always have you in mind in the writing, in the recording. I'm very much a live person, but it's a luxury to do something in a recording for a change. You don't have all that adrenaline and cold sweat before you go up to the podium, but I think that's an important part of it. An audio paper is a live event. This was very important to me.

Seth Weiner

As you were talking about Ricarda's piece, I thought about this really weird effect of listening to her recorded voice and watching her while she's not talking but instead speaking through this instrument. It seemed like a very intentional artistic move. Actually this kind of acoustic rippling of the accordion even changed the way I saw the space. Ricarda, I know you've used it before in some iteration, and that each time it becomes a different configuration, which I think is also a big part of how you work sculpturally. You take components and show them one way, and then they start being swallowed up and cannibalized and used in different forms with other things. I thought it was really nice in terms of the voice, of the embodiment of the voice, and the question of it being recorded and live. Having been recorded live, who's speaking through it?

Hui Ye

I often feel I have a kind of language disorder because I live constantly with German and English. Neither of them are my mother tongue, and I don't really have the opportunity to use Mandarin or Cantonese. Somehow I switch in between all these languages at the same time, which is pretty weird in my brain.

Fouad Asfour

Also in your paper, Ricarda, you mention Barthes saying that we have to change our listening so as to change language dramatically. When we listen to language we realize that we never remain in just "one" language. At the same time, we never work "across" languages, but inside of the struggle of hearing and listening. Sounding each other out across different forms, bodies, and practices, we use language, in the words of Ofelia García, "as a unitary meaning making system of the speaker." Like Ricarda says, you start writing in dialect to make yourself at home. You start with yourself to communicate across media and bodies. When Karen speaks about "jamming" research, I hear Barthes writing on the grain of the voice, asking how we can move outside the perceived ideas of language and towards sounding out our

und erweitert. Wenn ich einen Text lese, habe ich die Stimme der Autorin im Kopf. Wie aktivierst du diese Ebenen in deiner konzeptuellen Arbeit?

Christina Goestl

Wir haben alle als Medium das Schreiben oder einen Text eingesetzt, es gibt aber auch noch eine andere Ebene. Das ist die akustische Ebene, in der ein Element des Live-Events enthalten ist. Meine Arbeit ist eine Aufzeichnung, aber vor Augen hatte ich euch, den Ort, den Raum, die Wirkung des Halls im Auditorium.

Das ist etwas, das beim Schreiben sehr früh einsetzt. Beim Schreiben und Aufzeichnen denke ich immer an euch. Der Live-Auftritt entspricht mir sehr, aber zur Abwechslung etwas im Rahmen einer Aufzeichnung zu tun, ist Luxus. Man erspart sich das Adrenalin und das Lampenfieber, bevor man aufs Podium geht, wobei ich aber finde, dass das ein wichtiger Teil davon ist. Ein Audio Paper ist ein Live-Event. Für mich war das sehr wichtig.

Seth Weiner

Als von Ricardas Stück die Rede war, dachte ich an die sonderbare Wirkung, die entsteht, wenn man ihrer aufgezeichneten Stimme zuhört und sie dabei beobachtet, wie sie nichts sagt und stattdessen durch dieses Instrument spricht. Das hinterließ den Eindruck einer durchaus beabsichtigten künstlerischen Entscheidung. Diese akustische Verzerrung des Akkordeons hat meine Wahrnehmung des Raums tatsächlich verändert. Ricarda, ich weiß, dass du das woanders auch schon gemacht hast und dass die Konfiguration jedes Mal eine andere war, was vermutlich auch eine wichtige Rolle dabei spielt, wie du plastisch arbeitest. Du nimmst Komponenten her und zeigst sie auf eine Weise, und dann werden sie verschluckt und kannibalisiert und in anderer Form mit anderen Dingen verwendet. Ich fand das sehr schön, und zwar in Bezug auf die Stimme, die Verkörperung der Stimme und darauf, dass es live ist und aufgezeichnet wird. Wer ist bei dieser Live-Aufnahme zu hören?

Hui Ye

Ich habe oft das Gefühl, unter einer Art von Sprachstörung zu leiden, weil ich ständig im Deutschen und Englischen lebe. Keine der beiden Sprachen ist meine Muttersprache, und die Möglichkeit, Mandarin oder Kantonesisch sprechen zu können, ergibt sich so gut wie nie. Ich wechsle zwischen all diesen Sprachen hin und her, und zwar gleichzeitig, was sich in meinem Gehirn ziemlich schräg anfühlt.

Fouad Asfour

Ricarda, in deinem Audio Paper erwähnst du Roland Barthes, der sagt, dass wir anders zuhören müssen, um Sprache auf dramatische Weise zu ändern. Wenn wir jemanden sprechen hören, merken wir auch, dass wir nie in nur „einer“ Sprache bleiben. Zugleich arbeiten wir nie „sprachübergreifend“, sondern strengen

"unitary repertoires." At times it can also be about enjoying the liminalities of what it means to "understand" and to expand and oscillate around what we hear others say.

Ricarda Denzer

I also always want to ask people: when you drift away to somewhere else, where are you then? I have this idea that my thinking has a voice and this voice has a body. So my thinking has a body, which is moving in space. The idea of mind wandering, this other space which is also present.

Seth Weiner

The difference between recording voice versus writing? I'd say that writing in my practice is a less linear process than making sound. With sound I'm often stuck making decisions about what happens before and after. It's harder for me to go back into. Once it happens, it happens. It's very difficult to capture the same energy in the editing process or find and extend its form, enter back into its time. Whereas with text my thinking is less linear, funnily enough.

Karen Werner

I collaborated on a piece with Deanna Shoemaker called *What is collaboration*? And I ended up being the one who knew the sound editing software, and I feel like it had one level less collaboration than a written text would have had. Also, the language of the audio software has a big impact, given that one edits on a linear timeline. Whereas writing, I agree, allows our imagination to jump a bit more.

Christina Goestl

I'm very much a fan of getting together and talking live. It's about vibrations. Sound and voice—the most immediate feeling of vibration you can get is in a live moment. We function very much like fish. We have these mechanoreceptors that translate the vibrations to our nervous system, to our brain, and from the brain to the nervous system. It's the same with fish and humans and basically all living beings. It's most immediate in a live situation, and the pandemic has taught us that it's quite devastating not to get together. So what you said about drifting away—I have that a lot too. I don't get what's being talked about. I don't understand. But I'm inspired and I get all these wonderful feelings and I feel warm and alive and pulsating and I want to run home and write a book—you know, all these beautiful things. Also I really love to read aloud. In school I always wanted to read aloud, but I never get what I'm reading. I read perfectly, line by line by line by line by line. And everybody gets it and I don't. So I'm just a machine that translates the vibration, transmits it into the space.

Karen Werner

You spoke a bit about internalizing the room we're making

uns an, zu hören und zuzuhören. Wenn wir uns im Austausch über unterschiedliche Formen, Körper und Praktiken hinweg gegenseitig zuhören, setzen wir Sprache in den Worten von Ofelia García „als ein einheitliches sinngebendes System des Sprechers“ ein. Wie Ricarda sagt, beginnt man im Dialekt zu schreiben, um sich zu Hause zu fühlen. Man beginnt bei sich selbst, um medien- und körperübergreifend zu kommunizieren. Wenn Karen vom „Jammen“ der Forschung spricht, klingt bei mir Barthes' Text über die Körnung der Stimme an und die Frage, wie wir uns aus der üblichen Vorstellung von Sprache wegbewegen und unsere „gesamten sprachlichen Repertoires“ sondieren können. Manchmal kann es auch darum gehen, die Grenzzustände dessen zu genießen, was es heißt, „zu verstehen“, und das, was wir andere sagen hören, zu erweitern und in einer Art Pendelbewegung darum herum zu oszillieren.

Ricarda Denzer

Ich möchte andere auch immer fragen: Wenn du in Gedanken wegdriftest, wo bist du dann? Ich habe diese Vorstellung, dass mein Denken eine Stimme hat und diese Stimme einen Körper. Mein Denken hat also einen Körper, der sich durch den Raum bewegt. Dazu gehört auch die Vorstellung vom Wandern der Gedanken, und diesem anderen, dadurch präsenten Raum.

Seth Weiner

Was unterscheidet die Stimmaufzeichnung vom Schreiben? Ich würde sagen, bei mir ist das Schreiben ein weniger linearer Prozess als die Arbeit mit Sound. Beim Sound stecke ich oft fest, weil ich mich entscheiden muss, was vorher war und was danach kommt. Es fällt mir schwerer, noch einmal zurückzugehen. Was geschieht, geschieht. Beim Editing noch einmal dieselbe Energie aufzubringen oder ihre Form zu finden und zu erweitern, in ihre Zeit zurückzukehren, ist schwer. Beim Text hingegen denke ich witzigerweise weniger linear.

Karen Werner

Ich habe zusammen mit Deanna Shoemaker an einem Stück gearbeitet, das *What is Collaboration?* heißt. Am Ende war ich diejenige, die sich mit der Sound-Editing-Software auskannte, und für mich ist das so, als wäre, anders als beim Schreiben, eine Ebene in der Zusammenarbeit verloren gegangen. Außerdem hat die Sprache der Audio-Software einen großen Einfluss, da man auf einer linearen Timeline editiert. Das Schreiben, da stimme ich zu, erlaubt unserer Fantasie, sprunghafter zu sein.

Christina Goestl

Ich bin ein großer Fan von Zusammenkünften und Live-Gesprächen. Es geht um Schwingungen. Sound und Stimme – live spürt man die Schwingungen am unmittelbarsten. Wir funktionieren sehr ähnlich wie Fische. Wir haben diese Mechanorezeptoren, die die Schwingungen in unser Nervensystem, an unser Gehirn, und von unserem Gehirn in unser Nervensystem übertragen. Das ist bei

it for. Whom are we addressing? Who is our internalized, imagined audience?

Seth Weiner

We're all working in a format that is sort of bodily passive. It seems like everyone's working with a quality of voice that acts as a form of touch. Who is it for? I would say it doesn't really matter. Anyone who is on the other end of the speaker. My hope would be that it's fairly accessible though, and that sound can be a form of touch, a way of reaching out. If I make something that's more inert or sculptural, it's difficult. You can touch it, but it doesn't give back or respond to the physical conversation so directly.

Ricarda Denzer

I would even close this round by saying that we do our work for everybody who feels touched by it.

Fischen und Menschen so und im Grunde bei allen Lebewesen. Am unmittelbarsten ist es in einer Live-Situation, wobei uns die Pandemie gezeigt hat, wie entsetzlich es ist, wenn wir uns nicht mehr treffen können. Das, was du über das Wegdriften gesagt hast – das passiert mir auch oft. Ich verstehe nicht, wovon die Rede ist. Aber ich fühle mich inspiriert und werde in diese wunderbaren Gefühle versetzt und fühle mich warm und lebendig und pulsierend und will nach Hause rennen und ein Buch schreiben – ihr wisst schon, all das Schöne. Ich lese auch sehr gerne laut. In der Schule wollte ich immer laut vorlesen, verstand aber nie, was ich las. Ich lese ganz richtig, Zeile für Zeile für Zeile. Alle begreifen es, nur ich nicht. Ich bin also eine Maschine, die die Schwingung übersetzt, sie in den Raum überträgt.

Karen Werner

Du hast über die Verinnerlichung des Raums gesprochen, für den wir das alles machen. Wen sprechen wir an? Wer ist unser verinnerlichtes, imaginäres Publikum?

Seth Weiner

Alle von uns arbeiten in einem Format, das körperlich eher passiv ist. Es scheint, als würden wir alle mit einem Merkmal von Stimme arbeiten, das wie eine Berührung wirkt. An wen richtet sie sich? Ich würde sagen, das spielt eigentlich keine Rolle. An jeden und jede, die am anderen Ende zuhören. Ich hoffe nur, dass das, was wir machen, einigermaßen zugänglich ist und dass Sound eine Form von Berührung sein kann, eine Annäherung. Schwierig ist es, wenn ich etwas mache, das behäbiger oder plastischer ist. Man kann es berühren, aber da kommt nichts zurück, oder es reagiert nicht so unmittelbar auf das physische Gespräch.

Ricarda Denzer

Ich würde diese Runde damit abschließen, dass wir unsere Arbeit für alle machen, die sich davon berührt fühlen.

Brandon LaBelle

Listening, Thinking, Doing

Brandon LaBelle

Hören, Denken, Tun

Die Arbeit von Ricarda Denzer steht in Bezug zum Begriff „akustische Öffentlichkeit" („sonic publicness"), der auch Teil meiner Forschungsarbeit ist. Denzer arbeitet zwar meistens mit einem breiten Spektrum an Medien, doch oft kreisen ihre Arbeiten um das Thema Stimme. Für Denzer spielt vor allem die um uns herum gesprochene oder in uns sprechende Stimme eine zentrale Rolle; sie beschäftigt sich aber auch damit, wie sich die Stimme uns mitunter entzieht – oder anders gesagt, wie die Stimme nicht nur als Kommunikationsmittel dient, sondern auch ein Moment der Ablenkung und Verdrängung darstellt. Die Flüchtigkeit bzw. „Nichtverfügbarkeit" der Stimme wird dabei zum Ausgangspunkt und hier insbesondere die Frage, welche Anspannung der Körper erfährt, wenn er aus sich herauszutreten und an gesellschaftlichen Strömen teilhaben versucht. Insofern wird die Stimme hier als Material verstanden, eingespannt zwischen Denken und Sprechen, Dialog und Handeln; sie ist weniger ein kommunikatives Ereignis als vielmehr ein ständiger Aushandlungsprozess. Die Stimme, nach Denzers Verständnis, überwältigt.

Als Teil ihrer Arbeit macht sie sich obsessiv Notizen, die sie „Aufzeichnungen" nennt. Es handelt sich dabei um unterschiedliche Formen von Notizen, mit denen sie die Gespräche in ihrer Umgebung und parallel dazu ihre persönlichen Gedanken, Überlegungen und Assoziationen festhält. Die Aufzeichnungen bilden so eine bestimmte Situation ab: Indem sie nicht nur die Stimmen festhalten, die direkt mit ihr sprechen, sondern auch solche, die plötzlich aus dem Nichts auftauchen und ihre Aufmerksamkeit auf sich ziehen, oder solche, die in Form von Ereignissen und Eindrücken in ihre Gedanken einsickern, verweisen sie auf die Fluktuationen, Auslassungen, Sprünge und Intensitäten des Denkens und des Hörens (ein „Denken-Hören"). Sie markieren den

The notion of sonic publicness that I'm exploring finds a point of reference in the work of artist Ricarda Denzer. While mostly using a diversity of media, Denzer's practice often circles in and around the question of the voice. In particular, the voice that speaks around us, or within us, is a focal point for Denzer; yet she is also concerned with how the voice may elude us—voice, in other words, is defined not only as a communicative operation, but also as an event of distraction and displacement. The elusiveness or "unavailability" of the voice becomes a starting point, and in particular, how this comes to tense the body as it tries to show itself, as it attempts to participate within the flows of sociality. The voice, in this regard, is understood as a material stretched between thinking and speaking, conversing and acting; It is less a communicative event, and more a process of negotiation. For Denzer, the voice overwhelms.

As part of her work, Denzer obsessively produces what she refers to as "notations" (Aufzeichnungen). These are forms of note-taking that capture surrounding conversations, along with her personal thoughts, reflections, and references. The notations therefore map a given situation: tuning into not only the voices that speak to her directly, but also those that may suddenly appear, and that pull her attention, or that filter into her thoughts as so many events or impressions, the notations point toward the fluctuations, omissions, lapses, and intensities of thinking and of listening (a thinking-listening); they notate the meeting point between Denzer as an individual and the public environment around her—they are composites or *palimpsests* that capture the passing of voices as they move through her listening (and which capture her).

> The notations have to do with a type of documentary practice. The transfer of thoughts, ideas, questions, but mainly conversations, both held and found; interviews; texts; themes, including scribbles and doodles, accompany my audio-visual working process, which doesn't follow a script. The [notations] are, in a way, also a type of visualization or textualization of spoken language and show the chronology of a process and how we arrive at our ideas.[1]

These notations appear as colored or filled-in squares on graph paper, surrounded by words, captured phrases, references; a composite of what someone may be saying and the passing of time fills the pages. She may be speaking to someone or listening to others; there is a sort of compressed form of attention—Denzer concentrates and grows distracted at the same moment; it is an oscillation of focus, one that tunes us to the dynamic ways in which public life moves.

1 Denzer, R., Ricarda Denzer: *Perplexities* (Berlin: Revolver Publishing 2013), 187.

Berührungspunkt zwischen Denzer, dem Individuum, und der sie umgebenden Öffentlichkeit – sie sind Komposita oder *Palimpseste*, die die vorüberziehenden Stimmen einfangen, während sie durch ihr Gehör hindurchgehen (und von denen sie fasziniert ist).

> Die Aufzeichnungen sind eine Art von dokumentarischer Praxis, ein Transfer von Gedanken, Ideen, Fragen, aber vor allem von Gesprächen, eigenen wie gefundenen; Texte; Themen, einschließlich Kritzeleien, sind Teil meines audiovisuellen Arbeitsprozesses, der keinem Skript folgt. In gewisser Weise stellen sie [die Aufzeichnungen] auch eine Art von Visualisierung oder Textualisierung gesprochener Sprache dar und bilden die Chronologie eines Prozesses ab sowie die Art und Weise, wie wir zu unseren Ideen gelangen.[1]

Diese Aufzeichnungen enthalten bunte oder schwarz ausgefüllte Kästchen auf kariertem Papier, umgeben von Wörtern, aufgeschnappten Sätzen und Querverweisen. Die Seiten sind gefüllt mit Komposita aus dem, was jemand gerade sagt, und dem bloßen Vergehen der Zeit. Denzer kann währenddessen mit jemandem sprechen oder anderen zuhören; dabei herrscht eine komprimierte Form von Aufmerksamkeit – sie konzentriert sich und wird im selben Moment abgelenkt. Die Konzentration oszilliert gewissermaßen und stimmt uns so auf die Dynamik des öffentlichen Lebens ein.

Mich interessiert an dieser Praxis, wie Denzer es schafft, uns auf eine Eigenschaft von Öffentlichkeit hinzuweisen, die von etwas Unerwartetem geprägt ist, nämlich dem, was man zufällig aufschnappt. Denzer dazu: „In dem Moment, in dem ich etwas aufzeichne, bin ich mir dessen eigentlich gar nicht so bewusst. Ist es ein schönes Wort oder hat es eine besondere Bedeutung?[2] Die Aufzeichnungen stellen eine extreme suggestive „Visualisierung/Textualisierung" dar, nämlich inwiefern Subjektivität radikal von den Stimmen, die den Körper umgeben und zugleich in ihn eindringen, beeinflusst ist. Als akustische Landkarte fangen die Aufzeichnungen eine Vielheit ein, die in jedem Moment immer schon gegeben ist. In dieser Hinsicht vertieft das Hören nicht nur jede Form von Beziehung – als unmittelbare Begegnung –, sondern erweitert sie innerhalb eines Horizonts aus Immersion und Fragmentierung. Jeder öffentliche Dialog sollte daher stets so verstanden werden, als werde er von der Präsenz eines „da drüben" konterkariert und überschattet – der schieren Intensität akustischer Räumlichkeit.

Ebendiese Vielheit interessiert mich, und ich hebe sie deshalb hervor, weil sich damit auch ein Verständnis von globalen Beziehungen entwickeln lässt, das entscheidend von einem „da drüben" bzw. zufällig Mitgehörtem durchdrungen ist. Kann akustische Räumlichkeit als die Produktion einer solchen Vielheit – ein Raum

1 Denzer, R., Ricarda Denzer: *Perplexities*, Berlin: Revolver Publishing 2013, S. 187.
2 Ebd.

What interests me in this practice is how Denzer points us toward a condition of publicness, one immediately marked by something unexpected, that is, the overheard. "In the very moment when I note something down," Denzer says, "I'm not actually entirely aware of it. Is it a nice word or does it have a particular meaning?"[2] Denzer's notations produce an extremely suggestive "visualization/textualization" of how subjectivity is radically inflected by the voices that surround, and that equally move into the body; a type of sonic map, the notations capture a multiplicity always already embedded within the single moment. Listening, in this way, not only deepens relations, as proximate meeting, but also broadens them as a horizon of expanded immersion and fragmentation. The public expression of open dialogue thus must be countered or shadowed by the presence of the *over-there*—the sheer intensity of an acoustic spatiality.

It is precisely this multiplicity that interests me, and which I highlight so as to draw out an understanding of global relations as one fully flushed by the over-there and the overheard. Might acoustic spatiality, as that production of a more than one—a spatiality held between manifestation and evocation, of the near and the far—offer a path toward new public configurations? To forge a sense of "community" within the radically mobile, and ever departing, life of global relations? Can we follow sonority as the primary resonance that sets me apart, while always already weaving me into greater relations? The production of an event of radical sharing?

I want to turn to the work of Édouard Glissant, and his notion of a "poetics of relation," which may enable a fuller perspective onto this question of sharing and community. Glissant's theory of relation is developed through a question of colonialism and its effects onto language. Working within the context of the Caribbean, Glissant strives to overcome how we might understand the colonial question by specifically seeing in language a social arena. Foreign words, in delivering the power dynamics of a colonial ideology and history, perform an interruption onto the colonized: indigenous languages are arrested and suffused with the powers of imperial force. For Glissant, such a capture though produces surprising effects or opportunities for appropriation; by passing in and through the cultures of the colonized, such languages are inevitably contorted, brought under pressure by tactics that seek out resistance or navigation in and around foreign power. In other words, language is reshaped by acts of appropriation, usage, and integration within the ever-shifting and unsteady relations of the colonial project. Glissant terms such a process "creolization." Referring to the specific Creole languages of the Caribbean, which are contortions of the French language, Glissant applies this to a broader question, supporting an understanding of language as one of global relation.

2 Ibid.

3 Zitiert nach Brandon LaBelle, Restless Acoustics, Emergent Publics, in: Marcel Cobussen/Vincent Meelberg/Barry Truax (Hg.), *The Routledge Companion to Sounding Art*, London: Routledge 2017, S. 279–281.

zwischen Ausdruck und Beschwörung, zwischen Nahem und Fernem – den Weg zu neuen Öffentlichkeitskonfigurationen weisen? Kann sie im radikal mobilen und stets auf dem Sprung befindlichen Leben innerhalb von globalen Beziehungen einen Sinn von „Gemeinschaft" schaffen? Lässt sich Klanglichkeit als ein primärer Resonanzraum verstehen, in dem ich mich abgrenzen und zugleich in größere Zusammenhänge eingliedern kann? Lässt sich hier so etwas wie radikaler Austausch herstellen?

Ich möchte hier auf das Werk von Édouard Glissant und seinen Begriff der „Poetik der Beziehung" eingehen, da dies einen genaueren Blick auf die Themen Austausch und Gemeinschaft ermöglicht. Glissants Theorie der Beziehung erschließt sich über den Kolonialismus und dessen Auswirkungen auf die Sprache. Als Theoretiker aus dem karibischen Raum ging es Glissant um eine Überwindung unseres herkömmlichen Verständnisses von Kolonialität, indem er die Sprache als eine Art soziale Arena ansah. Die Sprache der Fremden stellt, insofern sie die Machtdynamik der kolonialen Ideologie und Geschichte transportiert, auf Seiten Kolonisierten einen Bruch dar: Die Sprache der Indigenen wird gleichsam angehalten und von den Kräften der imperialen Macht durchdrungen. In dieser Vereinnahmung erkennt Glissant jedoch überraschende Effekte bzw. Gelegenheiten für eine Aneignung: Indem diese Sprachen in die Kulturen der Kolonisierten eingehen bzw. durch sie hindurchgehen, werden sie unweigerlich verzerrt oder sind Widerstandstaktiken ausgesetzt, wie man sich innerhalb der fremden Macht bzw. um sie herumbewegen kann. Mit anderen Worten: Sprache wird umgeformt, und zwar durch Akte der Aneignung, des Gebrauchs und der Integration in die sich stets verlagernden und unbeständigen kolonialen Beziehungen. Glissant nennt diesen Prozess „Kreolisierung". Ausgehend von den spezifisch kreolischen Sprachen der Karibik, bei denen es sich um Verzerrungen des Französischen handelt, wendet Glissant dies auf größere Zusammenhänge an und tritt für ein Verständnis von Sprache ein, das für globale Beziehungen generell gilt.

Im Mittelpunkt von Glissants Poetik steht die Anfechtung der Theorie, Sprache stehe einer Vervielfachung der Beziehungen entgegen, die infolge der Migrationsströme und Wirtschaftssysteme der Moderne eintritt und zu zahlreichen Grenzüberschreitungen führt. Er sagt: „Die Verteidigung der Sprachen, die die Diversität sichern, ist daher untrennbar mit der Restabilisierung der Beziehungen zwischen den Gemeinschaften verbunden."[3] Insofern geht Glissants Projekt weit über das Thema Sprache hinaus; die Poetik der Beziehung zielt auf eine bestimmte Weltanschauung bzw. eine Theorie der globalen Beziehungen, mittels derer sich die Spannungen innerhalb jedes kolonialen Projekts (als imaginierter Singularität) begreifen lassen. Die Kreolisierung forciert einen Widerstandsmodus, indem sie die Hybridisierung von Formen

Central to Glissant's poetics is a refutation of language as a barrier to the proliferation of relationships, which following the migrancies and economies of modernity incite numerous border crossings. As he states, "[t]he defense of languages assuring Diversity is thus inseparable from restabilizing relations among communities."[3] In this regard, Glissant's project moves far beyond a question of language only; the poetics of relation aims for a certain worldview, expounding a theory of global relations by which to negotiate the inherent tensions to any colonial project (as an imagined singularity). Creolization spirits a mode of resistance by specifically embracing the hybridizations of form, and in particular, the power of migration: through the itinerant movements of global relations, culture gains in its ability to create powerful forms of dialogue, sharing, echoes—an echo-monde as Glissant states, which may expand Nancy's resonance to questions of national borders and post-colonial bodies.

I'm interested in Glissant's theories and how they may shape an understanding of the relational as not only about face-to-face conversation, or about the deliberations of public forums. In effect, Glissant sets the scene for a global model in which encounter and exchange occur within the gaps and upon the edges of formal relations; culture moves specifically through a transient behavior, appearing here, disappearing there, mutating and ending, embedding identities and communities within the force of becoming—within voices that might slur and err, capsize into silence or flood the scene with hyperbole. Ricarda Denzer's notebooks appear as maps of migratory events, and in doing so, they capture and literally notate the movements of voices, of sounds, and how they participate within a temporal flow of great intensity: she provides us with a sounding art performed on the page, of a deep listening that is equally diffuse, distracted, multiple. Such are the lessons: of acoustical expressions, tuning us to the far and the near, equally.

3 Cobussen/Vincent Meelberg/Barry Truax (Eds.), *The Routledge Companion to Sounding Art* (London: Routledge 2017), 279–281.

Excerpt from:
Brandon LaBelle, "Restless Acoustics, Emergent Public," in: Marcel Cobussen/ Vincent Meelberg/Barry Truax (Eds.), *The Routledge Companion to Sounding Art* (London: Routledge 2017), 279–281.

und insbesondere die Macht der Migration begrüßt: Infolge von globalen Wanderbewegungen ist Kultur eher in der Lage, kraftvolle Formen des Dialogs, des Austauschs und des Widerhalls zu schaffen – eine „echo-monde", wie Glissant sagt, die eine Erweiterung von Jean-Luc Nancys Ansatz in Bezug auf nationale Grenzen und postkoloniale Körper darstellt.

Mich interessiere insbesondere, inwiefern Glissants Theorie ein Verständnis des Relationalen befördert, das sich nicht nur um das Gespräch von Angesicht zu Angesicht oder um Überlegungen in öffentlichen Foren dreht. Tatsächlich bereitet Glissant die Bühne für ein globales Modell, demzufolge Begegnung und Austausch in den Zwischenräumen und an den Rändern formaler Beziehungen stattfinden. Kultur bewegt sich durch eine Reihe flüchtiger Stadien, taucht einmal hier auf, verschwindet dann wieder dort, mutiert, endet und setzt Identitäten und Gemeinschaften der Kraft des Werdens aus – Stimmen, die womöglich lallen und stammeln, in Schweigen verfallen oder sich in Übertreibungen ergehen. Die Notizbücher von Ricarda Denzer wirken wie Landkarten migratorischer Ereignisse, und gerade deshalb erfassen und halten sie im wahrsten Sinne des Worts die Bewegungen von Stimmen fest, von Klängen, und wie diese an einem zeitlichen Fluss von großer Intensität mitwirken: Denzer schafft so eine auf dem Blatt Papier aufgeführte Klangkunst, die von tiefem Hören [deep listening] zeugt, das gleichermaßen diffus, abgelenkt und vielseitig ist. Was wir daraus lernen, sind akustische Ausdrucksformen, die uns auf das Ferne und das Nahe gleichermaßen einstimmen.

Textausschnitt aus:

Brandon LaBelle, Restless Acoustics, Emergent Publics, in: Marcel Cobussen/Vincent Meelberg/Barry Truax (Hg.), *The Routledge Companion to Sounding Art*, London: Routledge 2017, S. 279–281.

Jaimini Patel

Pointing at the Moon

Jaimini Patel

Auf den Mond zeigen

„Geben wir ihm einen Namen. Und dann ist es ein Ding“ ist ein Versuch, ein fortlaufendes Gespräch zu führen und offen zu sein für alles. Mit der Namensgebung im August 2022 formalisierten wir unsere zuvor eher sporadischen Begegnungen, die sich auch mit großer Begeisterung um Bücher, Ideen und Kunst drehten – fast immer persönlich, in Covid-Zeiten via Zoom. Wir wollten uns im Abstand von zwei Wochen treffen, manchmal war es nicht ganz so oft, andere Male dafür häufiger. Dieser Raum ist ein Versuch, Bedingungen herzustellen und anzuerkennen, unter denen sich Fäden aufgreifen und entwirren lassen, und offen dafür zu sein, wo sie hinführen mögen. Die Tatsache, dass wir uns keine Agenda gaben und keine Ziele verfolgten, war enorm produktiv, denn sie förderte das Notwendige, Dringende, Ungelöste zutage und nahm unsere ganze Energie in Anspruch. Das Gespräch hilft uns, zu erkennen, was wir suchen, aber nur erahnen können. Manchmal benötigen wir andere, die uns zu einer Beschreibung drängen und auffordern, dem Flüchtigen Substanz zu verleihen bzw. zu registrieren, was wir vor Augen haben.

Mit diesem Text möchte ich vor allem das relationale und verworrene Wesen unserer Gespräche beschreiben, aus denen sich unser Ansatz zu Praxis, Forschung und Lehre herauskristallisiert. Damit Verbindungen entstehen können, gehe ich auch auf deinen Wunsch nach einem Buch ein, das porös und improvisiert bleiben soll. Auf entspannte Weise aufmerksam zu sein, ist eine Fähigkeit, die sich beim Meditieren entwickeln lässt. Mich verblüfft, dass Improvisation eine Art von Zuhören und Sich-darauf-Einstimmen verlangt, die das zentrale Element deiner Arbeit bildet. Du sprichst vom Akustischen als von etwas Fließendem/Fluidem, und

Let's give it a name. And then it's a thing endeavors to allow whatever may emerge through sustained conversation. In August 2022, through this act of naming, we formalized our previously sporadic meetings, which involved getting over-excited about books, ideas, and art, mostly in person, and in Covid times on Zoom. We try to meet fortnightly, but it sometimes ends up being less frequent and sometimes more. This space is an attempt to give urgency and recognition to conditions for gathering and unraveling threads and being open to where they might lead. The absence of agendas or outcomes has been enormously generative, nurturing what is necessary, pressing, unresolved, and absorbs our energy. The conversations help us to recognize what we chase but can only glimpse. Sometimes we need others to press us for a description and give flesh to the evanescent or register what is in front of us.

In writing this I am keen to capture the relational and entangled nature of our conversations through which our approach to practice, research, and pedagogy materialize. I also respond to your desire for this book to remain porous and improvisational, allowing connections to happen. Being alert in a relaxed way is a skill that can be developed through meditation. I'm struck by how improvisation requires a type of listening and tuning in that is key to your work. You talk about the sonic as liquid/fluid, and the way in which not knowing the source or origin affects what is received—an echo, a fragment. I think you mentioned holes. Doubts and pauses tend to be squeezed out of art discourse and academia, which seems strange because in both they are like old friends. A constant shuffle between clarity and obscurity. Looking back over my notes from our meetings, I notice how we hop around in our conversations—one thing connects to many others—nearby and far-reaching. Conversation allows for mess, and through it we arrive somewhere else. It involves paying attention to reciprocal sensory cues. Such interactions can also occur with material, ourselves, imaginary protagonists from the past/present/future, and imaginary exchanges with real protagonists. In writing, other types of arrangement and assembly occur; within academia, a further layer of convention is added.[1]

I think back to the Gloria Anzaldua essay "and now let us shift … conocimiento … inner work, public acts" (Anzaldua, 2015: 540–576), which you introduced me to years ago, and the way in which the reader is addressed as *you*. It's a powerful way to make the personal political. I read the essay with Misreading, an artist collective, to create a performative work together. In this way we influence and become involved in each other's lives and work. The value of these exchanges is increasingly important, as discovery and thinking happen through collaboration. This brings me to pedagogy as a creative practice, around which many of our

1 These conventions are deeply problematic, stifling, and exclusionary. The consensus of a narrow group of individuals decides what constitutes viable knowledge, how it should be communicated, and who can access it. Murris writes: "a visibly upset student who commented that my posthumanist teaching 'had pulled the stop out of his bath' … Perhaps it would have helped if I had pointed out that it is not about what is *in* the bath, but that we need to turn our attention as educators to the bath itself? … What is inside and outside this container, the measuring apparatus that holds the water? Who is the 'we' that decides what is in the bath and counts as the body of knowledge worth having?" (Murris, 2022: 4). My intention is to push against these conventions, and while I reluctantly use some I also want to draw attention to them. See Sara Ahmed, *Living a Feminist Life* (Durham: Duke University Press, 2017) on the politics of citation and inequity of citational practices that reproduce knowledge, Katherine McKittrick, *Dear Science and Other Stories* (Durham: Duke University Press, 2021) on how black intellectuals negotiate prevailing systems of knowledge, Karen Barad, *Meeting the Universe Halfway: Quantum Physics and the Entanglement of Matter and Meaning* (Durham: Duke University Press, 2007), ix–xiii, on entanglement and acknowledgement.

darüber, wie sich die Unkenntnis der Quelle bzw. des Ursprungs darauf auswirkt, was wahrgenommen wird – ein Echo, ein Fragment. Ich glaube, du hast auch Lücken erwähnt. Und dass Momente des Zweifels und Innehaltens tendenziell im künstlerischen Diskurs und in der akademischen Welt unterdrückt werden, was seltsam scheint, da sie doch in beiden Fällen wie alte Freunde sind. Ein permanentes Hin und Her zwischen Klarheit und Unklarheit. Beim Durchsehen meiner Notizen fällt mir auf, wie sprunghaft wir uns unterhalten – eine Sache stellt die Verbindung her zu vielen anderen, naheliegenden und weitreichenden. Das Gespräch lässt Unordnung zu, und erst dadurch kommen wir woanders an. Es wird dabei auf wechselseitige sinnliche Auslöser geachtet. Zu diesen Wechselwirkungen kann es auch mit Materialien kommen, mit uns selbst, mit imaginären Protagonist*innen aus Vergangenheit/Gegenwart/Zukunft und beim imaginären Austausch mit echten Protagonist*innen. Wenn man schreibt, stellen sich andere Anordnungs- und Aufbauweisen ein; im Kontext der akademischen Welt kommt noch eine weitere Konventionsebene hinzu.[1]

Mir fällt Gloria Anzalduas Aufsatz wieder ein, „and now let us shift … conocimiento … inner work, public acts" („und jetzt wechseln wir zu … *conocimiento* … innere Arbeit, öffentliches Handeln" (Anzaldua, 2015: 540–576), auf den du mich vor Jahren hingewiesen hast, und in dem die Leserin und der Leser – mit *you* – direkt angesprochen werden. Das ist ein starkes Mittel, das Persönliche politisch zu machen. Als Künstlerkollektiv *Misreading* lesen wir den Aufsatz, um eine performative Arbeit zu entwickeln. Durch die gemeinsame Lektüre beeinflussen wir uns gegenseitig und lassen uns auf das Leben und die Arbeit der jeweils anderen ein. Der Wert dieses gegenseitigen Austauschs wird immer wichtiger, denn das Entdecken und Denken finden in Zusammenarbeit statt. Das bringt mich zur Lehre als kreative Praxis, um die sich viele unserer Gespräche drehen. Um uns eingehender damit zu befassen, lesen wir im Slow-Reading-Modus *Karen Barad as Educator* (Murris, 2022). Es geht dabei um die Frage, wie das Lesen eines Textes unser Denken, Schreiben und Üben beeinflusst. Einen Text so sorgfältig lesen zu können, hat Seltenheitswert, bedenkt man das Tempo an den Universitäten und in der Kunstwelt. Die Soziologin Akwugo Emejulu nennt das ein „Wettrüsten" (Stuk Rood Vlees Podcast, Episode 32, 2019). Es ist schwindelerregend, überwältigend und von keinerlei nachhaltigem Wert. Wie einen Weg verhandeln, wenn Wissen, Kunst und Bildung auf ihren Geldwert reduziert werden? Wie Anzaldua möchte auch Emejulu eine Methode herausarbeiten, die anders an die Dinge herangeht, als wir es tun.

Es war ein Luxus, unsere erste Murris-Lektüre auf den Abschnitt „The World Kicks Back", und auf knapp eine Seite des ersten Kapitels „Troubling the Troubled Subject", zu fokussieren. Nach jedem der dichten Sätze entfaltet sich die Diskussion in

1 Diese Konventionen sind zutiefst problematisch, erdrückend und ausschließend. Der Konsens einer enggefassten Gruppe von Individuen entscheidet, was brauchbares Wissen ist, wie es kommuniziert werden soll und wer Zugriff darauf hat. Murris schreibt: „ein sichtlich bestürzter Student meinte, meine posthumanistische Lehre ‚habe den Stöpsel aus seiner Badewanne gezogen' … Vielleicht wäre es hilfreich gewesen, wenn ich betont hätte, dass es nicht darauf ankommt, was *in* der Badewanne ist, sondern dass wir als Lehrende unser Augenmerk auf das Bad an sich richten sollten … auf das, was im Inneren und außerhalb dieses Behälters ist, die Messapparatur, die das Wasser fasst. Wer ist dieses ‚wir', das entscheidet, was sich in der Wanne befindet und als der Wissensstand gilt, den zu erlangen sich lohnt?" (Murris, *Karen Barad as Educator*. S. 4.) Ich beabsichtige, an diesen Konventionen zu rütteln, und obwohl ich manche ungern einsetze, möchte ich auch das Augenmerk auf sie richten. Vgl.: Sara Ahmed, *Living a Feminist Life*, Durham: Duke University Press 2017 zur Politik der Zitation und Ungleichheit der Zitierpraktiken, die Wissen reproduzieren; Katherine McKittrick, *Dear Science and Other Stories*, Durham: Duke University Press 2021 dazu, wie schwarze Intellektuelle vorherrschende Wissenssysteme verhandeln; Karen Barad, *Meeting the Universe Halfway: Quantum Physics and the Entanglement of Matter and Meaning*, Durham: Duke University Press 2007, S. ix–xiii zu Verflechtung und Anerkennung.

conversations circulate. To consider this more methodically, we are slow-reading Murris's *Karen Barad as Educator* (Murris, 2022). We want to interrogate how we read, think, write, and practice through a text together. It is rare to be able to read something this carefully given the pace of academia and the art world. Sociologist Akwugo Emejulu refers to it as an "arms race" (Stuk Rood Vlees Podcast, episode 32, 2019). It's dizzying, overwhelming, and unsustainable. How do we negotiate a way through when knowledge, art, and education are reduced to capital? Like Anzaldua, Emejulu tries to carve out a different way to do things, as we do.

It was a luxury to focus our first reading of Murris on the section "The World Kicks Back," no more than a page of the first chapter, "Troubling the Troubled Subject." Each dense sentence unfolds discussion in multiple directions, not because of its opaqueness or impenetrability but through pertinent insights. We could only begin to touch the surface of topics such as the ethics of referencing indigenous knowledge. We see something else in each re-reading. Murris writes: "Reading this book involves getting entangled with the ethics and politics of what it means to know, teach, and learn" (Murris, 2022: 1). We were already elbow deep in grappling with what agential realism means to us as artists and teachers. This much-used theoretical term can become decorative or diluted. As we examine it, we find that post-humanist methodology describes how we approach teaching—continually renegotiating in each encounter, much like your way of listening, or "listening thinking," as you call it. It's to be *practiced* rather than *applied*, like agential realism for Murris.

You ask if theory affects how I talk about practice or seek to position it. For me it is key in informing the work, but to use it to describe it would be incongruous. For you it is the same. You mentioned Trinh T. Minh-ha's "speaking nearby" rather than "speaking about" (Trinh T., 1992: 87). I enjoyed your analogy of not wanting to embarrass the artwork by saying "It's like this" in case it is listening. I feel this, not only talking about my work but also that of other artists and students. It goes towards understanding my apprehension about talking about your work and instead focusing on your approach. The contingent is instrumental to practice; it discloses what makes it what it is. It's a curious thing we do—talking around the work. Do we get closer to it by not pinning it down and taming it? Are we able to see it from different angles in its fugitivity? Trying to follow a thought you say, "I'm thinking aloud." Once again, the text is making us do what it seeks. "This philosophical attitude is one of the collaborative enquiries, thinking aloud together, generating cascading questions, embracing silence, and taking deep breaths in 'temporary resting places'" (Murris, 2022: 2).

mehrere Richtungen – nicht, weil er unklar oder undurchdringlich gewesen wäre, sondern wegen der relevanten Erkenntnisse. Themen wie die Ethik des Verweisens auf indigenes Wissen konnten wir gerade einmal an der Oberfläche berühren. Bei jeder neuerlichen Lektüre erkennen wir etwas anderes. Murris schreibt: „Beim Lesen dieses Buchs muss man sich auf die Ethik und Politik dessen einlassen, was es bedeutet, zu wissen, zu lehren und zu lernen" (Murris, 2022: 1). Wir setzten uns bereits intensiv damit auseinander, was „agentialer Realismus" für uns Künstler*innen und Lehrende bedeutet. Dieser häufig benutzte theoretische Begriff kann zum Dekor bzw. verwässert werden. In unserer Auseinandersetzung damit stellen wir fest, dass die posthumanistische Methode unseren Ansatz zur Lehre beschreibt – als eine bei jeder Begegnung stattfindende, kontinuierliche Neuverhandlung, in etwa so, wie du zuhörst bzw. „zuhörend denkst", wie du es nennst. Es muss *praktiziert* werden und nicht *angewandt*, wie der agentiale Realismus im Fall von Murris.

Du möchtest wissen, ob die Theorie Einfluss darauf hat, wie ich über die eigene Arbeit spreche bzw. versuche, sie zu positionieren. Die Theorie bildet eine wesentliche Grundlage meiner Arbeit, aber sie zu ihrer Beschreibung einzusetzen, wäre unvereinbar. Du siehst das genauso. Du erwähntest Trinh T. Minh-ha und ihr „speaking nearby" (in der Nähe sprechen) anstelle von „speaking about" (Trinh T., 1992: 87). Mir gefiel deine Analogie, dass du das Kunstwerk nicht in Verlegenheit bringen möchtest, indem du sagst, „das ist so", da es ja zuhören könnte. Ich spüre das, nicht nur, wenn ich über meine eigene Arbeit spreche, sondern auch über die Arbeit anderer Künstler*innen und Studenten*innen. Mir werden so meine Bedenken klarer, wenn ich *über* deine Arbeit spreche; stattdessen möchte ich das Augennmerk mehr auf den Ansatz legen, der dahintersteckt. Entscheidend für die Praxis ist das Kontingente; es verdeutlicht, was die künstlerische Praxis zu dem macht, was sie ist. Es ist ungewöhnlich, was wir da tun – um die Arbeit herumreden. Kommen wir ihr näher, indem wir sie nicht auf etwas festlegen und dadurch bändigen? Können wir sie in ihrer Flüchtigkeit aus verschiedenen Blickwinkeln sehen? Beim Versuch, einen Gedanken weiterzuverfolgen, sagst du, „ich denke laut nach". Abermals veranlasst uns der Text, das zu tun, worum er sich bemüht. „Diese philosophische Haltung ist eine der kollaborativen Fragestellungen, ein gemeinsames lautes Nachdenken, das Erzeugen kaskadenförmiger Fragen, das Annehmen von Stille und ein tiefes Luftholen an ‚temporären Rastorten'." (Murris, 2022: 2)

> Innehalten – dem Atem nachgehen – in Form einer expandierenden Gestalt – die sich schrittweise verändert – die gegen die Bauchwand drückt – sie nach außen wölbt – du wirst dir deines Körpers wieder bewusst.

> Pausing—observing the breath—in the form of an expanding shape—that changes gradually—pressing up against the walls of the stomach—moving it outwards—you are reminded of your body.

"Speaking nearby" gives the work agency. Trinh T. Minh-ha writes about the use of indirect language: "a speaking that does not objectify, does not point to an object as if it is distant from the speaking subject or absent from the speaking place. A speaking that reflects on itself and can come very close to a subject without, however, seizing or claiming it. A speaking in brief, whose closures are only moments of transition opening up to other possible moments of transition—these are forms of indirectness well understood by anyone in tune with poetic language" (Trinh T., 1992: 87). Thinking about how this relates to teaching, I'm reminded of the chapter "Pedagogy of Buddhism," in Eve Kosofsky Sedgwick's *Touching Feeling* (2003), which I mentioned in an earlier conversation. The author is careful to point out her Western understanding of Buddhist teachings, which nevertheless is more comprehensive than my own. Sedgwick talks about the considerable Buddhist thought on "knowing" and "realizing," and this recognition as both an end and a means as well as an active ongoing practice (Sedgwick, 2003: 167). I enjoy the skill with which humor is used to examine illness and death and the everyday to introduce complex ideas. Theory and practice like knowing and being as one. The attempts by Sedgwick and her cat to teach each other lead to a discussion of language and the non-linguistic, which in Buddhist writing is referred to as "pointing at the moon." *Teaching* is the finger pointing at the moon. Sedgwick introduces us to "thusness and suchness" and the eighth-century Japanese monk Kukai's assertion that Buddhist teaching is beyond speech but cannot be revealed without speech (Sedgwick, 2003: 170). When we bring our work in dialogue with an audience or in pedagogy there is also the constant interplay between immediacy and ungraspability described here. Maybe this is another text to slow-read with you.

I wonder what insights and patterns a diagram tracking the subjects of our conversations would reveal. Notation, repetition, and documenting are methods we both use in our work—attempts to capture something through labor. Since our first Zoom meeting I have been rubbing a section of a roll of yellow carbon paper onto the same piece of unprimed linen. In doing so I record something. Exactly what, I don't know. I can't see the negative marks left on the carbon paper or the positive ones that accumulate on the linen while I'm making them. Much like life. I know that you use painting as a tool to listen more intently. These activities that channel attention are like throwing out a broad fine net.

„Speaking nearby" verleiht der Arbeit Handlungsmacht. Trinh T. Minh-ha schreibt über die indirekte Sprache als „ein Sprechen, das nicht objektifiziert, nicht auf ein Objekt verweist, so als bliebe es auf Distanz zum sprechenden Subjekt oder abwesend vom sprechenden Ort. Ein Sprechen, das auf sich selbst reflektiert und einem Subjekt sehr nahekommen kann, ohne es jedoch völlig in Beschlag zu nehmen oder Anspruch darauf zu erheben. *A speaking in brief*, ein Andeuten, dessen Abschlüsse nur Momente des Übergangs darstellen, die sich anderen möglichen Momenten des Übergangs öffnen – das sind indirekte Formen, die alle verstehen, die auf eine poetische Sprache eingestimmt sind" (Trinh T., 1992: 87). Wenn ich darüber nachdenke, inwieweit sich das auf die Lehre bezieht, fällt mir das in einem früheren Gespräch erwähnte Kapitel „Pedagogy in Buddhism" in Eve Kosofsky Sedgwicks *Touching Feeling* (2003) ein. Die Autorin verweist vorsorglich auf ihr westliches Verständnis der buddhistischen Lehre, das dennoch umfassender ist als mein eigenes. Sedgwick spricht über die Bedeutung, die „Wissen" und „Erkennen" im buddhistischen Denken einnehmen, wahrgenommen sowohl als Zweck wie auch als Mittel und kontinuierliche Praxis (Sedgwick, 2003: 167). Mir gefällt, wie geschickt Humor eingesetzt wird, um Themen wie Krankheit und Tod und das Alltägliche zu behandeln und komplexe Gedanken einzuführen. Theorie und Praxis als Einheit wie Wissen und Sein. Die Versuche Sedgwicks und ihrer Katze, einander etwas beizubringen, führen zur Erörterung von Sprache und dem Nichtsprachlichen, das in den buddhistischen Schriften als „auf den Mond zeigen" bezeichnet wird. Die *Lehre* ist der Finger, der auf den Mond zeigt. Sedgwick macht uns mit „So-Sein und Solchheit" bekannt und mit der These des japanischen Mönchs Kukai aus dem achten Jahrhundert, wonach die buddhistische Lehre über das Sprechen hinausgeht, aber ohne Sprache nicht gelehrt werden kann (Sedgwick, 2003: 170). Wenn wir mit unserer Arbeit in einen Dialog mit einem Publikum treten oder sie in der Lehre einsetzen, findet ebenfalls dieses ständige Wechselspiel zwischen der hier beschriebenen Unmittelbarkeit und Unerfassbarkeit statt. Vielleicht wäre das ein weiterer Text für eine langsame Lektüre mit dir.

Ich frage mich, welche Erkenntnisse und Muster bei einem *Diagram Tracking* der Themen herauskämen, über die wir gesprochen haben. Notizen, Wiederholung und Dokumentation sind Methoden, die wir beide in unserer Arbeit einsetzen – Versuche, etwas durch schöpferisches Tun einzufangen. Seit unserem ersten Zoom-Treffen reibe ich mit gelbem Kohlepapier auf demselben Stück nicht ungrundierter Leinwand. Auf diese Weise zeichne ich etwas auf. Was genau, weiß ich nicht. Ich kann weder den negativen Abdruck auf dem Kohlepapier sehen noch den positiven auf dem Leinen. Wie das Leben. Ich weiß, dass du das Malen als Mittel

You listen through a parallel activity that enables you to suspend judgement and the need to immediately make meaning from words. It's a way to be fully present, tuned to the subtlest of cues, like following a sound as it recedes into nothing or the breath as it makes room for the next. I have one of your potato prints hanging in my living room. I imagine the sound of it being made, the movement towards silence as paint and moisture are absorbed. I love this work and never tire of looking at it. I see it as a distillation of your practice, rooted in materiality and the body, in which listening is a practice that expands beyond sound. It is a way of bringing and holding attention.

Further reading

Andaluza, G. 2015. *Light in the Dark/Luz en lo Oscuro: Rewriting Identity, Spirituality, Reality*. Durham: Duke University Press.

Kosofsky Sedgwick, E. 2003. *Touching Feeling: Affect, Pedagogy, Performativity*. Durham: Duke University Press.

Murris, K. 2022. *Karen Barad as Educator: Agential Realism and Education*. New York: Springer.

Trinh T., M. 1992. *Framer Framed. Film Scripts and Interviews*. Abingdon: Routledge.

einsetzt, um aufmerksamer zuzuhören. Diese Aktivitäten, die die Aufmerksamkeit kanalisieren, erinnern an das Auswerfen eines breiten feinmaschigen Netzes. Du hörst mittels einer Parallelaktivität zu, die es dir ermöglicht, vorläufig kein Urteil fällen und den Worten nicht augenblicklich eine Bedeutung abgewinnen zu müssen. Das ist eine Möglichkeit, vollkommen anwesend zu sein, eingestimmt auf die subtilsten Zwischentöne, als lauschte man einem Klang bis an sein Ende oder folgte einem Atemzug bis zu dem Moment, da er dem nächsten weicht. In meinem Wohnzimmer hängt ein Kartoffeldruck von dir. Ich stelle mir den Klang vor, während er entsteht, und dann sein allmähliches Verklingen, während Farbe und Feuchtigkeit absorbiert werden. Ich liebe diese Arbeit und werde nie müde, sie anzusehen. Ich sehe sie als Destillation deiner in Materialität und Körper verankerten Praxis, die Zuhören als eine Praxis versteht, die weit über den Klang hinausgeht. So kann man Aufmerksamkeit entgegenbringen und aufrechterhalten.

Weiterführende Literatur

Anzaldua, G. (2015), *Light in the Dark/Luz en lo Oscuro: Rewriting Identity, Spirituality, Reality*, Durham: Duke University Press.

Kosofsky Sedgwick, E. (2003), *Touching Feeling: Affect, Pedagogy, Performativity*, Durham: Duke University Press.

Murris, K. (2022), *Karen Barad as Educator: Agential Realism and Education*, New York: Springer.

Trinh T., M. (1992), *Framer Framed. Film Scripts and Interviews*, Abingdon: Routledge.

Works 2013–2023

Arbeiten 2013–2023

About The House – Silence Turned into Objects is an art project in the form of an exhibition by Ricarda Denzer. Proceeding from the life and work of the British-American writer Wystan Hugh Auden (1907–1973)—one of the great poets of the twentieth century, who from 1958 onward lived mainly in Kirchstetten, Lower Austria—work by twelve artists dealing in different ways with language was shown in Kirchstetten, as well as in and around Auden's house. The theme is listening and the voice, together with language as action and its transformation into visual, spatial, and socio-political dimensions.

About The House – Silence Turned into Objects ist ein Kunstprojekt von Ricarda Denzer in Form einer Ausstellung: Ausgehend vom Leben und Werk des britisch-amerikanischen Schriftstellers Wystan Hugh Auden (1907–1973), einem der großen Lyriker des 20. Jahrhunderts, der von 1958 an großteils im niederösterreichischen Kirchstetten lebte, werden im Ort sowie im und beim Auden-Haus Arbeiten von zwölf Künstler*-innen gezeigt, die sich auf unterschiedliche Weise mit dem Thema Sprache beschäftigen. Es geht um das Hören und um die Stimme sowie um Sprache als Handlung und deren Transformation in visuelle, räumliche und gesellschaftspolitische Dimensionen.

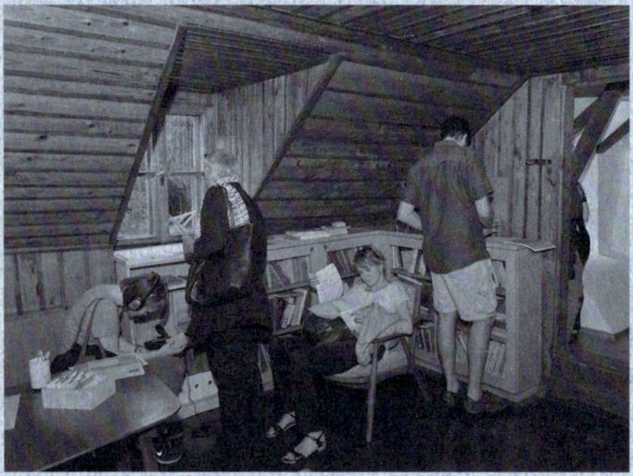

Exhibition view
About the House – Silence Turned into Objects, 2013
Ultra-red, *Politics (in Private)*

Ausstellungsansicht
About the House – Silence Turned into Objects, 2013
Ultra-red, *Politics (in Private)*

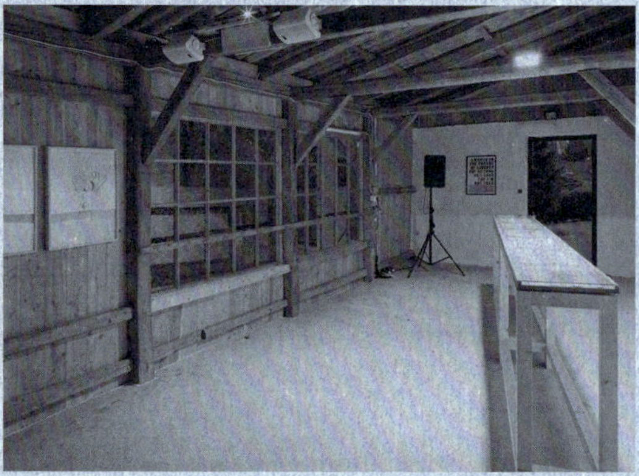

Exhibition view
About the House – Silence Turned into Objects, 2013
Imogen Stidworthy, *Topography of a Voice*; Simone Forti, *Song of the Vowels*; Sharon Hayes, *I March in the Parade of Liberty But as Long as I Love You I'm Not Free*

Ausstellungsansicht
About the House – Silence Turned into Objects, 2013
Imogen Stidworthy *Topography of a Voice*; Simone Forti, *Song of the Vowels*; Sharon Hayes, *I March in the Parade of Liberty but as Long as I Love You I'm Not Free*

Art in public space,
Kirchstetten, Lower Austria,
curated by Ricarda Denzer

With work by Fatih Aydoğdu, Simone Forti, Sharon Hayes, Olga Karliková, Pamelia Kurstin, Brandon LaBelle, Jonathan Quinn, Annette Stahmer, Imogen Stidworthy, Ultra-red, and Marcel Broodthaers's *Interview with a Cat*

Kunst im öffentlichen Raum
Kirchstetten, Niederösterreich,
kuratiert von Ricarda Denzer

Mit Arbeiten von Fatih Aydoğdu, Simone Forti, Sharon Hayes, Olga Karliková, Pamelia Kurstin, Brandon LaBelle, Jonathan Quinn, Annette Stahmer, Imogen Stidworthy, Ultra-red und Marcel Broodthaers' *Interview with a Cat*

Ricarda Denzer's *Subjektives Auden-Archiv* [Subjective Auden Archive], in the public space of Kirchstetten, includes an audio drama for a car radio (in W. H. Auden's VW Beetle, parked on the village square), a photographic installation with archive material (in the display window of the local post office), the 1936 film *Night Mail* (in the station waiting room), and the work *Wystan* (in public space). Alternating passages from the work of W. H. Auden, interviews with him, conversations with village residents, and letters can be read on a flip-dot panel visible from both railway and road. This magnet-controlled display panel, usually used in transportation systems—for example as an arrivals board on rail platforms—was placed on a grassy area by the tracks. As a result, the sentences on the panel-lit displays seem to be collaged into the surroundings, like subtitles contrasting with or questioning the landscape: "In the garden he loved the wilderness, the chaos."

Ricarda Denzers *Subjektives Auden-Archiv* im öffentlichen Raum von Kirchstetten beinhaltet neben einem Hörspiel für ein Autoradio (des VW-Käfers von W. H. Auden, geparkt auf dem Dorfplatz) eine Fotoinstallation mit Archivmaterialien (in der Auslage des örtlichen Postamts), den Film *Night Mail* aus dem Jahr 1936 (im Warteraum des Bahnhofs), die Arbeit *Wystan* (im öffentlichen Raum). Auf einem aus dem Zug wie von der Straße aus sichtbaren Flip-Dot-Panel sind wechselnde Textpassagen aus dem Werk W. H. Audens, aus Interviews mit dem Autor und Gesprächen mit Dorfbewohner*innen sowie aus Briefen zu lesen. Die durch Magnete gesteuerte Anzeigetafel, die üblicherweise im Verkehrswesen – zum Beispiel als Auskunftstafel an Zuggleisen – eingesetzt wird, wurde auf einem Wiesenstück neben den Gleisen platziert. So erscheinen die Sätze auf der Tafel wie in die Umgebung hinein collagierte, zum Teil das Landschaftsbild kontrastierende oder befragende Untertitel: „Im Garten hat er die Wildnis, also das Chaos geliebt."

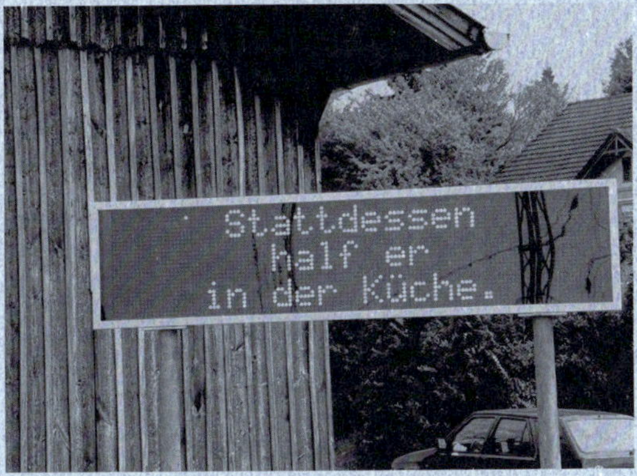

en *Wystan*, magnet-controlled flip-dot panel, light; temporary art in public space, Kirchstetten, Lower Austria, 2013

de *Wystan*, von Magneten gesteuertes Flip-Dot-Panel, Licht. Temporäre Kunst im öffentlichen Raum, Kirchstetten, Niederösterreich, 2013

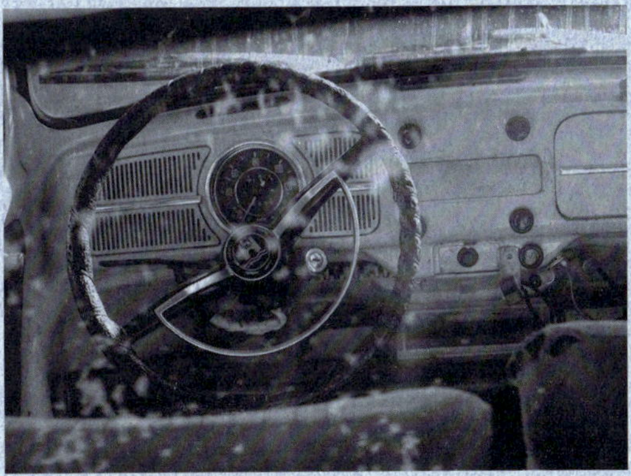

en Audio drama for a car radio, 1 h 32 min, VW Beetle; temporary art in public space, Kirchstetten, Lower Austria, 2013

de Hörspiel für ein Autoradio, 1 h 32 min, VW Käfer, 2013. Temporäre Kunst im öffentlichen Raum, Kirchstetten, Niederösterreich

Temporary art in public space, Kirchstetten, Lower Austria

Audio drama for a car radio, VW Beetle, video, photomontage, archive material, magnet-controlled flip-dot panel, light

en

Temporäre Kunst im öffentlichen Raum Kirchstetten, Niederösterreich

Hörspiel für ein Autoradio, VW-Käfer, Video, Fotomontage, Archivmaterialien, von Magneten gesteuertes Flip-Dot-Panel, Licht

de

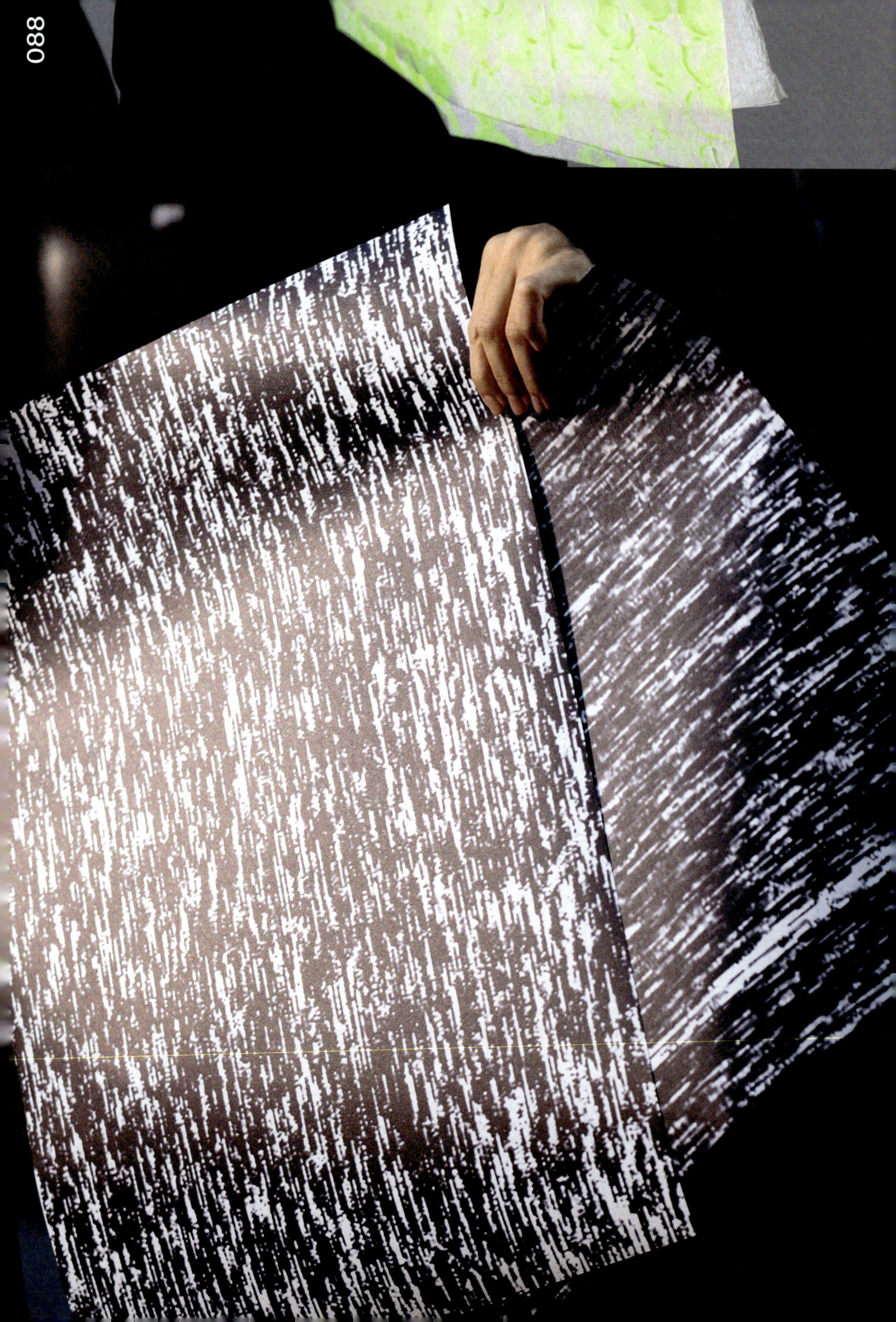

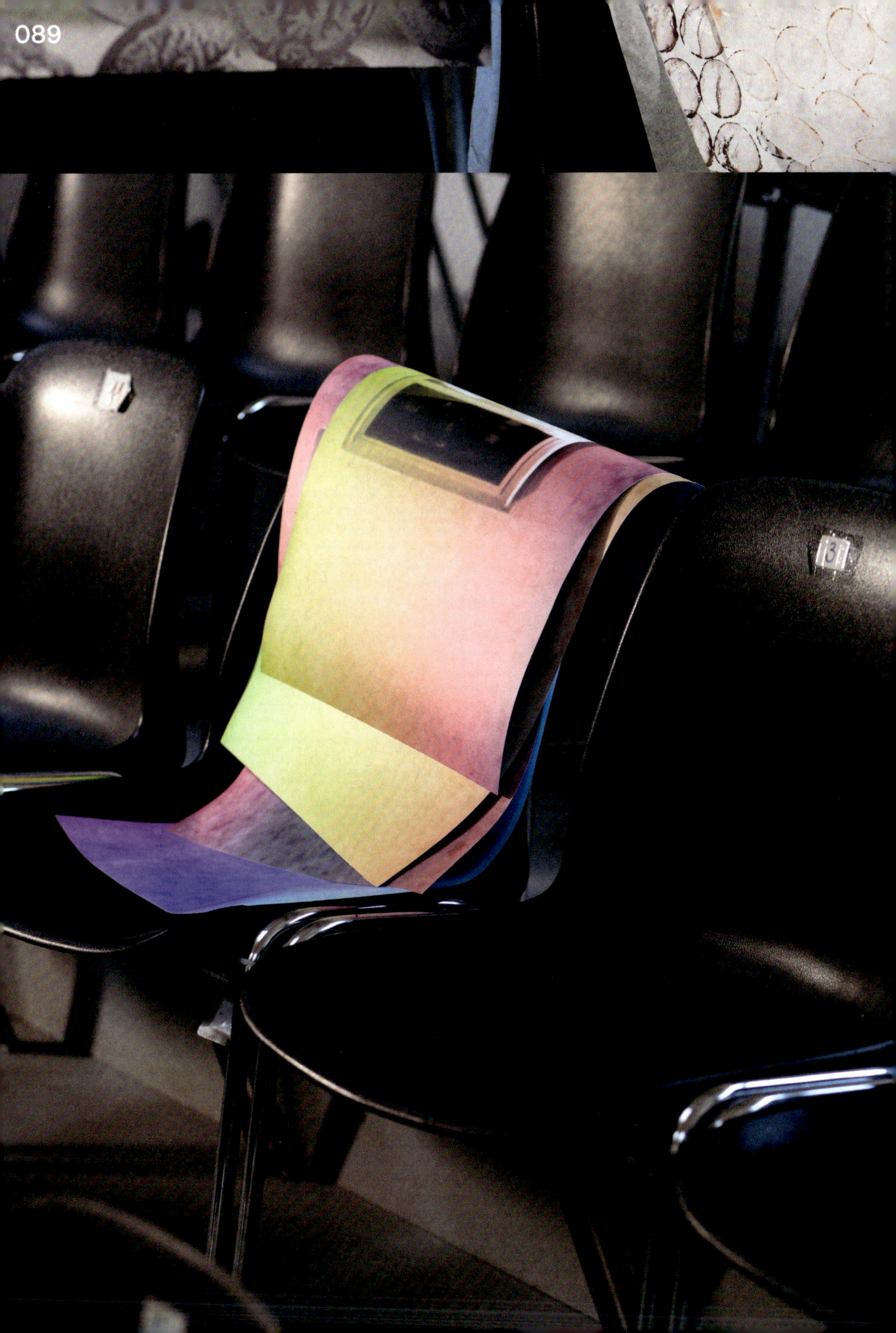

The soundscape of a city like Istanbul is so loud and varied that you usually try to block it out. In the apartment where Ricarda Denzer lived during her residency in 2013, she listened to it very closely, in keeping with her interest in sound, voice, language, and what they have to say: the calls of street vendors offering their wares by day, but also the noise of demonstrators in May 2013, initially protesting against a building project in Gezi Park, later more generally against Recep Tayyip Erdoğan's increasingly authoritarian government.

The camera's view from the apartment window determines the video frame: we hear the vendors, but also see processions of demonstrators and police, hear people running away, and follow the deployment of tear gas through both the images and the camera work, which is not always even and focused.

With her view from the window, Denzer deliberately positions herself as a witness to the protests, not as an insider. She recounts police violence, the protestors' courage, and the solidarity of a neighbor, who every evening signaled to activists fleeing from the police that his door was open—*kapı açık*.

Video, sound, 13 min

Screening during the exhibition *Senses of Place in a Multicentered Society* (In der Kubatur des Kabinetts – der Kunstsalon im Fluc, 2014), curated by Ursula Maria Probst

With work by Nikola Hansalik, Ricarda Denzer, Ryo Ikeshiro, Evelyn Loschy, Anja Manfredi, Jaime Ruiz Otis, Toni Schmale, Walter Seidl / Stefan Geissler

en

Die Geräuschkulisse in einer Großstadt wie Istanbul ist so laut und vielfältig, dass man sie üblicherweise lieber auszublenden versucht. In dem Apartment, das Ricarda Denzer während ihrer Residency 2013 bewohnte, hat sie gemäß ihrem Interesse an Sound, Stimme, Sprache und dem, was diese zu erzählen haben, sehr genau hingehört: auf die Rufe von Straßenhändlern, die dort tagsüber ihre Waren feilbieten, aber auch auf die Geräusche der Demonstrierenden, die im Mai 2013 zunächst gegen ein Bauprojekt auf dem Gelände des Gezi-Parks und bald generell gegen die immer autoritärer werdende Regierung von Recep Tayyip Erdoğan protestierten.

Der Kamerablick aus dem Fenster des Apartments gibt im Video den Blickausschnitt vor: Man hört die Verkäufer, sieht aber auch Züge von Demonstrierenden und Polizisten, hört davonlaufende Menschen und bekommt beim Betrachten den Einsatz von Tränengas nicht nur im Bild, sondern auch durch die Kameraführung mit, die nicht immer gerade und fokussiert ist.

Denzer positioniert sich mit ihrem Blick aus dem Fenster ganz bewusst als Zeugin – und nicht als Insiderin – des Protests: Sie erzählt von der Gewalt der Polizei, dem Mut der Protestierenden und der Solidarität eines Nachbarn, der den vor der Polizei fliehenden Aktivist*innen jeden Abend signalisierte, dass seine Tür offen – *kapı açık* – ist.

Video, Sound, 13 min

Vorführung im Rahmen der Ausstellung *Senses of Place* in a Multicentered Society (In der Kubatur des Kabinetts – der Kunstsalon im Fluc, 2014), kuratiert von Ursula Maria Probst

Mit Arbeiten von Nikola Hansalik, Ricarda Denzer, Ryo Ikeshiro, Evelyn Loschy, Anja Manfredi, Jaime Ruiz Otis, Toni Schmale, Walter Seidl / Stefan Geissler

de

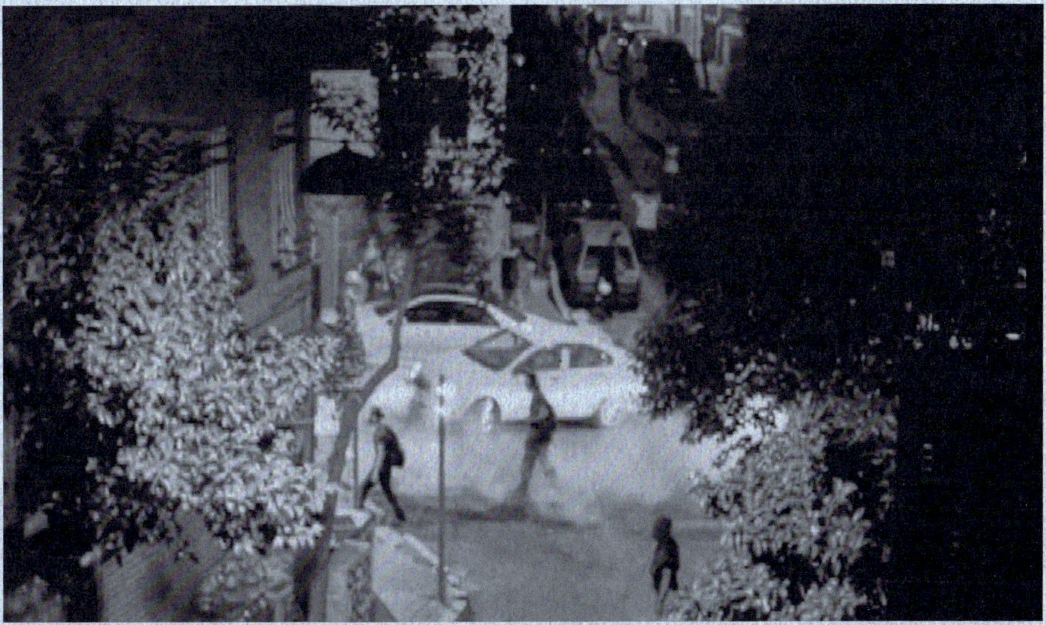

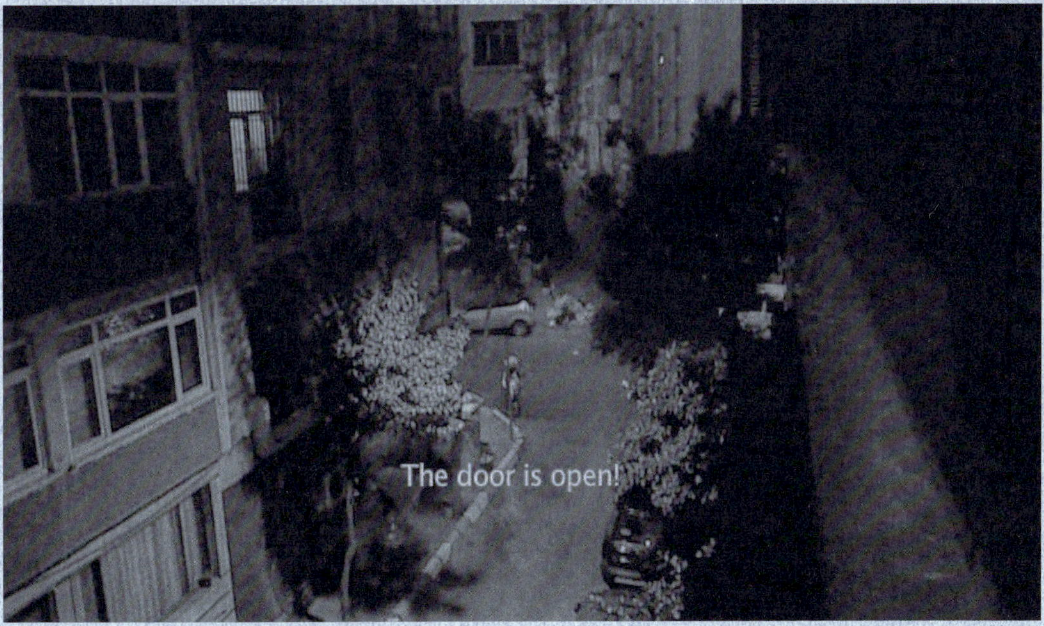

en Video stills from *Kapı açık*, video, sound, 13 min, 2013

de Videostills *Kapı açık*, Video, Sound, 13 min, 2013

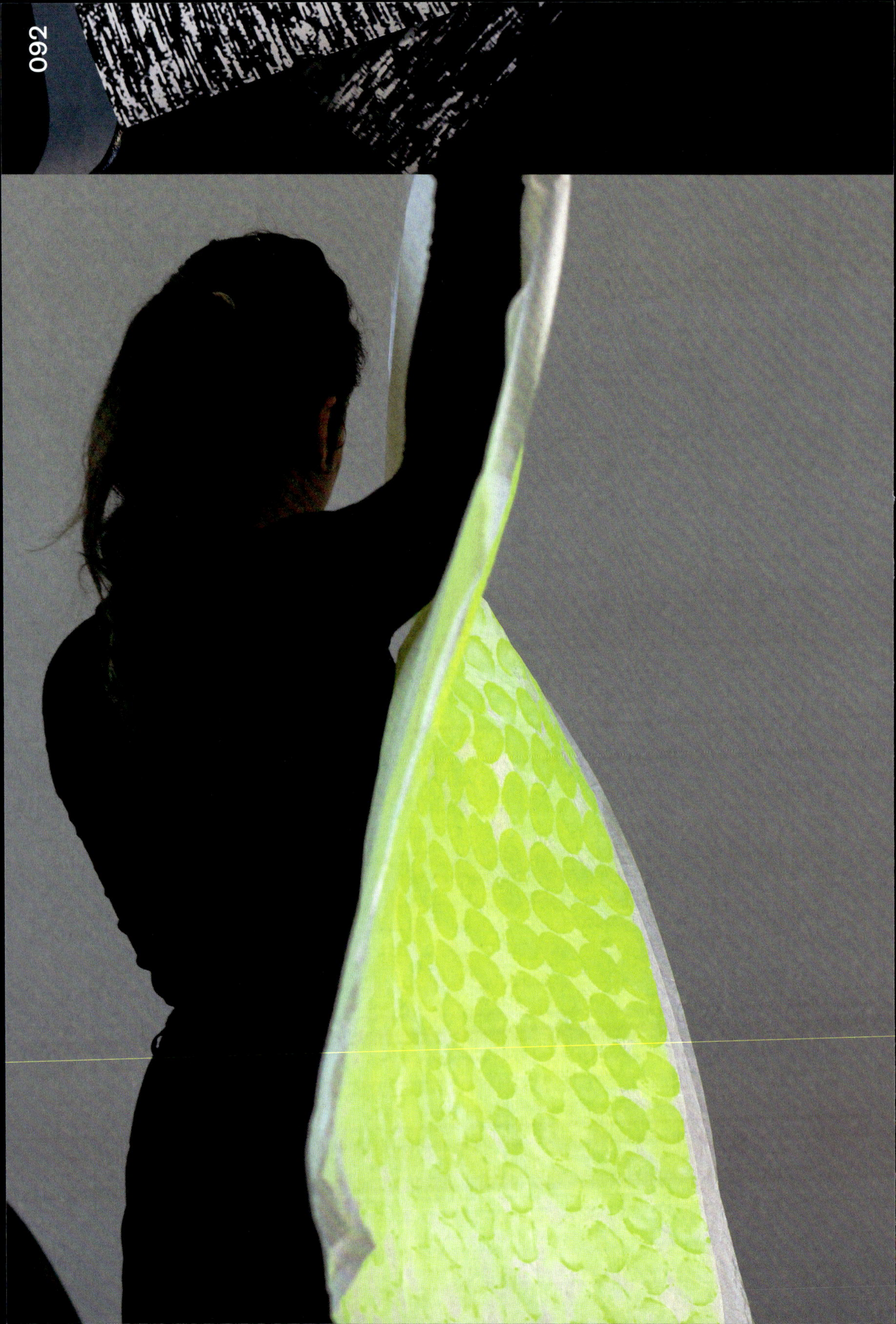

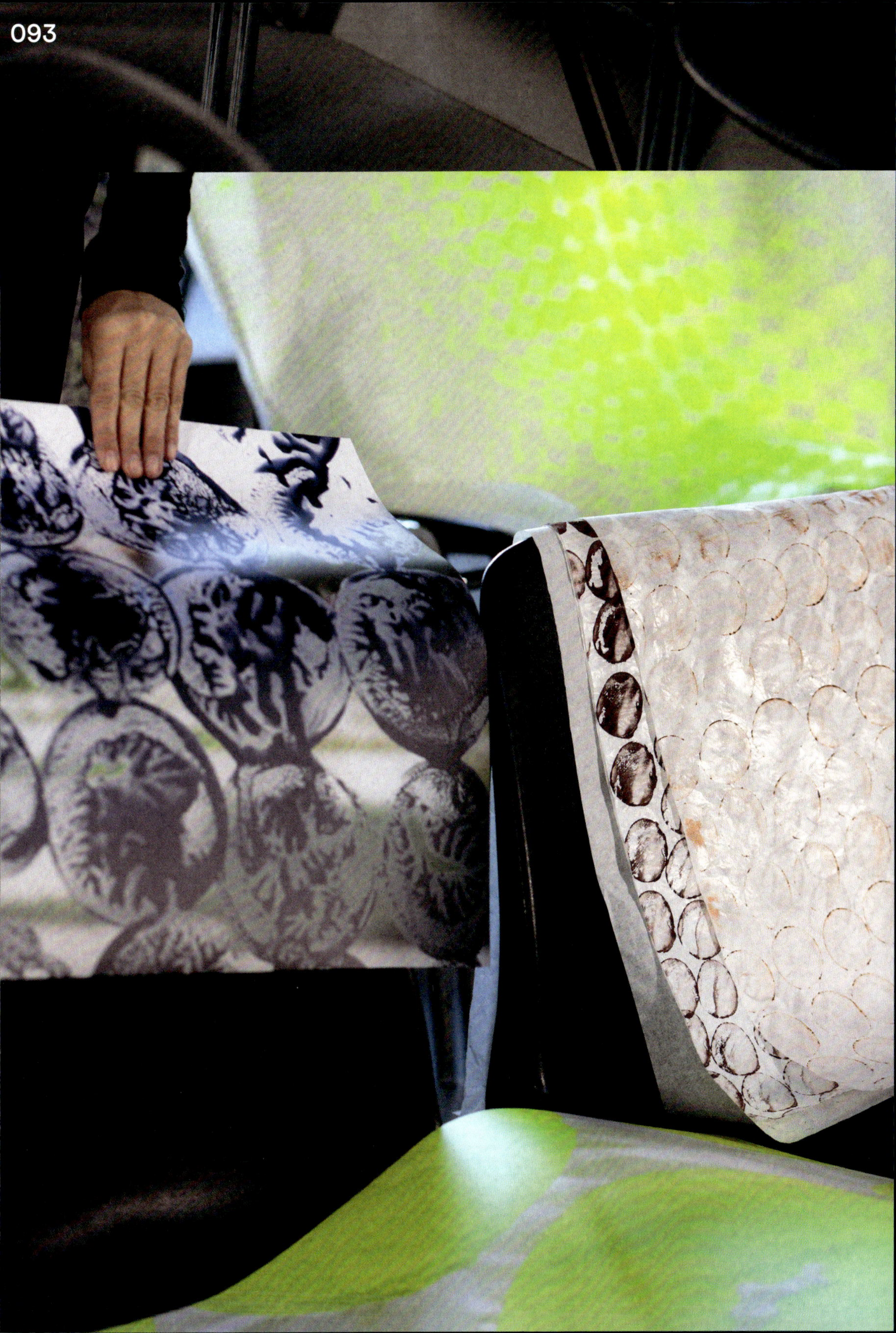

The history and ongoing interplay of capital, collecting, art, and their instrumentalization are central to the exhibition *Cumuli – Trading Places*, which takes its starting point from Canaletto's painting *Campo di Rialto*. Contrasting with the kind of art-dealing heyday recorded in this large historical work from the mid-eighteenth century, Denzer juxtaposes a small everyday gesture on the Campo di Rialto, in the form of a clay sculpture made on the spot, a selfie taken during the production process, and a specially commissioned painting of it.

With her "image" of a knee-print on a piece of clay on the Rialto, Denzer asks what defines the value of a work of art. Is it the artwork's local specificity and authenticity? Is it the production process and material? Or might it be the possibility of added value and tradability, which are created "in the consensus of imaginary values in which production and distribution appear to remain 'an open space that always leave you outside'"? (Ricarda Denzer, in reference to Michel Foucault's *Of Other Spaces. Utopias and Heterotopias*.)

Die Geschichte und das bis heute anhaltende Zusammenspiel von Kapital, Sammeln, Kunst und deren Instrumentalisierung standen im Zentrum der Ausstellung *Cumuli – Trading Places*, die das Gemälde *Campo di Rialto* des Malers Canaletto als Ausgangspunkt nahm. Während dieser Mitte des 18. Jahrhunderts quasi eine „Hochzeit" des Kunsthandels festhielt, setzt Denzer diesem großen historischen Werk eine kleine Alltagsgeste am Campo di Rialto entgegen, von der eine vor Ort gefertigte Tonskulptur, ein Selfie während des Produktionsprozesses und ein davon in Auftrag gegebenes Gemälde zeugen.

Mit dem „Bild" ihres Knieabdrucks auf einem Stück Ton auf dem Rialto-Platz fragt Denzer danach, was den Wert eines Kunstwerks ausmacht: Sind es seine Ortspezifik und Authentizität? Sind es der Produktionsprozess und das Material? Oder sind es die Möglichkeiten der Wertschöpfung und Handelbarkeit, die „im Konsens imaginärer Werte geschaffen werden, in denen Produktion und Verteilung ein ‚offener Ort zu bleiben scheinen, dem gegenüber man stets eine Außenposition einnimmt'"? (Ricarda Denzer in Anlehnung an Michel Foucaults Thesen in *Die Heterotopien. Der utopische Körper*)

Project for the exhibition *Cumuli – Trading Places*, *an exhibition project by Camelot*, Verein zur Förderung von Kunst und Kultur am Rosa-Luxemburg-Platz, Berlin; Kunsthalle Memmingen; Galerie 5020, Salzburg, 2016

With work by Paolo Chiasera, Clegg & Guttmann, Ricarda Denzer, Tomáš Džadoň, Heike Gallmeier, Robert Gschwantner, Stef Heidhues, Axel Hoedt, Ralf Hoedt, Candice Lin, Nora Mertes, Alexej Meschtschanow, Gianni Moretti, Jana Müller, Regine Müller-Waldeck, Tom Nicholson, Katrin Plavcak, Jochen Plogsties, Nika Radić, Gregor Schmoll, Tilo Schulz, Christian Schwarzwald, Stephanie Syjucio, Simon Wachsmuth, Moira Zoitl

Projekt im Rahmen von *Cumuli – Trading Places*, ein Ausstellungsprojekt von Camelot, Verein zur Förderung von Kunst und Kultur am Rosa-Luxemburg-Platz, Berlin; Kunsthalle Memmingen; Galerie 5020, Salzburg, 2016

Mit Arbeiten von Paolo Chiasera, Clegg & Guttmann, Ricarda Denzer, Tomáš Džadoň, Heike Gallmeier, Robert Gschwantner, Stef Heidhues, Axel Hoedt, Ralf Hoedt, Candice Lin, Nora Mertes, Alexej Meschtschanow, Gianni Moretti, Jana Müller, Regine Müller-Waldeck, Tom Nicholson, Katrin Plavcak, Jochen Plogsties, Nika Radić, Gregor Schmoll, Tilo Schulz, Christian Schwarzwald, Stephanie Syjucio, Simon Wachsmuth, Moira Zoitl

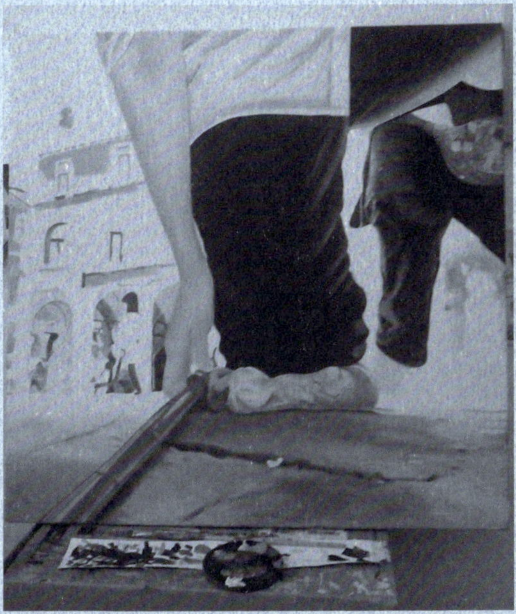

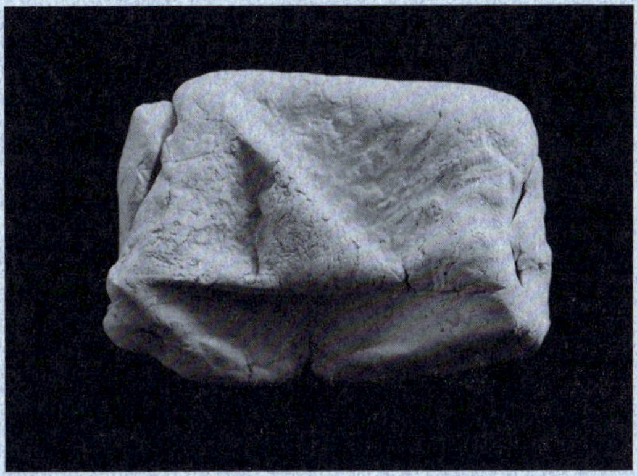

en Detail
Anderswo Woanders,
in the exhibition *Cumuli – Trading Places*, 2015;
photograph of a commissioned painting
(by Parihan Keles, 68 × 70 cm,
acrylic and oil on canvas);
floor sculpture, clay, 17 × 13 × 5 cm

de Detailansicht
Anderswo Woanders,
Ausstellung *Cumuli – Trading Places*, 2015;
Fotografie einer Auftragsmalerei
(von Parihan Keles, 68 × 70 cm,
Akryl und Öl auf Leinwand);
Bodenplastik, Ton, 17 × 13 × 5 cm

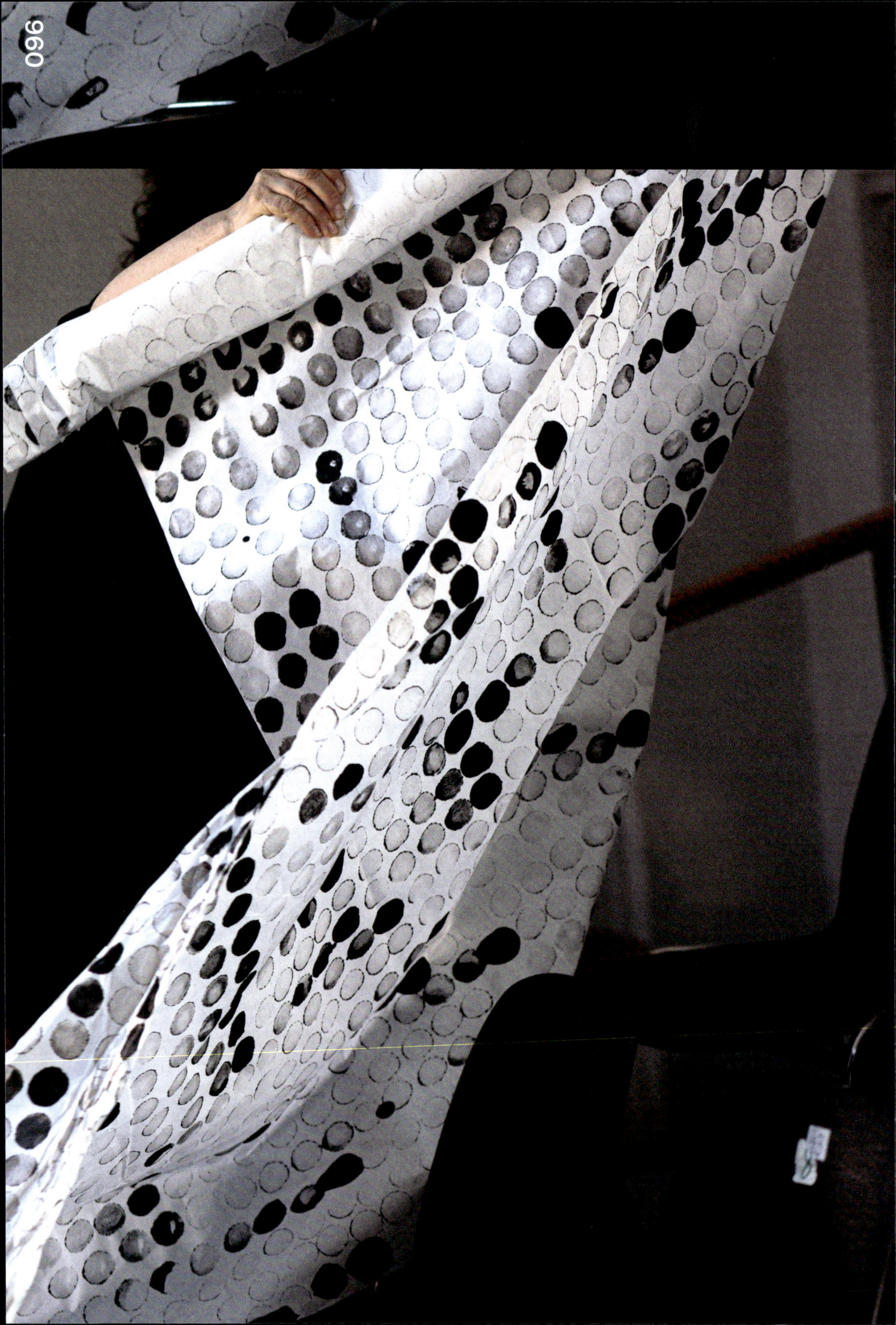

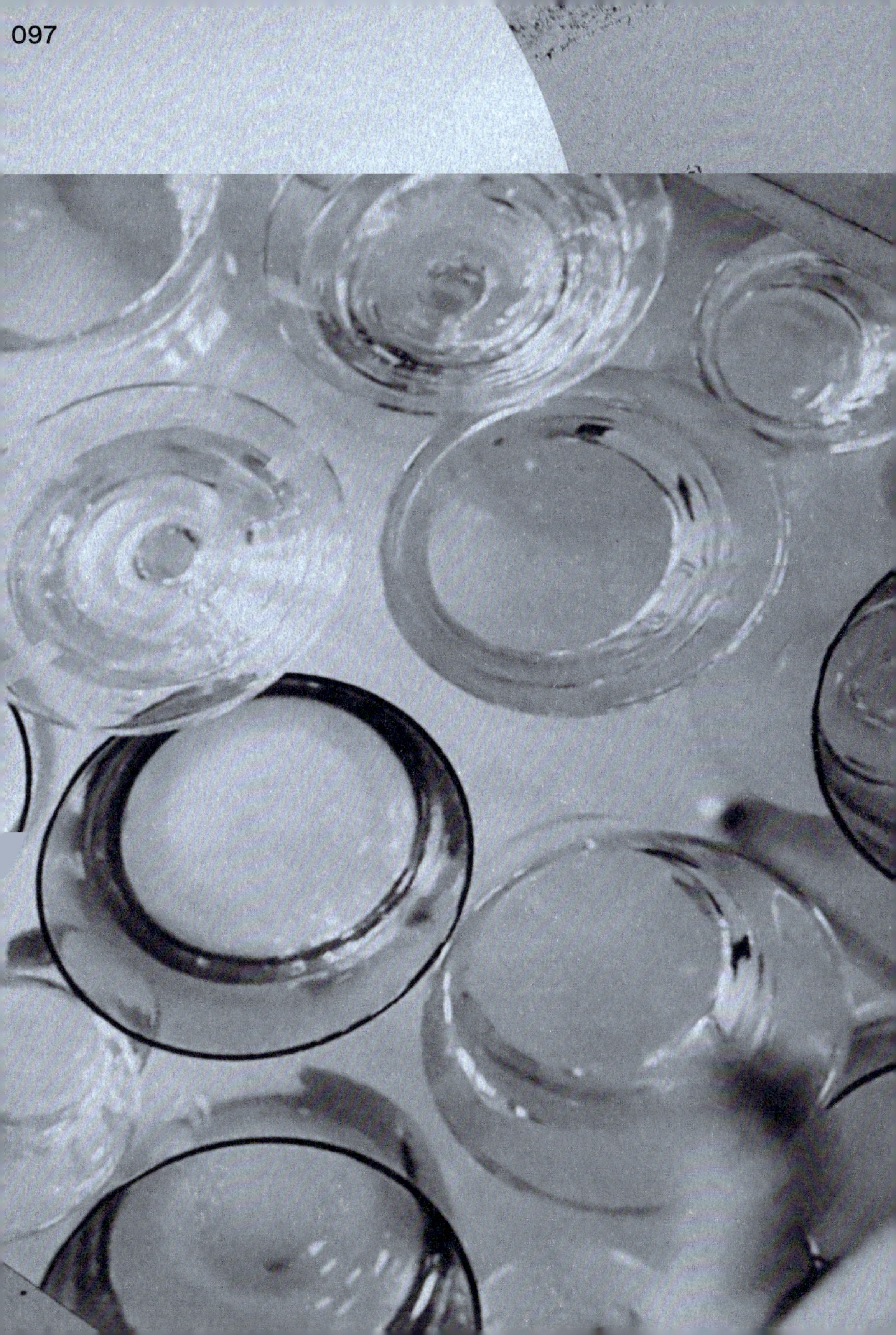

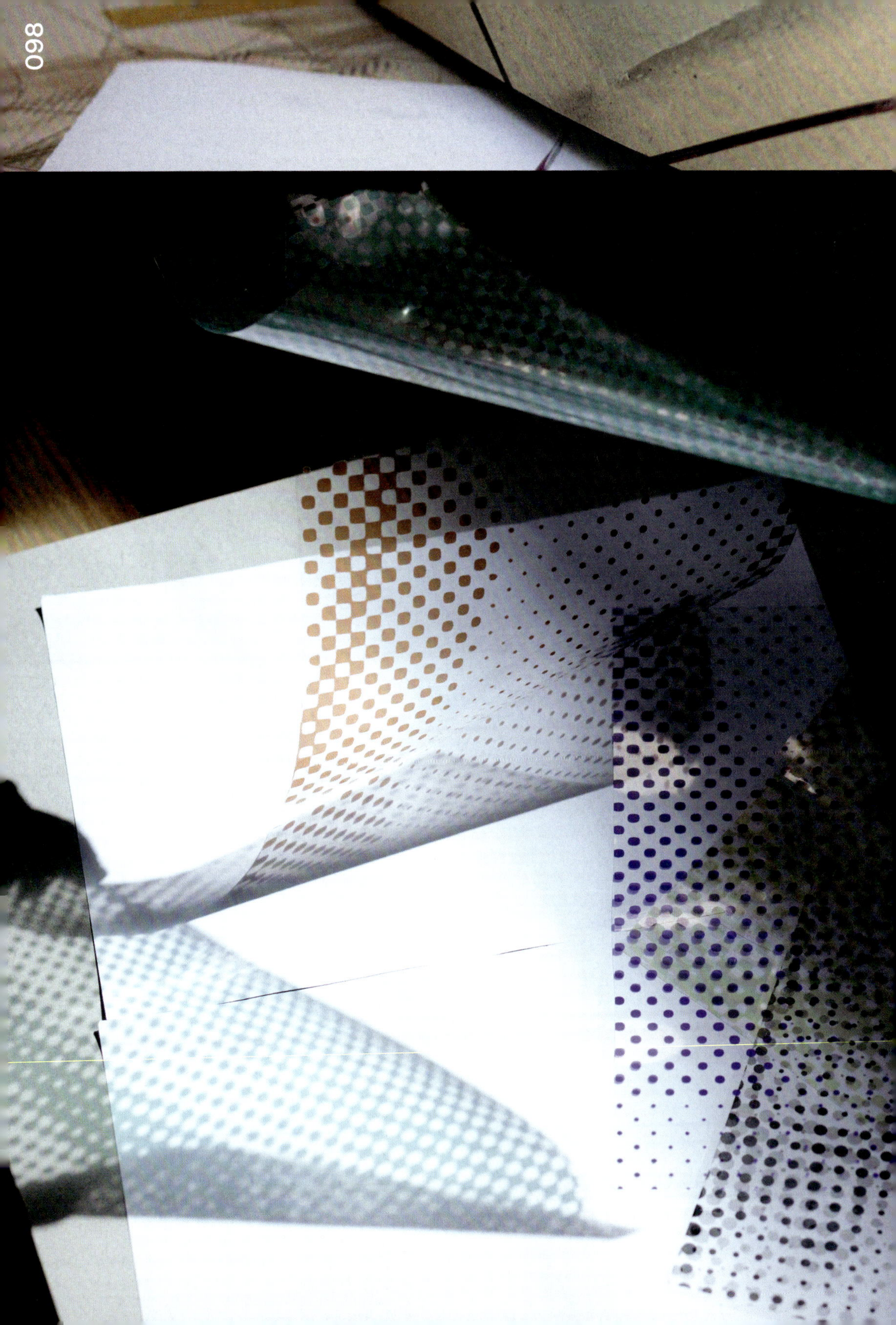

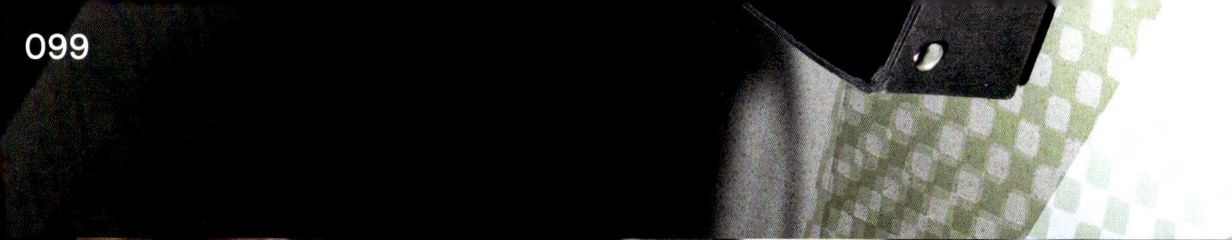

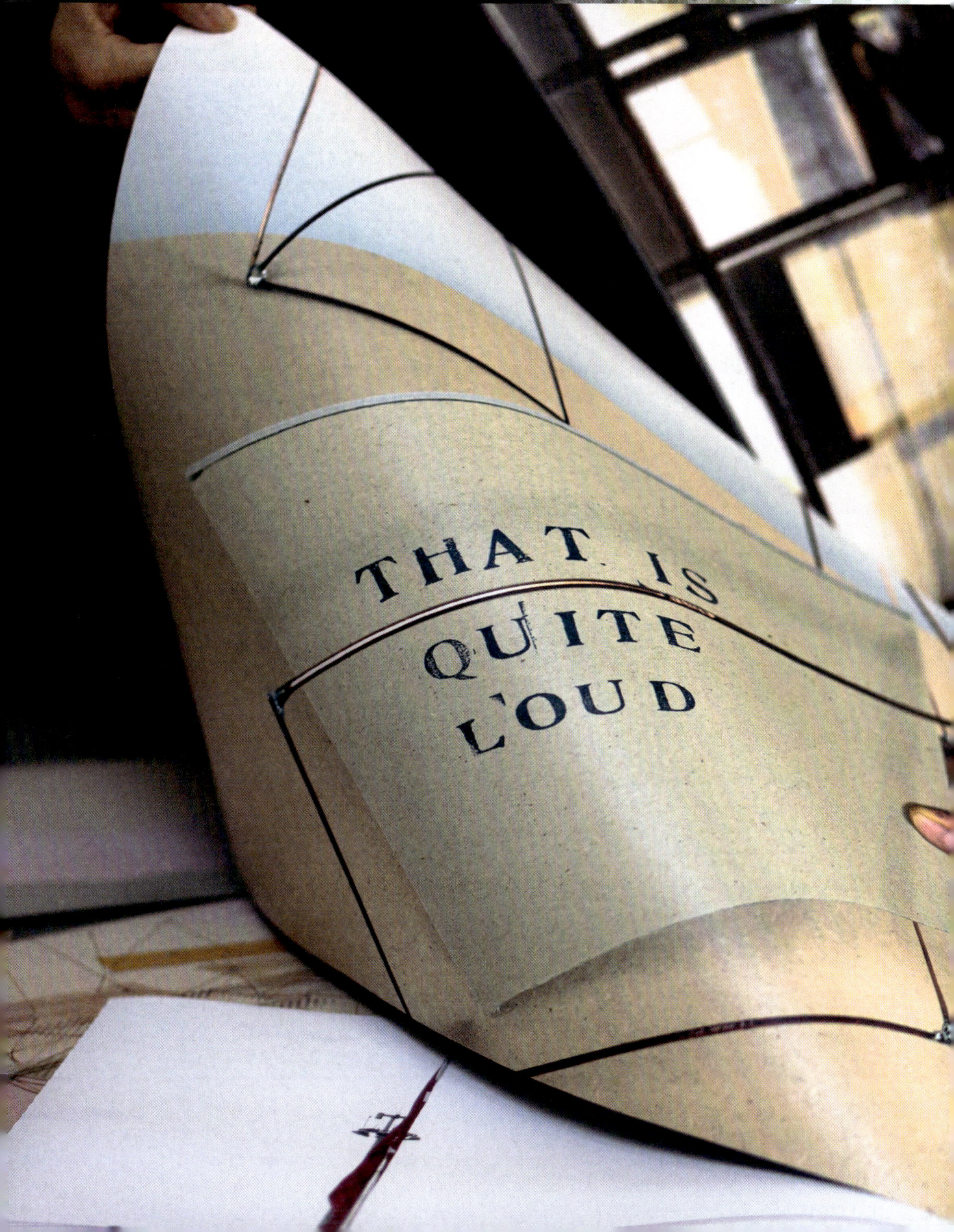
THAT IS
QUITE
LOUD

Schwebendes [Hovering] grew out of photographs Ricarda Denzer took at Atatürk Kültür Merkezi, an important cultural center on Taksim Square in Istanbul, during the 2013 Gezi Park protests. The modernist building, already empty at that point, was emblematic of the utopia of a secular society, and for a short time served protestors both as a symbol and as a place to present their political banners.

In the exhibition *Speech Acts. Vom Sprechen als politischem Handeln* [Speech Acts. Speaking as Political Action] Denzer sets out a narrative around her photographs of the protest, while also reflecting on her own standpoint and the form of narrative adopted. Her visual model is Paul Klee's painting *Schwebendes* [Hovering] (1930), which depicts a spatial form that breaks with both the logic of perspectival vision and the idea of linear chronologies and rational spatial connections.

Denzer recreated this complex structure in her installation as the model for her attempt to create a multi-perspective, non-linear narrative.

The video in the installation incorporates a further plane for viewing the photographs, moving beyond the protest that is documented to consider speech as political action. Rather than simply being hung on the wall, the photographs from Atatürk Kültür Merkezi are presented to the video camera by a group of young school pupils in a kind of performance. Denzer sees their dialogs—which address not simply what the images depict but also the pupils' shared activity—as embodying the actual meaning of speech acts, as defined by Hannah Arendt: Arendt describes speaking as a form of action, in which we "thread ourselves into a network of relationships. We never know what arises from this," (Hannah Arendt in conversation with Günther Gaus, in the television interview series *Zur Person*, 1964).

Ausgangspunkt der Arbeit *Schwebendes* sind Fotografien, die Ricarda Denzer während der Gezi-Park-Proteste 2013 im *Atatürk Kültür Merkezi*, einem bedeutenden Kulturzentrum am Taksim-Platz in Istanbul, aufgenommen hat. Das modernistische, damals bereits leerstehende Gebäude stand für die Utopie einer säkularen Gesellschaft und diente den Protestierenden für kurze Zeit sowohl als Symbol als auch als Präsentationsort für ihre politischen Banner.

In der Ausstellung *Speech Acts. Vom Sprechen als politischem Handeln* breitete die Künstlerin eine Erzählung rund um diese Aufnahmen des Protestes aus, nicht ohne ihren eigenen Standpunkt und die Form der Erzählung zu reflektieren: Als „Bild" dafür diente ihr das Gemälde *Schwebendes* (1930) von Paul Klee, das ein räumliches Gebilde zeigt, welches mit der Logik des perspektivischen Sehens ebenso wie mit der Vorstellung linearer Chronologien und rationalen räumlichen Verbindungen bricht.

In ihrer Installation hat Denzer diese komplexe Struktur nachgebaut, um ein Modell für ihren Versuch einer multiperspektivischen, nicht-linearen Erzählung zu schaffen.

Die Videokomponente der Installation enthält noch eine weitere Ebene der Betrachtung der Fotografien, die über den dokumentierten Protest hinaus eine Vorstellung vom Sprechen als politischem Handeln liefert: Die Fotografien aus dem *Atatürk Kültür Merkezi* hängen nicht einfach an der Wand, sondern werden von einer Gruppe junger Schüler*innen vor der Videokamera präsentiert und erfahren so eine Art Aufführung: Ihre Dialoge, die sich nicht allein um das Dargestellte, sondern auch um das gemeinsame Tun drehen, verkörpern aus Denzers Sicht den eigentlichen Sinn von Sprechakten, wie Hannah Arendt ihn definiert hat: Arendt beschreibt Sprechen als eine Form des Handelns, bei dem wir *„unseren Faden in ein Netz der Beziehungen schlagen. Was daraus wird, wissen wir nie."* (Hannah Arendt im Gespräch mit Günter Gaus, *Zur Person*, 1964)

Installation in the exhibition *Speech Acts Vom Sprechen als politischem Handeln* [Speech Acts. Speaking as Political Action], Forum Stadtpark, steirischer herbst, Graz, 2015, curated by Georgia Holz

With work by Michael Baers, Ricarda Denzer, Sharon Hayes, and Elske Rosenfeld

Video screening at mumok Kino, Vienna, 2016, Hua Art Museum, Shenzhen, China, 2018, Kamel Lazaar Foundation (KLF) Tunis, Tunisia, 2019

Installation im Rahmen der Ausstellung *Speech Acts Vom Sprechen als politischem Handeln*, Forum Stadtpark, steirischer herbst, Graz, 2015, kuratiert von Georgia Holz

Mit Arbeiten von Michael Baers, Ricarda Denzer, Sharon Hayes und Elske Rosenfeld

Videovorführungen im mumok Kino Wien, 2016, Hua Art Museum, Shenzhen, China, 2018, The Kamel Lazaar Foundation (KLF) Tunis, Tunisia, 2019

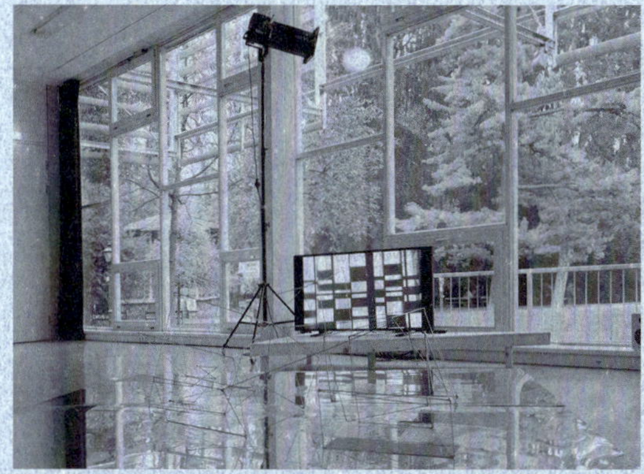

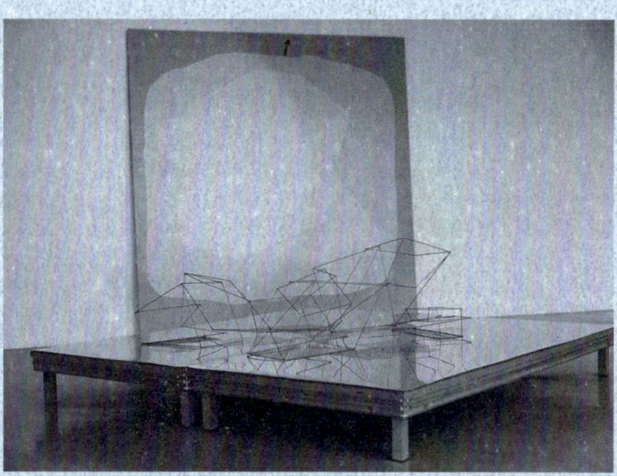

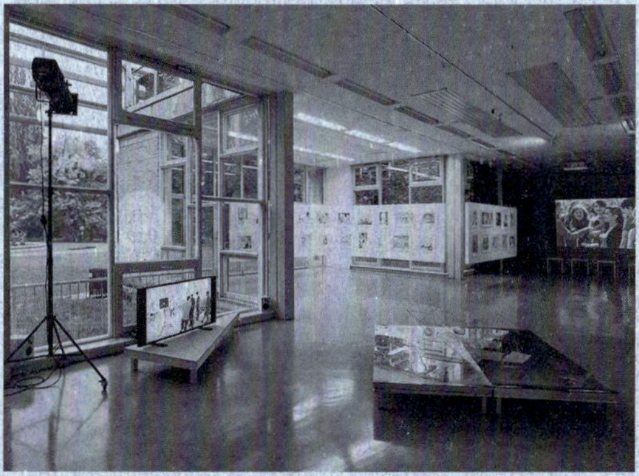

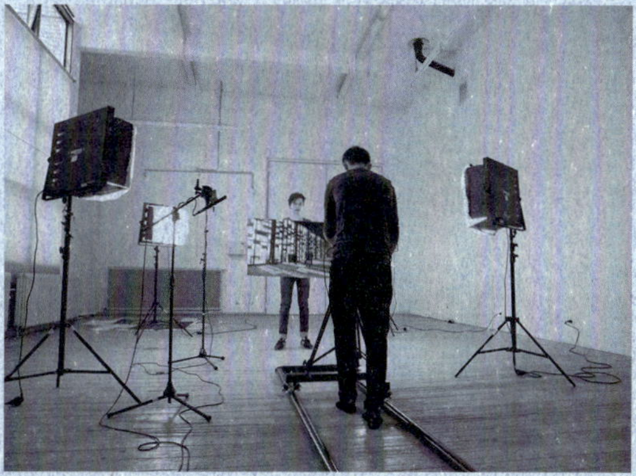

98–99, 102, 106–107, 110–111, 112–113 ←

en Exhibition view
Schwebendes, in the exhibition *Speech Acts*,
Forum Stadtpark, steirischer herbst, Graz, 2015

Video/audio installation, 16 min, stage structure, mirror foil, wooden construction, floodlights, laminated color print, *Sprachobjekt*: color print on foil, welding rod, solder

Recording team: Can Noa Denzer, Claus Diwisch, Alexander Mörtl, Andreas Rippl, Marian Wagner

de Ausstellungsansicht
Schwebendes, Ausstellung *Speech Acts*,
Forum Stadtpark, steirischer herbst, Graz, 2015

Video-/Audio-Installation, 16 min, Bühnenelement, Spiegelfolie, Holzkonstruktion, Scheinwerfer, Farbprint kaschiert, *Sprachobjekt*: Farbprint auf Folie, Schweißstäbe, Lötzinn

Aufnahmeteam: Can Noa Denzer, Claus Diwisch, Alexander Mörtl, Andreas Rippl, Marian Wagner

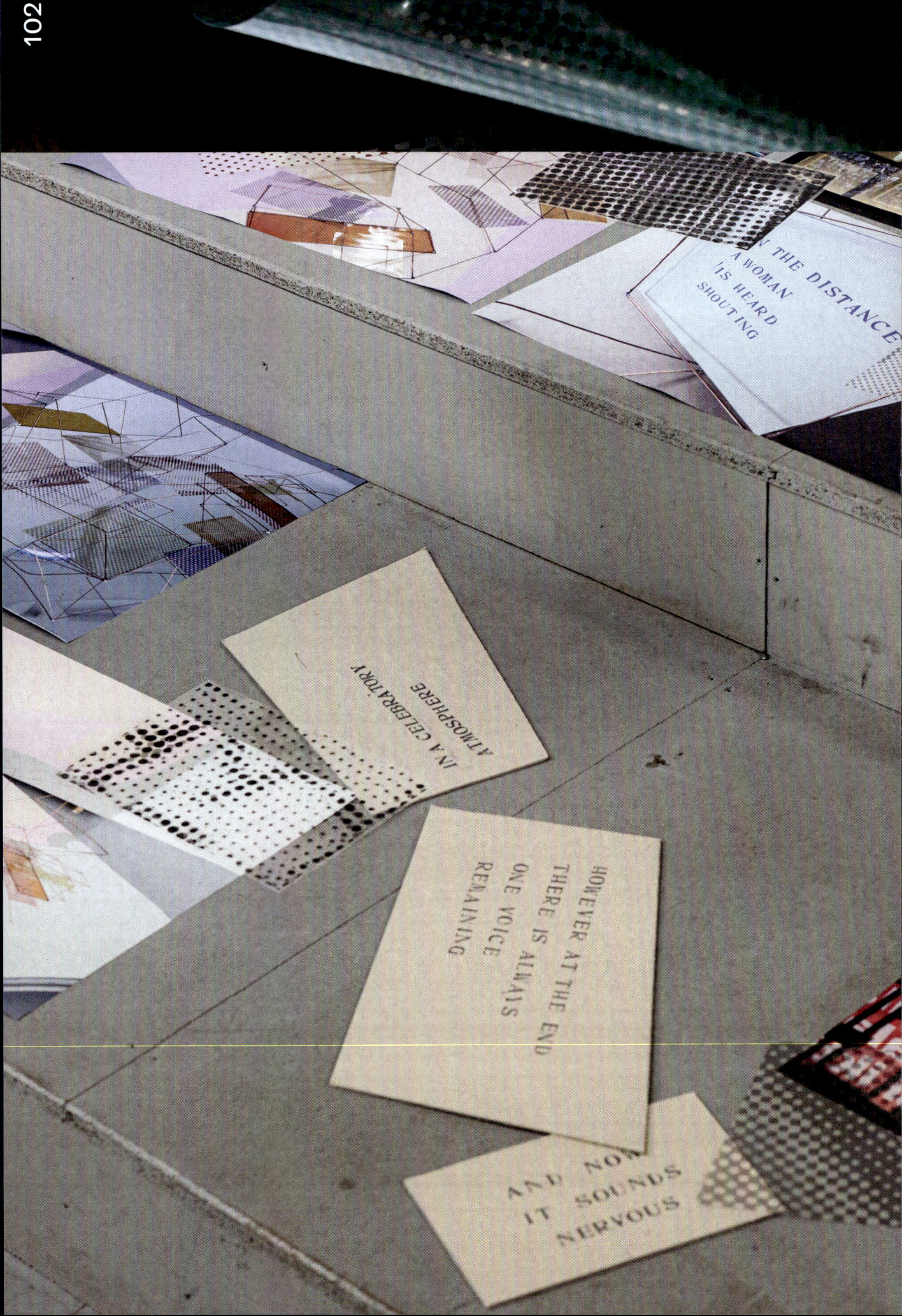
N THE DISTANCE
A WOMAN
IS HEARD
SHOUTING
IN A CELEBRATORY
ATMOSPHERE
HOWEVER AT THE END
THERE IS ALWAYS
ONE VOICE
REMAINING
AND NO
IT SOUNDS
NERVOUS

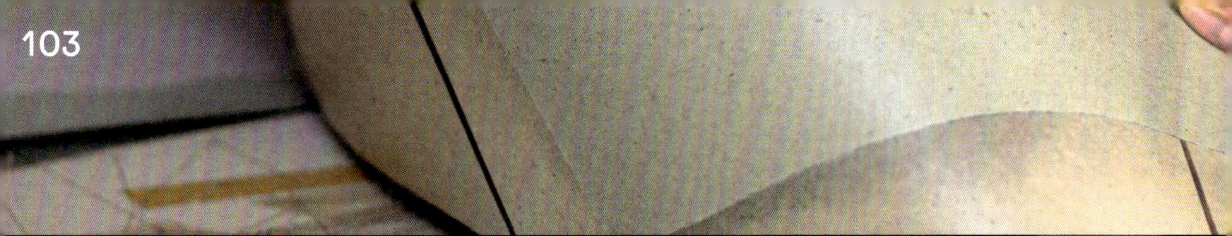

Ricarda Denzer's audiovisual installation *restore* (2008) took as its starting point the story of Rose Dugan, an American aviation pioneer, who in 1916 was the first to fly over Santa Fe, with Vera van Blumenthal, who later became her lover, as a passenger. The latter, a Russian dealer in applied arts, planned to export Czech lace to Pasadena. The two women settled in New Mexico and became a couple. Their collaboration with potters from San Ildefonso Pueblo, where they provided workshops for handicraft production as well as marketing strategies and financial support, ultimately led to the founding of the Indian Arts Fund, followed in 1922 by the first Santa Fe Indian Market, which has become the world's largest art fair for indigenous art.

In the exhibition *Resist: be modern (again)*, which illuminated the groundbreaking practice of artists, designers, and writers from the 1920s and 30s, Denzer built on her contribution to the 2008 Site Santa Fe Biennial, adding further images of traditional pueblo pottery from the early 1900s by influential ceramic artist Maria Martinez. The video images show a vase by Maria Martinez that entered the collection of what is now Weltmuseum Wien, in 1955.

Denzer's audiovisual work on the art trade links Santa Fe with 1920s Vienna, the Arts and Crafts Movement, the Wiener Werkstätte (Vienna Workshop), and a generation of Viennese collectors who were forced to flee or were murdered by the Nazis.

Ausgangspunkt von Ricarda Denzers audiovisueller Installation *restore* (2008) war die Geschichte von Rose Dugan, einer amerikanischen Flugpionierin, die zusammen mit ihrer Passagierin und späteren Geliebten, Vera van Blumenthal, 1916 als erste über Santa Fe flog. Die russische Kunstgewerbehändlerin van Blumenthal plante, tschechische Spitze nach Pasadena zu exportieren. Die beiden Frauen ließen sich in New Mexico nieder und wurden ein Paar. Ihre Zusammenarbeit mit Töpfern aus dem San Ildefonso Pueblo, wo sie neben Workshops auch Marketingstrategien und finanzielle Unterstützung für die Produktion des Kunsthandwerks anboten, führte schließlich zur Gründung des Indian Arts Fund und 1922 zum ersten Santa Fe Indian Market, der inzwischen größten Kunstmesse indigener Kunst der Welt.

Für die Ausstellung *Resist: be modern (again)*, in der zeitgenössische Positionen die wegweisenden Praktiken von Künstlerinnen, Designerinnen und Schreiberinnen der 1920er- und 1930er-Jahre beleuchteten, hat Denzer den ursprünglich für die Site Santa Fe Biennale 2008 realisierten Beitrag um weitere Aufnahmen der traditionellen Pueblo-Keramik der einflussreichen Keramikkünstlerin Maria Martinez aus den frühen 1900er-Jahren erweitert. Die Videobilder zeigen eine Vase von Maria Martinez, die 1955 in die Sammlung des heutigen Weltmuseums Wien gelangte.

Denzer verbindet in ihrer audiovisuellen Arbeit über das Thema des Kunsthandels den Ort Santa Fe mit dem Wien der 1920er-Jahre und der Arts and Craft-Bewegung, der Wiener Werkstätte, Art Nouveau und einer Generation von Wiener Sammlerfamilien, die fliehen mussten oder von den Nazis ermordet wurden.

Part of the exhibition *Resist: be modern (again)*, curated by Stefanie Seibold and Alice Maude-Roxby, John Hansard Gallery, Southampton, UK, 2019

With work by Becky Beasley, Madeleine Bernstorff, Tessa Boffin, Ricarda Denzer, Andrea Geyer, Moira Hille, Alice Maude-Roxby, Nick Mauss, Ursula Mayer, Falke Pisano, Ingrid Pollard, Tanoa Sasraku-Ansah, Katie Schwab, Stefanie Seibold, Megan Francis Sullivan, S. Louisa Wei, Riet Wijnen, Gillian Wylde, and a contribution from the curator Beatriz Herráez

Im Rahmen der Ausstellung *Resist: be modern (again)*, kuratiert von Stefanie Seibold und Alice Maude-Roxby, John Hansard Gallery, Southampton, UK, 2019

Mit Arbeiten von Becky Beasley, Madeleine Bernstorff, Tessa Boffin, Ricarda Denzer, Andrea Geyer, Moira Hille, Alice Maude-Roxby, Nick Mauss, Ursula Mayer, Falke Pisano, Ingrid Pollard, Tanoa Sasraku-Ansah, Katie Schwab, Stefanie Seibold, Megan Francis Sullivan, S. Louisa Wei, Riet Wijnen, Gillian Wylde und einem Beitrag der Kuratorin Beatriz Herráez

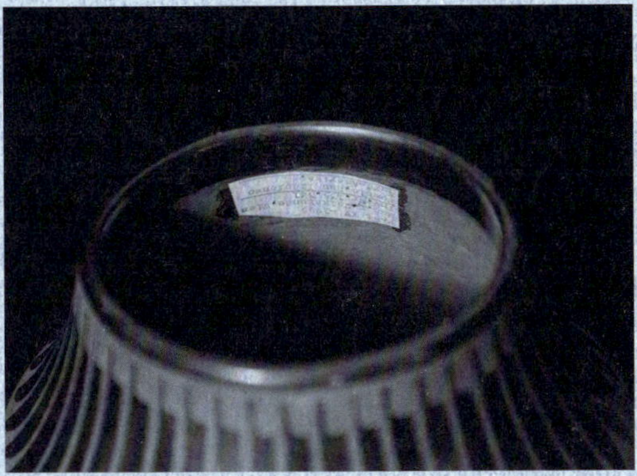

en Detail
restore (restore), 2008/2019, black ceramic by Maria Martinez (early 1900s), from the collection of the Weltmuseum Wien

de Detailansicht
restore (restore), 2008/2019, Schwarze Keramik von Maria Martinez (frühe 1900er-Jahre), aus der Sammlung des Weltmuseum Wien

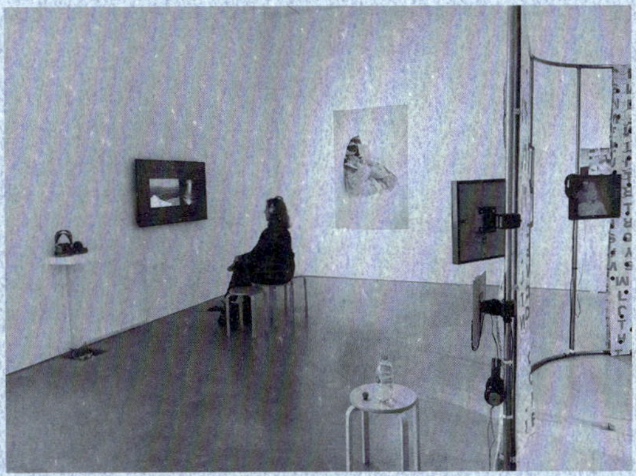

en Exhibition view
restore (restore) in the exhibition *Resist: be modern (again)*
John Hansard Gallery, Southampton, UK, 2019
Video/sound 34 min; *Pink Toxic Cloud*, 2008, C-print, matt (122 × 173 cm)

de Ausstellungsansicht
restore (restore) im Rahmen der Ausstellung *Resist: be modern (again)*
John Hansard Gallery, Southampton, UK, 2019.
Video/Sound 34 min, *Pink Toxic Cloud*, 2008, C-print, matt (cc 122 × 173 cm)

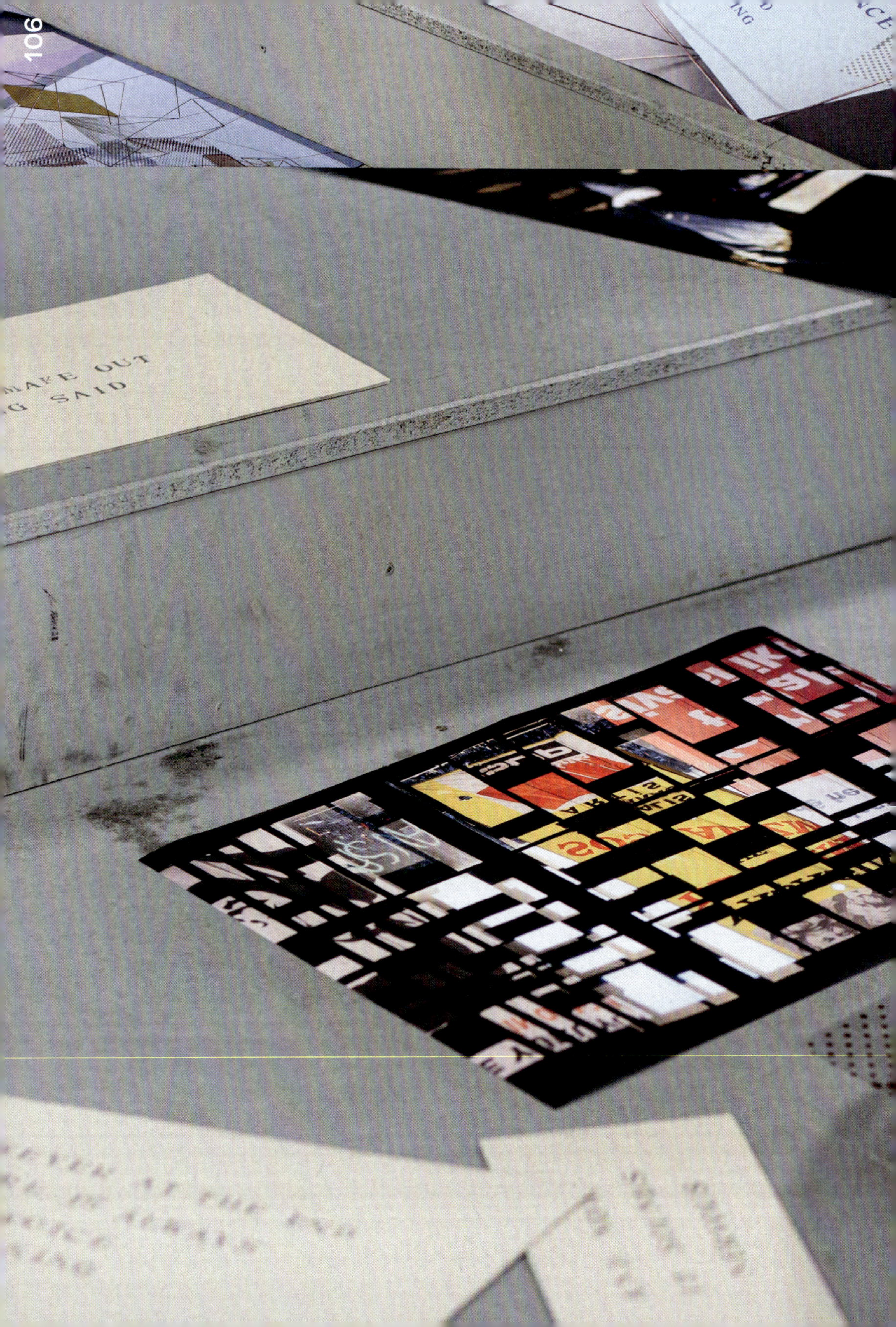

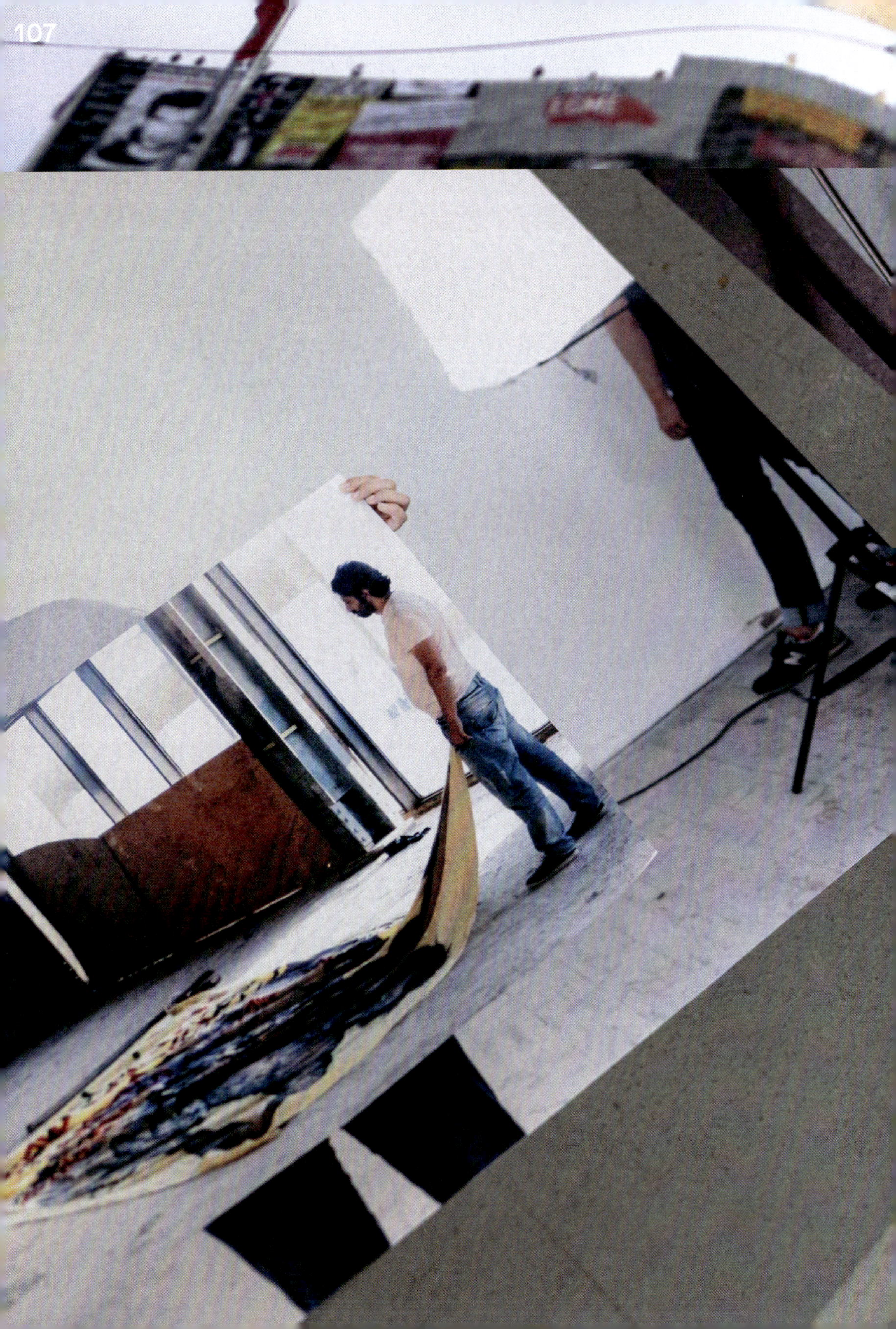

As in the game of telephone, in which a story is whispered from one player to the next, being modified and reinterpreted as it is repeated, Denzer focuses on different aspects of her work in the light of the specific space(s) and site of every exhibition venue. Recurring forms are supplemented by new materials and contexts; certain aspects are emphasized, others omitted. Denzer's examination of oral materiality and forms of narrative was continued in a sequence of linked exhibitions between 2014 and 2023 in Berlin, Innsbruck, Salzburg, Stockholm, Klagenfurt, Helsinki, Kufstein, and Vienna.

Ähnlich wie bei dem Spiel Stille Post, bei dem eine Geschichte flüsternd von Mund zu Ohr im wiederholten Erzählen abgewandelt und umgedeutet wird, rückt Denzer an jedem Ausstellungsort raum- und ortsspezifisch unterschiedliche Aspekte ihrer Arbeit in den Vordergrund. Wiederkehrende Formen werden durch neue Materialien und Zusammenhänge ergänzt, manches wird hervorgehoben, anderes weggelassen. Denzers Fragstellung nach der Materialität des Mündlichen sowie nach Formen der Erzählung fand aufeinanderfolgend zwischen 2014 und 2023 eine verbindende Weiterführung in Ausstellungen in Berlin, Innsbruck, Salzburg, Stockholm, Klagenfurt, Helsinki, Kufstein und Wien.

Potato prints have been a recurring element in Ricarda Denzer's work since 2014. In an active, meditative process, Denzer imprints paint onto paper with the cut surface of a potato until it stops leaving a visible mark, generally moving from left to right, but also following other patterns. This contemplative low-tech procedure creates a pattern of dots or a grid that can be produced by hand anywhere, in contrast to other often elaborate printing techniques.

For Ricarda Denzer, engaging in this activity is related to a performative "carrying on," a continual process of recording that helps her to reflect. The potato print is like a placeholder text, an interim stage, as she considers a key question while developing her works: "What is the story to tell?"

The viewer can also read the prints as visual translations of acoustic phenomena, in which "listening is a practice that expands beyond sound [as] a way of sparking and holding attention" (Jaimini Patel). In addition, the printed patterns also reveal intensities, rhythms, or compositional means such as fadeouts.

Ein wiederkehrendes Element in der Arbeit von Ricarda Denzer sind ab 2014 Kartoffeldrucke. Dabei wird von der Künstlerin in einem tätig-meditativen Prozess mit der Schnittfläche einer Kartoffel – meist von links nach rechts oder auch anderen Mustern folgend – so lange Farbe auf das Papier gedruckt, bis diese keinen sichtbaren Abdruck mehr hinterlässt. Das Ergebnis dieses kontemplativen Lowtech-Druckverfahrens ist ein Punkte- oder auch Rastermuster, das im Unterschied zu anderen, oft aufwändigen Drucktechniken überall manuell produziert werden kann.

Der Künstlerin geht es beim Ausüben dieser Tätigkeit um ein performatives „Weitermachen“, ein stetes Aufzeichnen, das ihr beim Nachdenken hilft. Der Kartoffeldruck ist für sie eine Art Blindtext, ein Zwischenstadium, während sie in der Entwicklung ihrer Arbeiten der Frage nachgeht, welche Geschichte es zu erzählen gilt: „What is the story to tell?“

Als Betrachter*in kann man die Drucke auch als visuelle Übersetzungen akustischer Phänomene lesen, bei der „das Zuhören eine Praxis ist, die sich über den Klang hinaus ausdehnt als eine Art, die Aufmerksamkeit zu wecken und zu halten“. (Jaimini Patel)

Darüber hinaus erkennt man in den gedruckten Mustern Intensitäten, Rhythmen oder gestaltende Mittel wie Fadeouts.

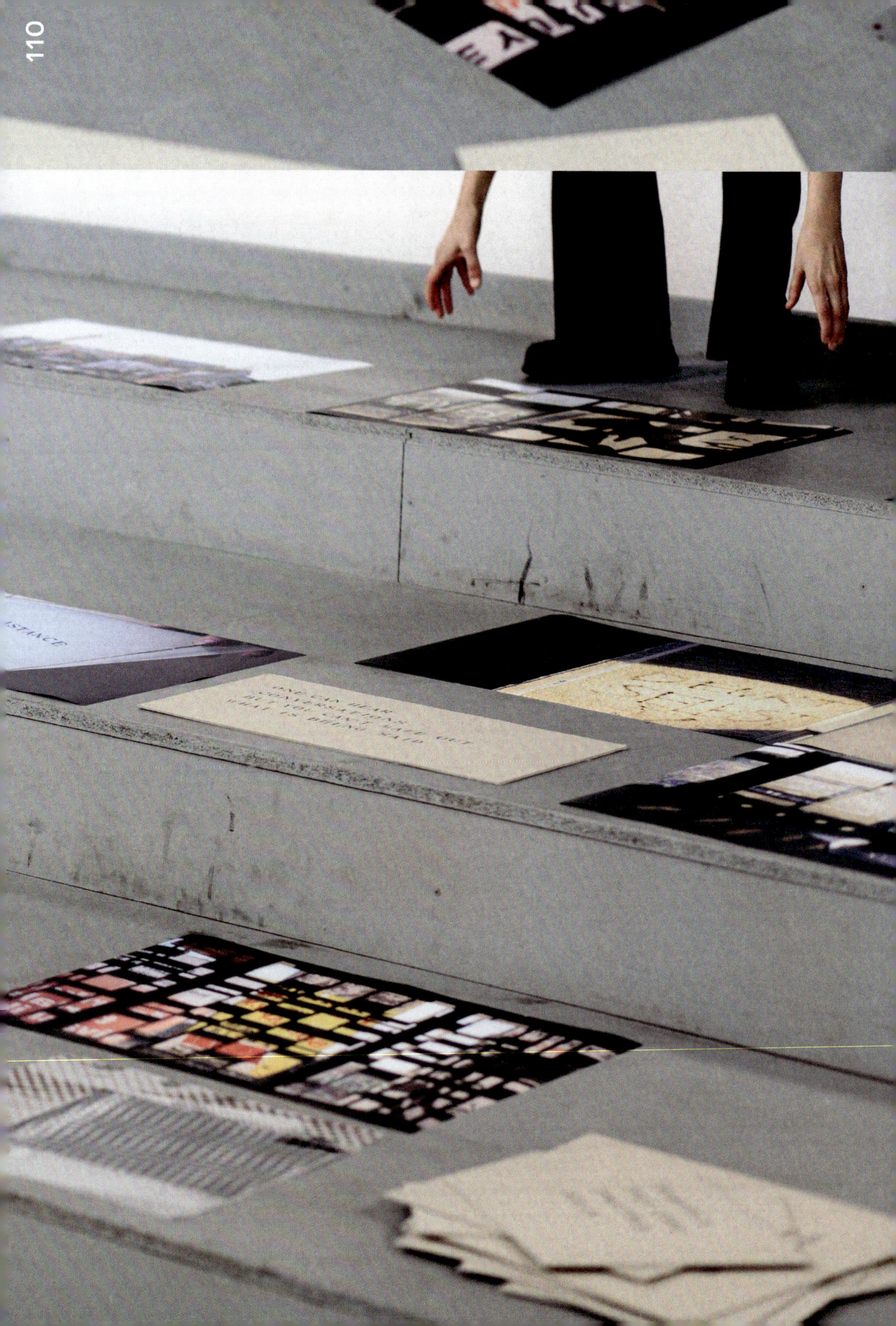

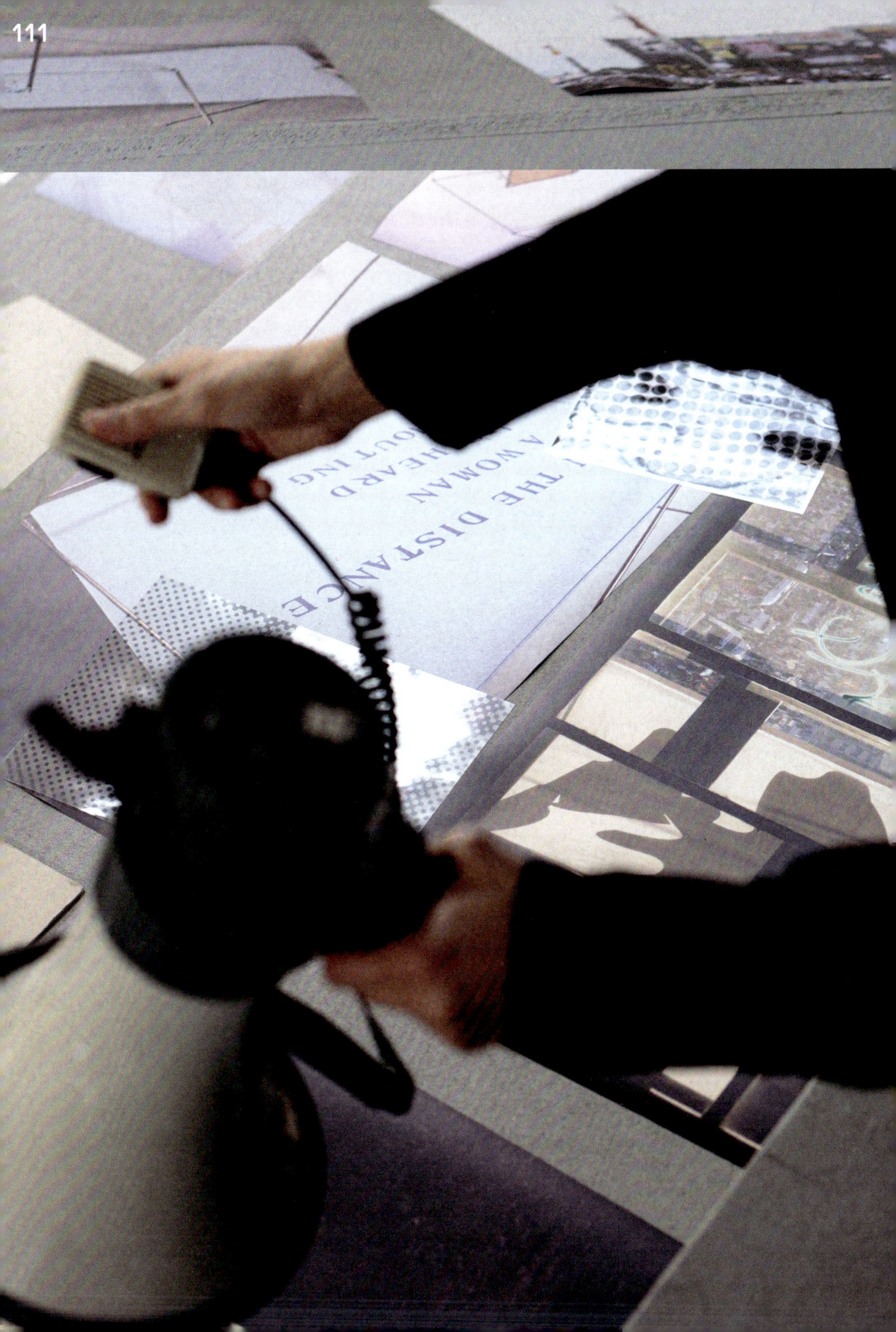
THE DISTANCE
A WOMAN
HEARD
SHOUTING

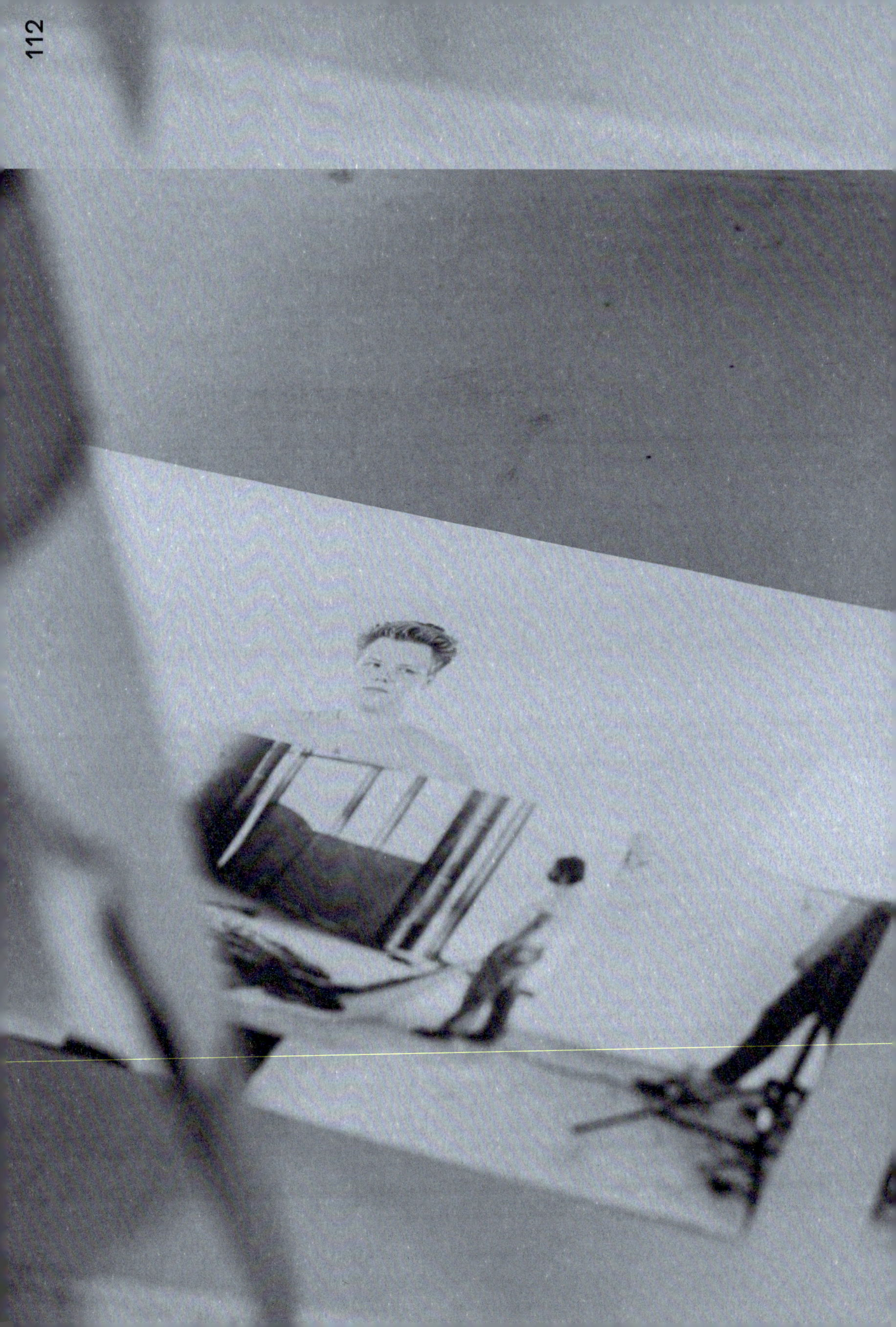

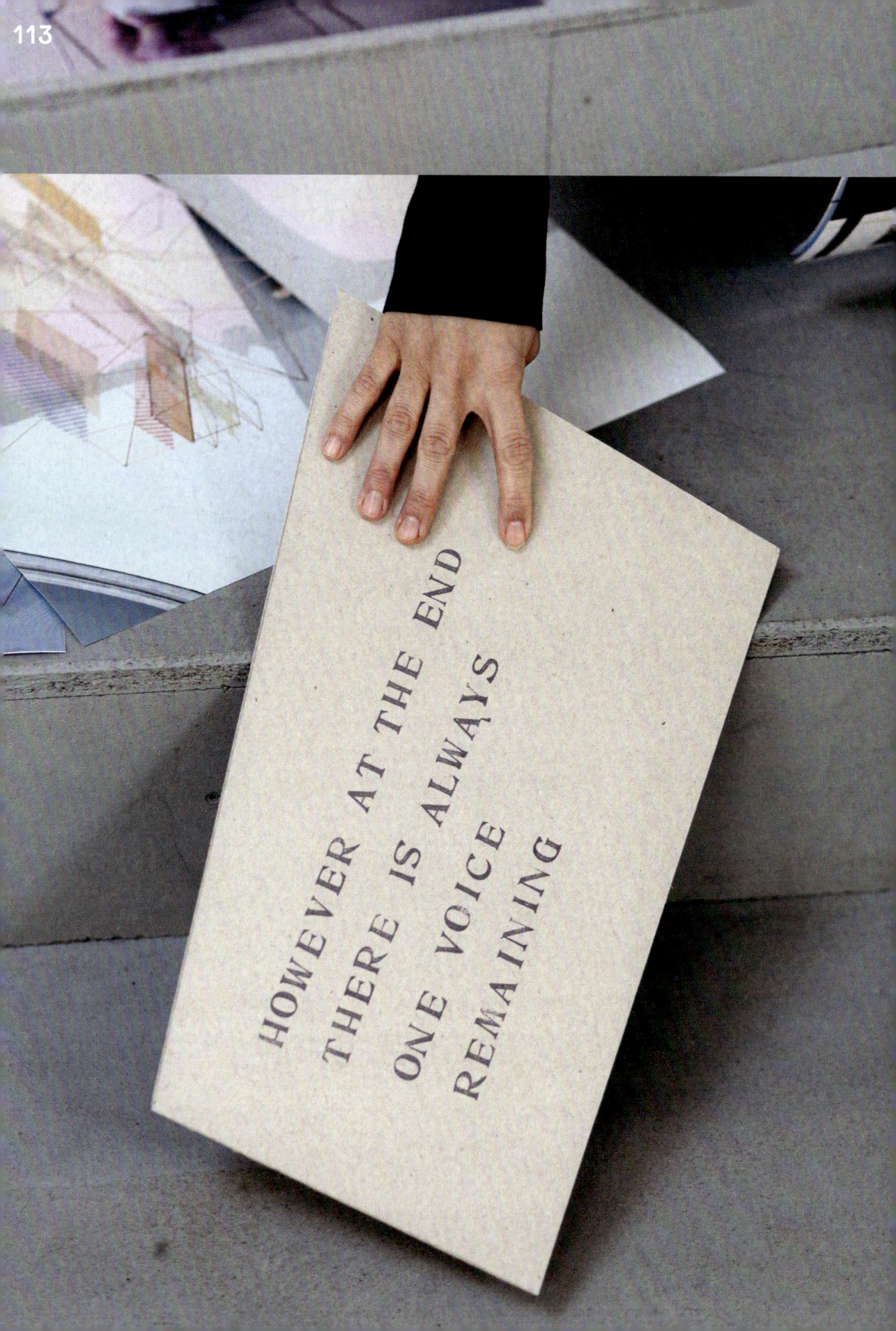
HOWEVER AT THE END
THERE IS ALWAYS
ONE VOICE
REMAINING

In the series *Präsenz eines anderen Ortes* [Presence of Another Place], Ricarda Denzer refers to a quotation from Franz Xaver Bayer about the way in which "humming, warbling, whistling" can open up spaces that connect the interior with the exterior, the corporeal with the incorporeal.

In the exhibition *The Inner Acoustics*, at the Errant Bodies art space in Berlin, Denzer used thin tissue paper to make a potato print that also passed through the paper and directly onto the wall. The imprinted form tells of physical presence, yet also of the ephemerality of voice and language, or rather the momentary nature of every recording. Like a cover or trace of the "original," the paper lies on the floor, relating to the imprint by recounting the differences between the source (of a noise, for example) and its perception through hearing/seeing.

In the video *Summen Trällern Pfeifen* [Humming Warbling Whistling] Denzer sensitizes viewers and listeners to these sometimes very fine distinctions: the artist's ink-stained fingers, which link both works, circle the dampened edges of glasses filled with water, making them hum. Occasional black, grey, or white wipes from left or right fade out not the sound but the images. They introduce rhythm into the visual level, on which image and sound are recurrently out of sync, until at some point a crackling and rustling overlays the glass harp. We see hands wrapping the glasses in newspaper after playing, as if for an impending move.

In der Serie *Präsenz eines anderen Ortes* greift Ricarda Denzer ein Zitat von Franz Xaver Bayer auf, demzufolge „Summen, Trällern, Pfeifen" Räume eröffnen können, die das Innen mit dem Außen verbinden, das Körperliche mit dem Nicht-Körperlichen.

Im Rahmen der Ausstellung *The Inner Acoustics* im Kunstraum Errant Bodies in Berlin hat sie einen ihrer Kartoffeldrucke durch dünnes Seidenpapier gedruckt und dabei den Kartoffeldruck auch direkt auf die Wand übertragen. Der Abdruck erzählt von körperlicher Präsenz, aber auch von der Flüchtigkeit von Stimme und Sprache beziehungsweise von der Momenthaftigkeit jeder Aufzeichnung. Wie die Hülle oder auch Spur des „Originals" liegt das Papier auf dem Boden, wo es im Verhältnis zum Abdruck von den Abweichungen zwischen der Quelle (zum Beispiel eines Geräusches) und deren Wahrnehmung im Prozess des Hörens/Sehens erzählt.

In der Videoarbeit *Summen Trällern Pfeifen* sensibilisiert Denzer die Betrachter*innen und Hörer*innen für diese teils sehr feinen Unterschiede: Mit tintenverschmierten Fingern, die die beiden Arbeiten verbinden, fährt die Künstlerin mit Kreisbewegungen die Ränder von befeuchteten, mit Wasser gefüllten Gläsern entlang, bis diese gemeinsam zu klingen beginnen. Zwischendurch „faden" schwarze, graue und weiße Blenden von links oder rechts kommend nicht den Sound, aber die Bilder aus. Sie rhythmisieren die Bildebene, auf der Bild und Ton immer wieder asynchron sind, bevor irgendwann ein Knistern und Rascheln das Spiel der Glasorgel überlagert: Zu sehen sind Hände, die die Gläser nach dem Spiel, wie für einen bevorstehenden Umzug, in Zeitungspapier verpacken.

Video installation for the exhibition *The Inner Acoustics*, curated by Brandon LaBelle, Errant Bodies, 2015

With work by Ricarda Denzer, Brandon LaBelle, Ines Lechleitner, Annette Stahmer, Imogen Stidworthy

Video-Installation im Rahmen der Ausstellung *The Inner Acoustics*, kuratiert von Brandon LaBelle, Berlin, Errant Bodies, 2015

Mit Arbeiten von Ricarda Denzer, Brandon LaBelle, Ines Lechleitner, Annette Stahmer, Imogen Stidworthy

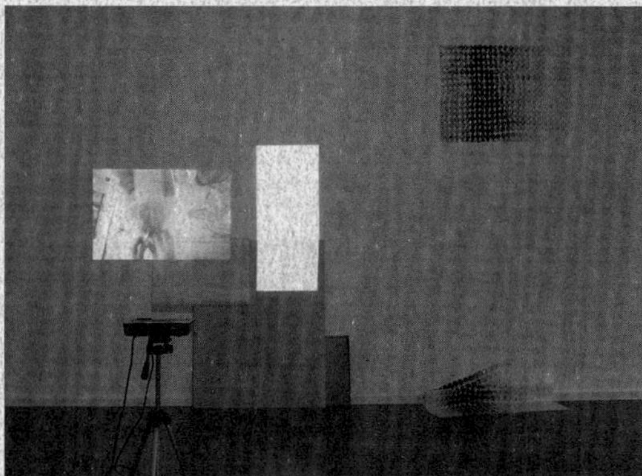

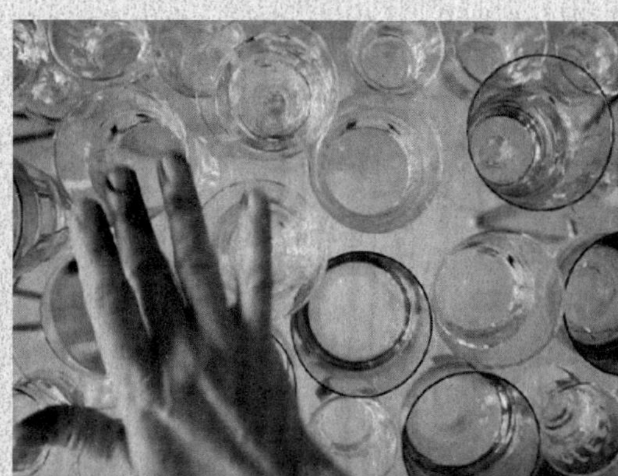

97 ←

Exhibition view
Summen Trällern Pfeifen, in the exhibition
The Inner Acoustics, Errant Bodies, Berlin, 2015

Ausstellungsansicht
Summen Trällern Pfeifen, Ausstellung
The Inner Acoustics, Errant Bodies, Berlin, 2015

O.T. [Untitled], potato print with black ink on the wall and 20 g tissue paper, 50 × 70 cm

O. T., Kartoffeldruck auf Wand mit schwarzer Tinte und Papier 20 g 50 × 70 cm

Summen, Trällern Pfeifen [Humming Warbling Whistling], audio/video loop, 15 min

Summen Trällern Pfeifen, Audio-/Videoloop, 15 min

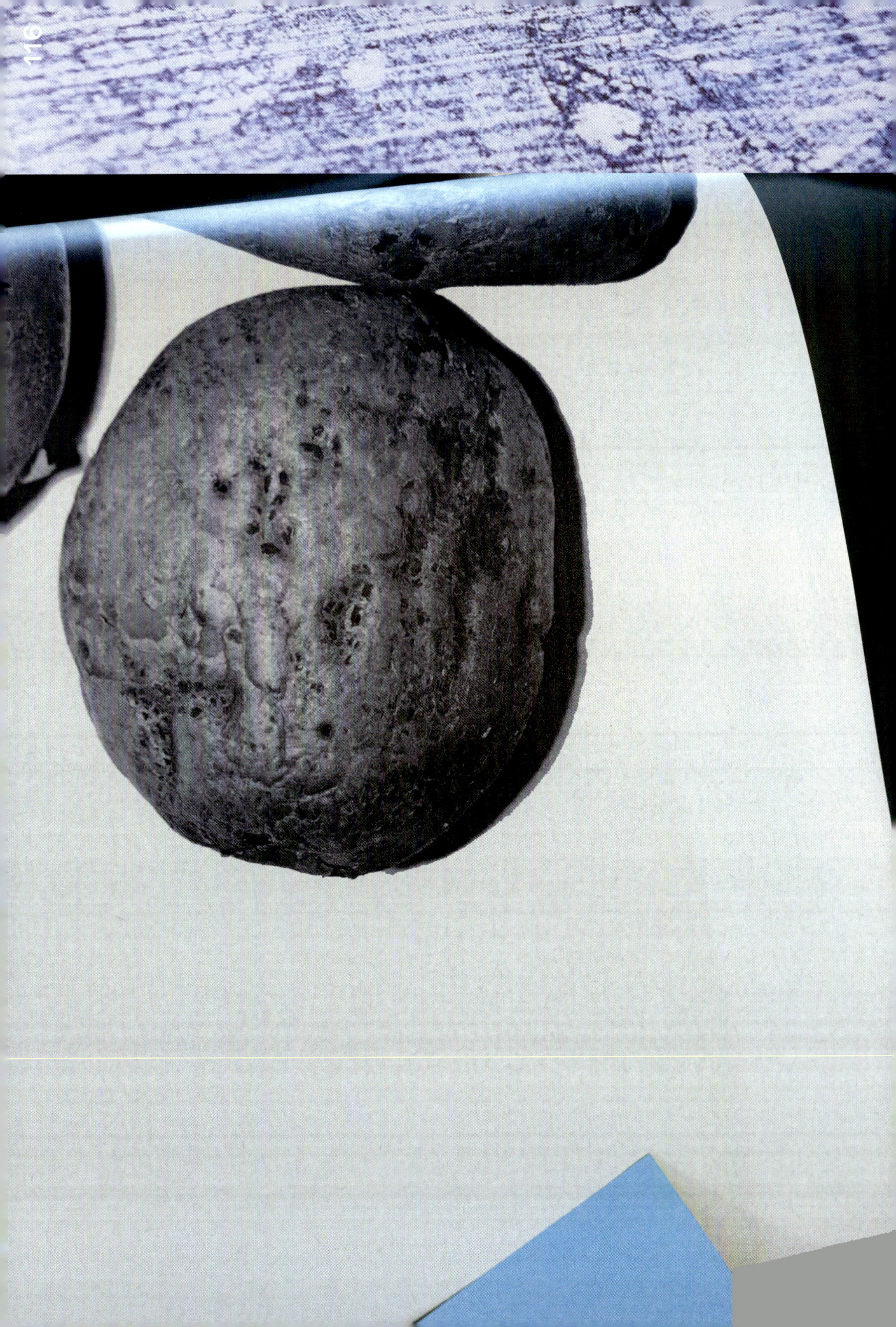

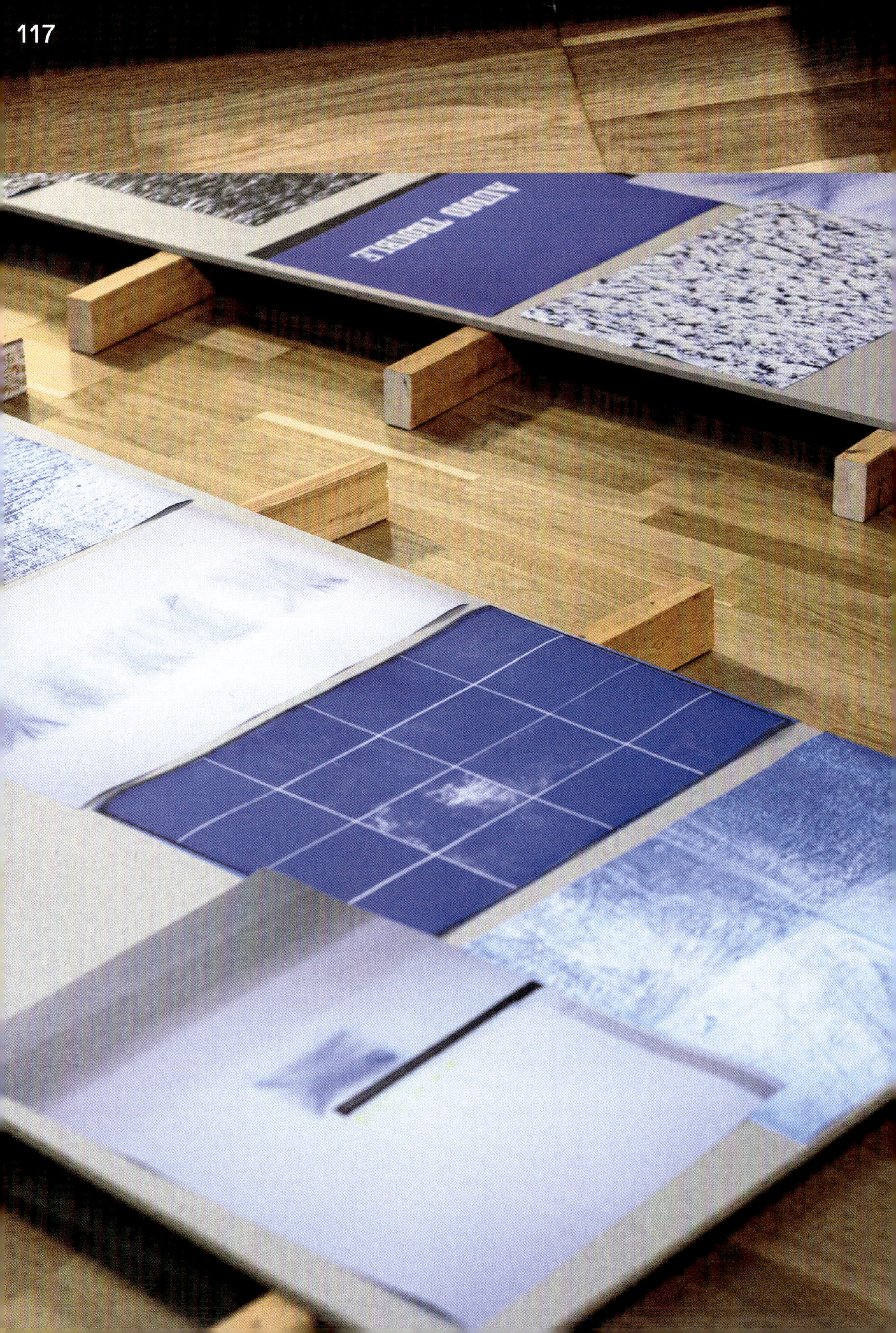
AUDIO TROUBLE

Reusing and building on images, motifs, sounds, compositional means, and themes forms an important part of Ricarda Denzer's artistic practice. In the exhibition *Die Kunst der Frau* [The Art of Women], a "barter exhibition" that referenced a 1932 format and slogan devised by the Austrian Association of Women Artists (VBKÖ), the potato print transferred to the wall testifies to physical presence and its inscription into a space in which numerous stories of twentieth-century women artists in the archives are still waited to be rediscovered, retold, and continued.

Die Wiederaufnahme und Weiterentwicklung von Bildern, Motiven, Sounds, gestalterischen Mitteln und Themen ist wichtiger Teil der künstlerischen Praxis von Ricarda Denzer. Im Rahmen der Ausstellung *Die Kunst der Frau*, die sich als „Tauschausstellung" auf ein Format und Motto der VBKÖ von 1932 bezog, erzählt der an der Wand affichierte Kartoffeldruck von körperlicher Präsenz und deren Einschreibung in einen Raum, in dem in den Archiven noch zahlreiche Geschichten von Künstlerinnen des 20. Jahrhunderts auf ein Wiederentdecken, Weitererzählen und Fortschreiben warten.

Die Kunst der Frau [The Art of Women], VBKÖ Vienna, 2016, curated by Barbara Steiner

With work by Maren Blume / Franziska Kabisch, Catharina Bond, Ricarda Denzer, Carola Dertnig, Veronika Dirnhofer, Barbara Eichhorn, Lizzy Fidler, Hilde Fuchs, Julia Gaisbacher, Helmut / Johanna Kandl, Brigitte Kovacs, Maria Hahnenkamp, Christian Helbock / Markus Lobner, Christine and Irene Hohenbüchler, Ruth Kaaserer, Anna Meyer, Lilo Nein, Marion Porten, Isa Rosenberger, Johannes Schweiger, Sekretariat für Geister, Archivpolitiken und Lücken (Nina Höchtl / Julia Wieger), Tatia Skhirtladze, Esther Straganz, Ingeborg Strobl

Die Kunst der Frau, VBKÖ Wien, 2016, kuratiert von Barbara Steiner

Mit Arbeiten von Maren Blume / Franziska Kabisch, Catharina Bond, Ricarda Denzer, Carola Dertnig, Veronika Dirnhofer, Barbara Eichhorn, Lizzy Fidler, Hilde Fuchs, Julia Gaisbacher, Helmut / Johanna Kandl, Brigitte Kovacs, Maria Hahnenkamp, Christian Helbock / Markus Lobner, Christine und Irene Hohenbüchler, Ruth Kaaserer, Anna Meyer, Lilo Nein, Marion Porten, Isa Rosenberger, Johannes Schweiger, Sekretariat für Geister, Archivpolitiken und Lücken (Nina Höchtl / Julia Wieger), Tatia Skhirtladze, Esther Straganz, Ingeborg Strobl

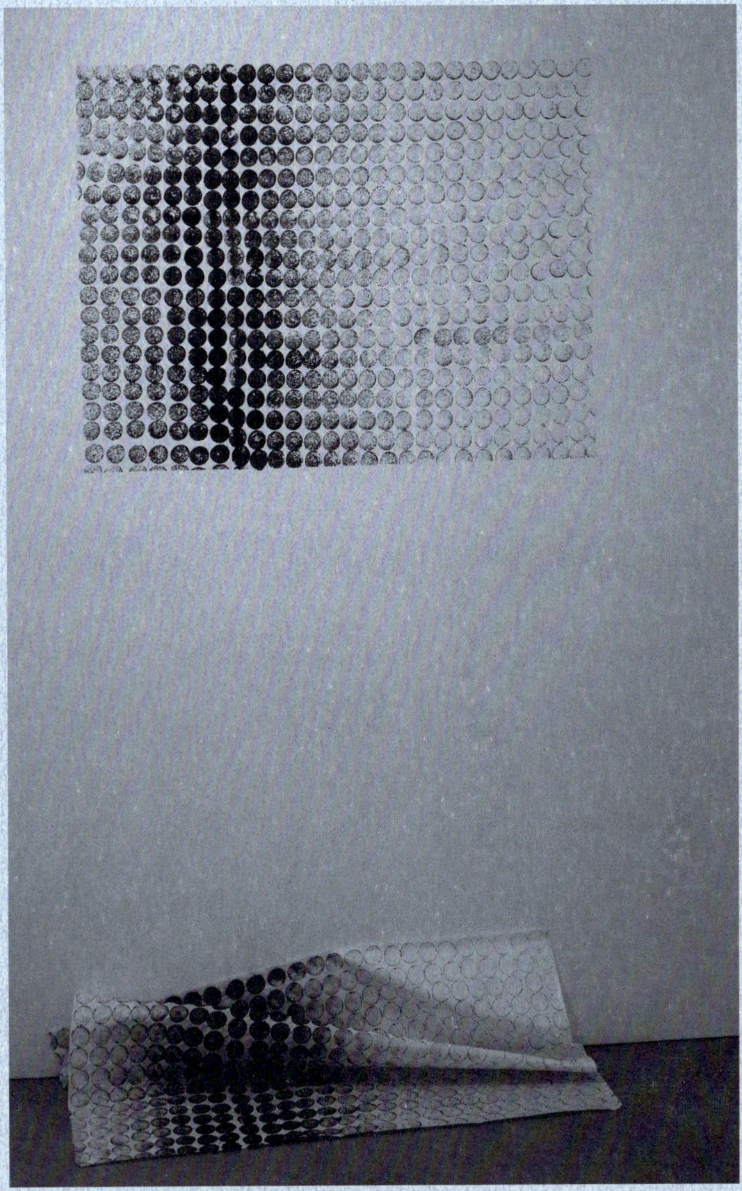

en Potato print, black ink on wall and 20 g paper 50 × 70 cm

de Kartoffeldruck, schwarze Tinte auf Wand und Papier 20 g 50 × 70 cm

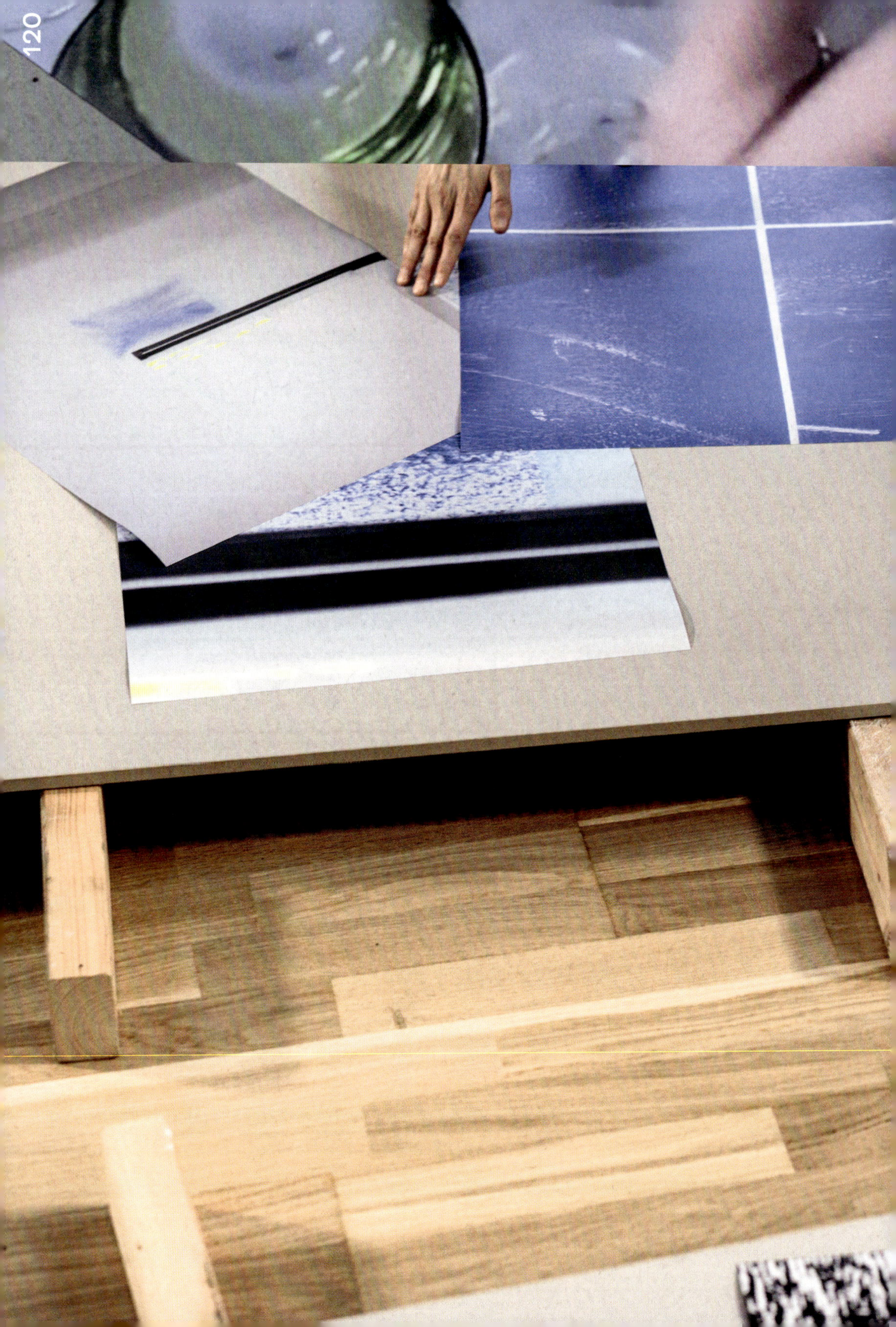

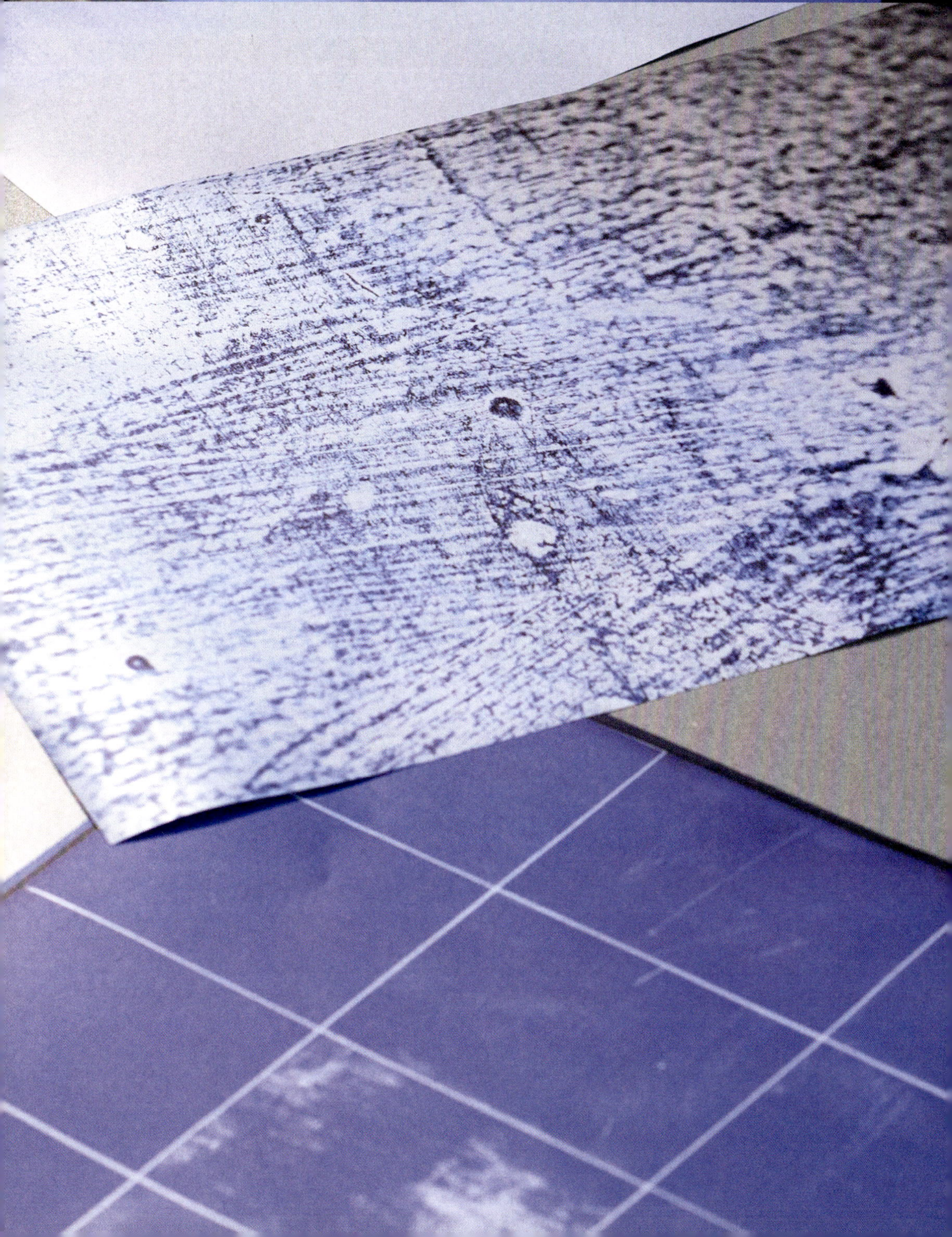

Echo, oder die Abweichung vom Original [Echo, or The Deviation from the Original] is the title of a multi-part assemblage for *Cross-Sections*. Having been invited to participate in this exhibition and research platform, Ricarda Denzer seized the opportunity to think about artistic research and continue exploring her "listening research practice."

The "original" here stands for the source, for the document and the origin. There is a smooth transition in the artistic process between happening upon an object, the documentary aspect of recording it in various modes, and recombination, that is, producing fiction through montage.

In this assemblage, objects appear like actors in a play in which the possible narratives only come into being thanks to the relationships between objects, material, and contexts. The central artistic stance is not to proceed from a clearly pre-defined idea or to make a piece *about* an issue, but to give form to the process of searching when researching the work, while at the same time reflecting on it.

In the exhibition the "alternative" forms and media used for recording include blueprints, which Denzer traces directly from her studio wall, and the artist's typical placeholder texts in the form of potato prints, for which she uses ocher or neon-yellow pigments. From this underpinning, the narrative branches out via the found material, ranging from the mines of the Forest of Dean in England, where ocher was quarried, to Hagia Sophia in Istanbul, where Denzer spotted a star-shaped ornament that took on central significance in her work. Found material—such as the color ocher, images, bronze objects, or blueprints—is incorporated as a source of inspiration and arranged without stipulating its precise geographic origin.

Echo, oder die Abweichung vom Original titelt der erste Teil einer mehrteiligen Assemblage im Rahmen von *CrossSections*. Ricarda Denzer nahm die Einladung zu der Ausstellungs- und Forschungsplattform zum Anlass, um über den Prozess künstlerischer Forschung nachzudenken und ihre Beschäftigung mit einer „hörenden Recherchepraxis" prozessual fortzuführen.

Das „Original" steht hier für die Quelle, für das Dokument und den Ursprung. Im künstlerischen Prozess ist die Bewegung zwischen dem Vorfinden eines Objektes, dem dokumentarischen Moment durch diverse Aufzeichnungen und dem neuen Zusammenfügen, also der Produktion von Fiktion durch Montage, fließend.

Objekte treten in dieser Assemblage wie Darsteller*innen in einem Stück auf, in dem sich die möglichen Erzählungen erst im Bezug der Objekte, Materialien und Zusammenhänge zueinander ergeben. Zentral ist die künstlerische Haltung, im Arbeitsprozess nicht schon von einer Idee, einer klaren Vorstellung auszugehen oder eine Arbeit *über* ein Thema zu realisieren, sondern der Suchbewegung im Zuge der Recherche eine Form zu geben und diese gleichzeitig auch zu reflektieren.

Zu den „alternativen" Aufzeichnungsformen und -medien gehören in der Ausstellung Blaupausen, die Denzer direkt von ihrer Atelierwand abpaust, sowie die für die Künstlerin typischen Blindtexte in Form von Kartoffeldrucken, für die sie Ockerpigmente oder auch neongelbe Pigmente verwendet. Von hier verzweigt sich die Erzählung über die vorgefundenen Materialien in die Bergbauhöhlen des Forest of Dean in England, wo die Ockerpigmente abgebaut werden, bis zur Hagia Sophia in Istanbul, wo der Künstlerin ein sternenförmiges Ornament auffiel, das in der Folge in den Mittelpunkt ihrer Arbeit rückte. Vor Ort Vorgefundenes – etwa die Farbe Ocker, Bildmaterial, Bronzeobjekte oder Blaupausen – werden als Impuls aufgenommen und arrangiert, ohne dabei die Herkunftsorte konkret zu benennen.

Audiovisual assemblage on the interdisciplinary platform *CrossSections*, Kunsthalle Exnergasse Vienna, 2018/2019, Konstfack Stockholm, 2019, Exhibition Laboratory, University of Arts Helsinki, 2019, curated by Başak Şenova

With work by Heba Y. Amin, Nisrine Boukhari, Benji Boyadgian, Yane Calovski, Ramesch Daha, Ricarda Denzer, Nikolaus Gansterer, Inma Herrera, Barbara Holub, Otto Karvonen, Ebru Kurbak, Bronwyn Lace, Marcus Neustetter, Behzad Khosravi Noori, Egle Oddo, Isa Rosenberger, Lina Selander, Tamsin Snow, Timo Tuhkanen

Audiovisuelle Assemblage im Rahmen der interdisziplinäre Plattform *CrossSections* Kunsthalle Exnergasse, 2018/2019, Konstfack Stockholm, 2019, Exhibition Laboratory, University of Arts Helsinki, 2019, kuratiert von Başak Şenova

Mit Arbeiten von Heba Y. Amin, Nisrine Boukhari, Benji Boyadgian, Yane Calovski, Ramesch Daha, Ricarda Denzer, Nikolaus Gansterer, Inma Herrera, Barbara Holub, Otto Karvonen, Ebru Kurbak, Bronwyn Lace, Marcus Neustetter, Behzad Khosravi Noori, Egle Oddo, Isa Rosenberger, Lina Selander, Tamsin Snow, Timo Tuhkanen

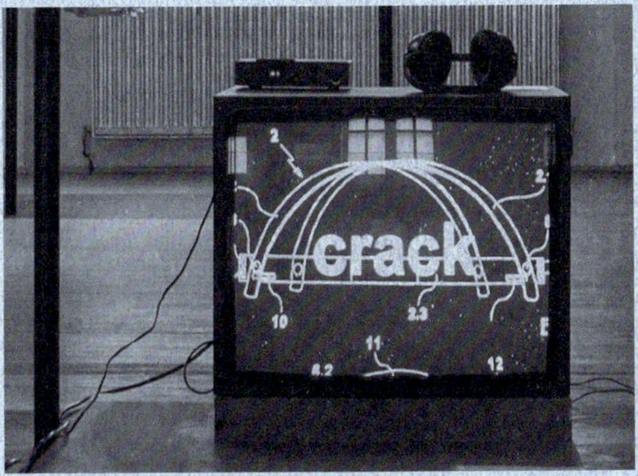

φ⊂ Interview with Elaine Morman, first women free-mineer in the Forest of Dean, audio/video, 20 min, 2015

ʊφ Interview mit Elaine Morman, erste *Freimineurin im Forest of Dean*, Audio/Video, 20 min, 2015

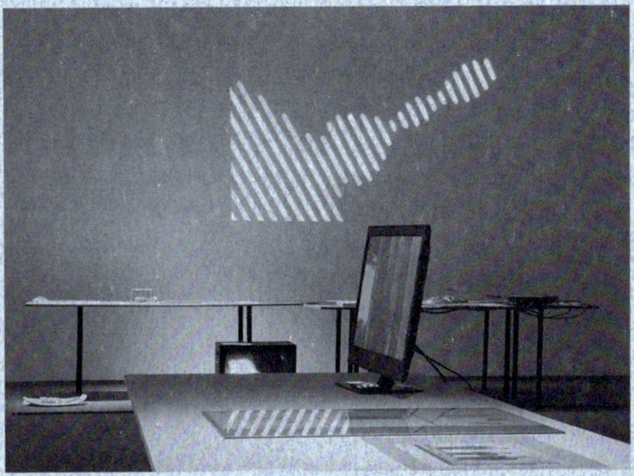

φ⊂ Exhibition view, *Echo, or The Deviation from the Original*, in the exhibition *CrossSections*, Kunsthalle Exnergasse, 2018/2019

ʊφ Ausstellungsansichten *Echo, oder die Abweichung vom Original*, Ausstellung *CrossSections*, Kunsthalle Exnergasse, 2018/2019

139 ←

φ⊂ *Stern* [Star], split-screen video loop, 2018

ʊφ *Stern*, Split Screen, Videoloop, 2018

156, 161, 162 ←

φ⊂ *Puddle*, video loop, 2018

ʊφ *Pfütze*, Videoloop, 2018

143 ←

φ⊂ *Stern* [Star], 2018, silicon-and-plaster form, 2018

ʊφ *Stern* 2018, Silikon- und Gipsform, 2018

116–117, 120–121 ←

φ⊂ *O. T.* [Untitled], framed blueprints of the studio wall, 2018

ʊφ *O. T.*, Blaupausen der Atelierwand gerahmt, 2018

145 ←

φ⊂ *Stern* [Star], print with text

ʊφ *Stern*, Grafik mit Text

193 ←

φ⊂ *O. T.* [Untitled], potato print with ocher pigments on 20 g paper

ʊφ *O. T.*, Kartoffeldrucke mit Ockerpigmenten auf Papier 20 g

156, 161, 162 ←

φ⊂ Ocher pigments from the Forest of Dean, mining "nelly" (forking branch with candle in a piece of clay), iron ore from the Forest of Dean

ʊφ Ockerpigmente aus dem Forest of Dean, „Nelly"-Astgabel mit Kerze in einem Stück Ton, Eisenerz aus dem Forest of Dean

128–129, 170 ←

φ⊂ Video loop, helmet-camera footage from the iron and ocher mines beneath the Forest of Dean, 2018

ʊφ Videoloop, Helmkameraaufnahmen der Eisen- und Ockerminen unterhalb des Forest of Dean, 2018

139←

φ⊂ Brass star, Istanbul workshop, 2018

ʊφ Messingstern, Werkstatt Istanbul, 2018

134 ←

φ⊂ *Condition of the Mouth*, slides, Condition Report, 2016

ʊφ *Condition of the Mouth*, Dias, Zustandsbericht, 2016

131 ←

φ⊂ Video animation, sound diagram, loop, 2016, realized by Can Denzer

ʊφ Videoanimation, Sounddiagramm, Loop, *2016*

162/163, 166, 170 ←

φ⊂ Interview with Elaine Morman, first women freemineer in the Forest of Dean, audio/video, 20 min, 2015

ʊφ Interview mit Elaine Morman, erste Freimineurin im Forest of Dean, Audio/Video, 20 min, 2015

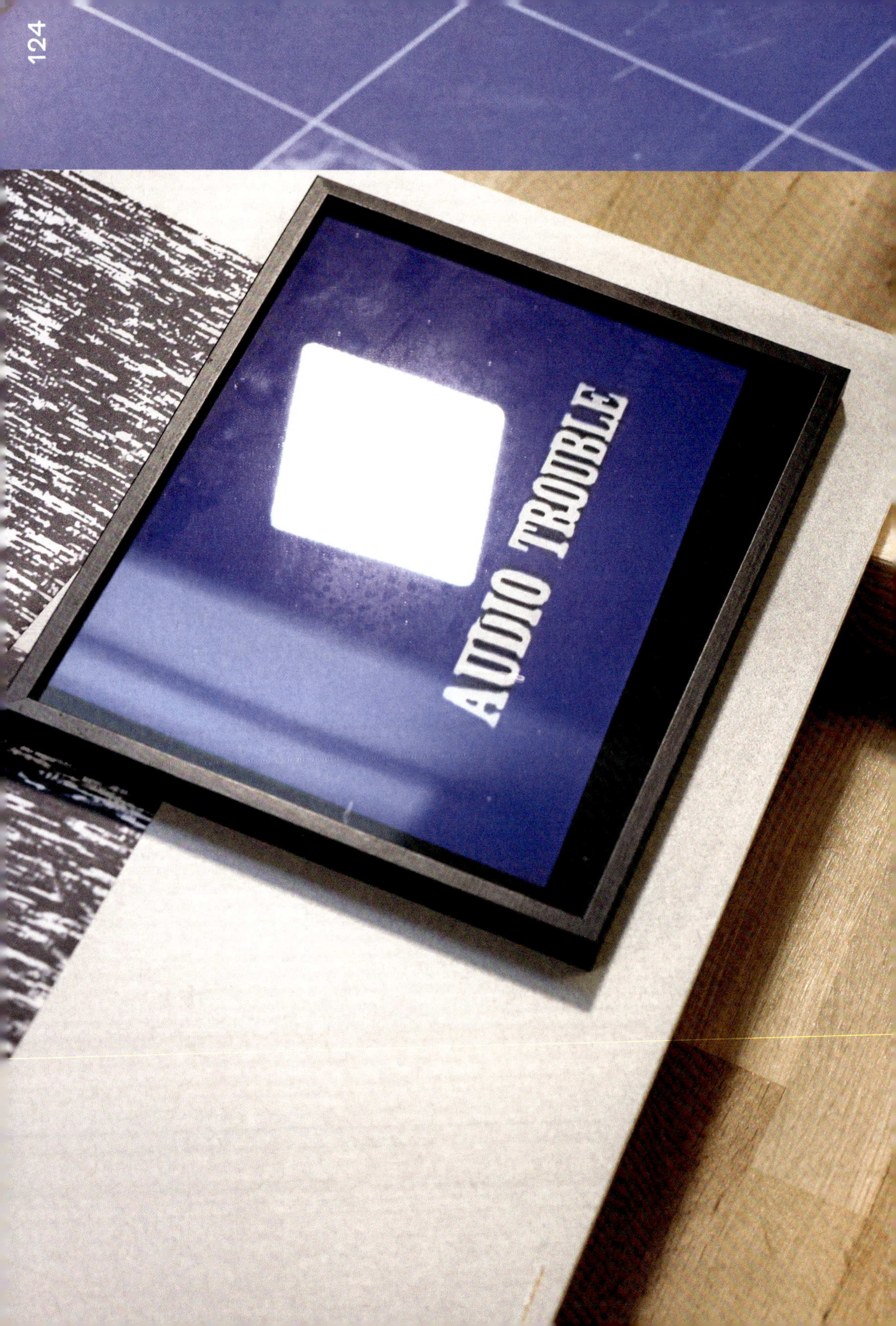
AUDIO TROUBLE

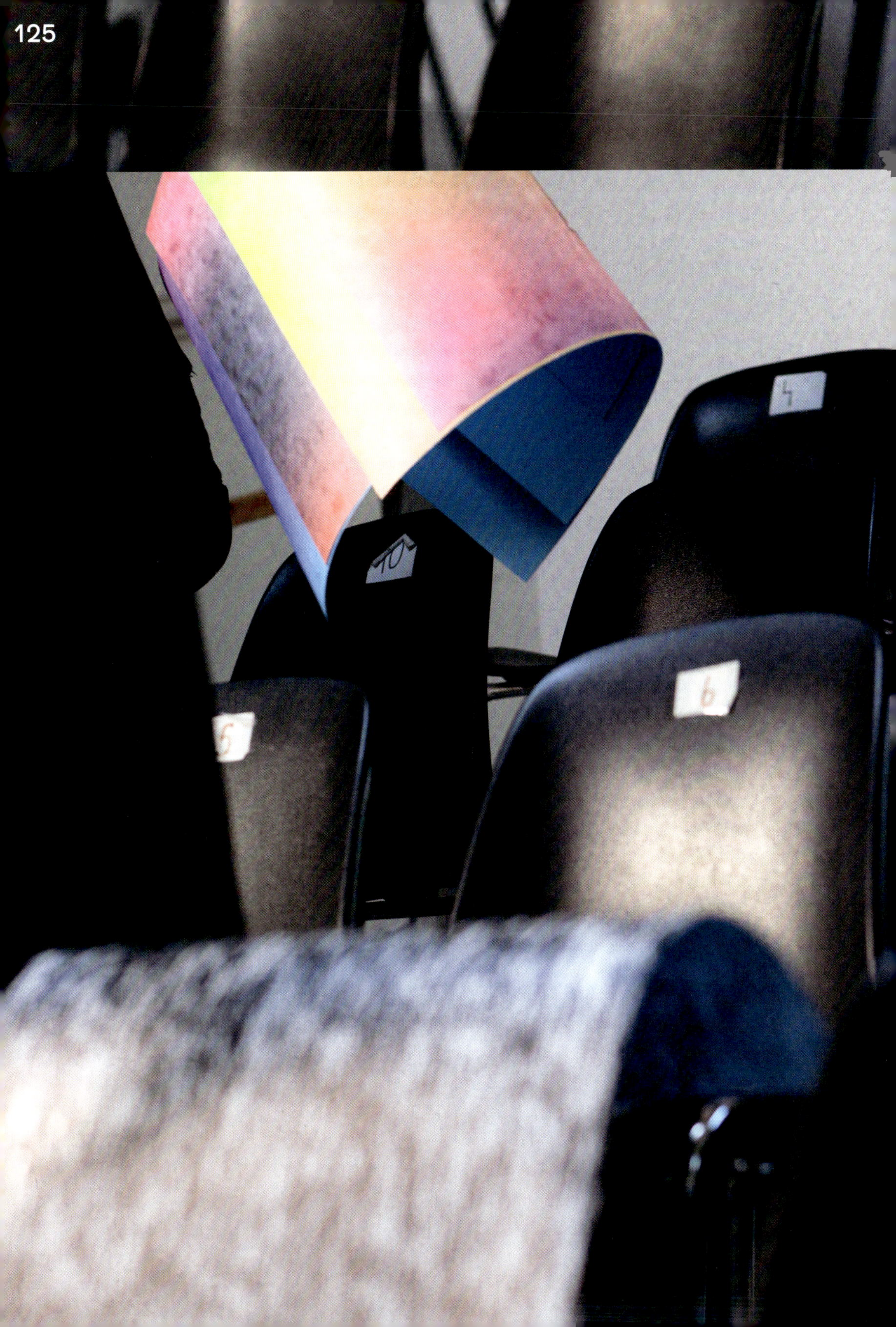

In her exhibition at Neue Galerie Innsbruck, Ricarda Denzer used temporarily installed walls in front of the windows as stages: as an actual stage with microphones on which she conducted an interview with philosopher Bernhard Braun on the meaning of iconoclasm in art history; and to display her objects, finds, and artworks. In the entrance area, part of the gallery's architecture is extended into the exhibition space. A star-shaped bronze object, referring to an ornament from Hagia Sophia that often recurs in Denzer's work, appears in several formats and variations: as a drawing on paper, a plaster-and-silicon replica, but also as a cast and finished bronze mask.

This ornament, introduced to cover the faces of the seraphim when the Byzantine church was transformed into a mosque, is reproduced in two casts that Denzer had made, one in bronze and one in brass. Both versions pick up on questions about the relationship between original, imagination, and interpretation.

The clicking of a flip-dot panel visualizes a dialogue between John Berger and Susan Sontag about storytelling, while ocher pigments, next to the abstraction of a sawn-off tree trunk, guide viewers to the Forest of Dean in England. Denzer creates a staging of these objects, along with other research material and images, on an elongated dais that accords them all equal status.

In her continuation of earlier thoughts and motifs, Denzer examines subtle shifts of meaning in variations resulting from a methodical exposure of strata—in the gallery, in Hagia Sophia, or in the Forest of Dean, where the ocher miners used an object that is initially puzzling in the exhibition: what is known as a "nelly" consists of a piece of clay with a candle stuck in a forked stick. It ensured miners, crawling on all fours with the stick in their mouths, had enough light and had their hands free to do their work.

In der Ausstellung in der Neuen Galerie Innsbruck verwendete Ricarda Denzer die vor den Fenstern temporär einbaubaren Wände als Bühnen: zum einen als tatsächliche „Stage" mit Mikrofonen, auf der sie im Zuge der Ausstellung ein Gespräch mit dem Philosophen Bernhard Braun über die Bedeutung von Ikonoklasmus in der Kunstgeschichte führte; zum anderen als Display für ihre Objekte, Fundstücke und bildnerischen Arbeiten. Im Eingangsbereich wird die vorgegebene Architektur der Vorsatzschalen der Galerie in den Raum hinein verlängert. Ein sternförmiges, bei ihr wiederkehrendes Bronzeobjekt, das auf ein Ornament in der Hagia Sophia verweist, taucht in mehreren Abwandlungen und Variationen auf: als Zeichnung auf Papier, als Abguss in Gips und Silikon, aber auch als fertig gegossene Bronzemaske.

Das Ornament, das seit der Umwandlung der byzantinischen Kirche in eine Moschee die Gesichter der Seraphim überdeckt, hat Denzer einmal als Bronze und einmal in Messing ausführen lassen. Die beiden Versionen schließen an Fragen nach dem Verhältnis von Original, Imagination und Interpretation an.

Das klackende Rauschen eines Flip-Dot-Panels visualisiert einen Dialog von John Berger und Susan Sontag über das Erzählen von Geschichten, während neben der Abstraktion eines abgeschnittenen Baumstamms Ockerpigmente die Betrachter*innen in den englischen Forest of Dean führen. All diese Objekte präsentiert Denzer neben anderen Recherche- und Bildmaterialien auf einem länglichen, jedes Objekt gleichwertig behandelnden Display.

In der Weiterführung früherer Überlegungen und Motive thematisiert Denzer subtil Bedeutungsverschiebungen durch Abwandlungen, die sich durch ein methodisches Freilegen von Schichten – in der Galerie, in der Hagia Sophia oder auch im Forest of Dean – ergeben. Dort benutzen Minenarbeiter beim Ockerabbau auch das Objekt, das hier zunächst Rätsel aufgibt: Die sogenannte „Nelly" besteht aus einem in eine Astgabel gedrückten Stück Ton mit einer Kerze – das ermöglicht den Minenarbeitern, auf allen Vieren zu kriechen, während sie mit der Astgabel im Mund genug Licht und die Hände frei zum Arbeiten haben.

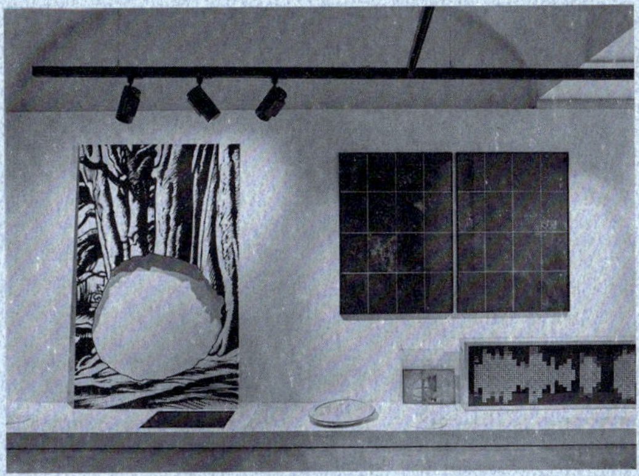

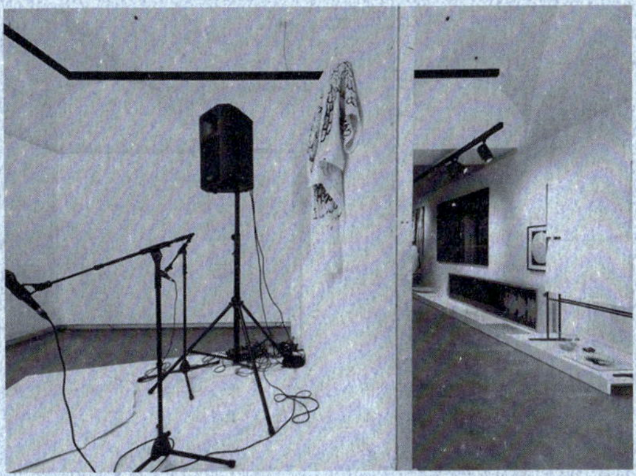

Φ⊏ Exhibition view, *Erste Fassung (Interpretation)*, solo exhibition, Neue Galerie Innsbruck, 2018

ʊΦ Ausstellungsansicht *Erste Fassung (Interpretation)*, Einzelausstellung, Neue Galerie Innsbruck, 2018

176–177←

Φ⊏ *Wald ohne Zentrum* [Wood without a Center], silkscreen print on canvas, 120 × 170 cm, 2018

ʊΦ *Wald ohne Zentrum*, Siebdruck auf Leinwand, 120 × 170 cm, 2018

Φ⊏ *To Tell a Story*, flip-dot panel, voice diagram ([soundless] dialogue: Susan Sontag & John Berger, 1983), 207 × 49 × 17 cm, 2018

ʊΦ *To Tell a Story*, Flip-Dot-Panel, Stimmendiagramm ([tonloser] Dialog: Susan Sontag & John Berger, 1983), 207 × 49 × 17 cm, 2018

144–145, 148 ←

Φ⊏ *Stern* [Star], drawings, 2018

ʊΦ *Stern*, Zeichnungen, 2018

Φ⊏ Cake stencils, ca. 1960

ʊΦ Tortenschablonen, ca. 1960

92–93 ←

Φ⊏ *O. T.* [Untitled], potato prints with neon pigments on 20 g paper

ʊΦ *O. T.*, Kartoffeldrucke mit Neonpigmenten auf Papier 20 g

Φ⊏ Copy of a historical roofing tile with dirt from the site where it was found (Archäologie Innsbruck)

ʊΦ Kopie eines historischen Dachziegels mit Originaldreck vom Fundort (Archäologie Innsbruck)

167 ←

Φ⊏ Color print on Hahnemühle paper, source: *Dokumentation Befundung Neue Galerie*, 2010 Photo: Pescoller Werkstätten GmbH, 2010/2018

ʊΦ Farbdruck auf Hahnemühle-Papier, Quelle: Dokumentation Befundung Neue Galerie, 2010 Foto: Pescoller Werkstätten GmbH, 2010/2018

135 ←

Φ⊏ *Heilig, Heilig, Heilig* [Holy, Holy, Holy], stage from the gallery's wall cladding, microphones, amplifier, loudspeakers, costume: *Seraphim*, 2018

ʊΦ *Heilig, Heilig, Heilig*, Bühne aus den Verschalungswänden der Galerie, Mikrofone, Verstärker, Soundboxen, Kostüm: *Seraphim*, 2018

138, 142 ←

Φ⊏ *Reflections on a Star-Shaped Masque* bronze object, 2018, realized by Dorota Rapacz

ʊΦ *Reflections on a Star-Shaped Masque*, Bronzeobjekt, 2018

174–175, 177 ←

Φ⊏ *Ohne Zentrum* [Without a Center], mirror object, 2018

ʊΦ *Ohne Zentrum*, Spiegelobjekt, 2018

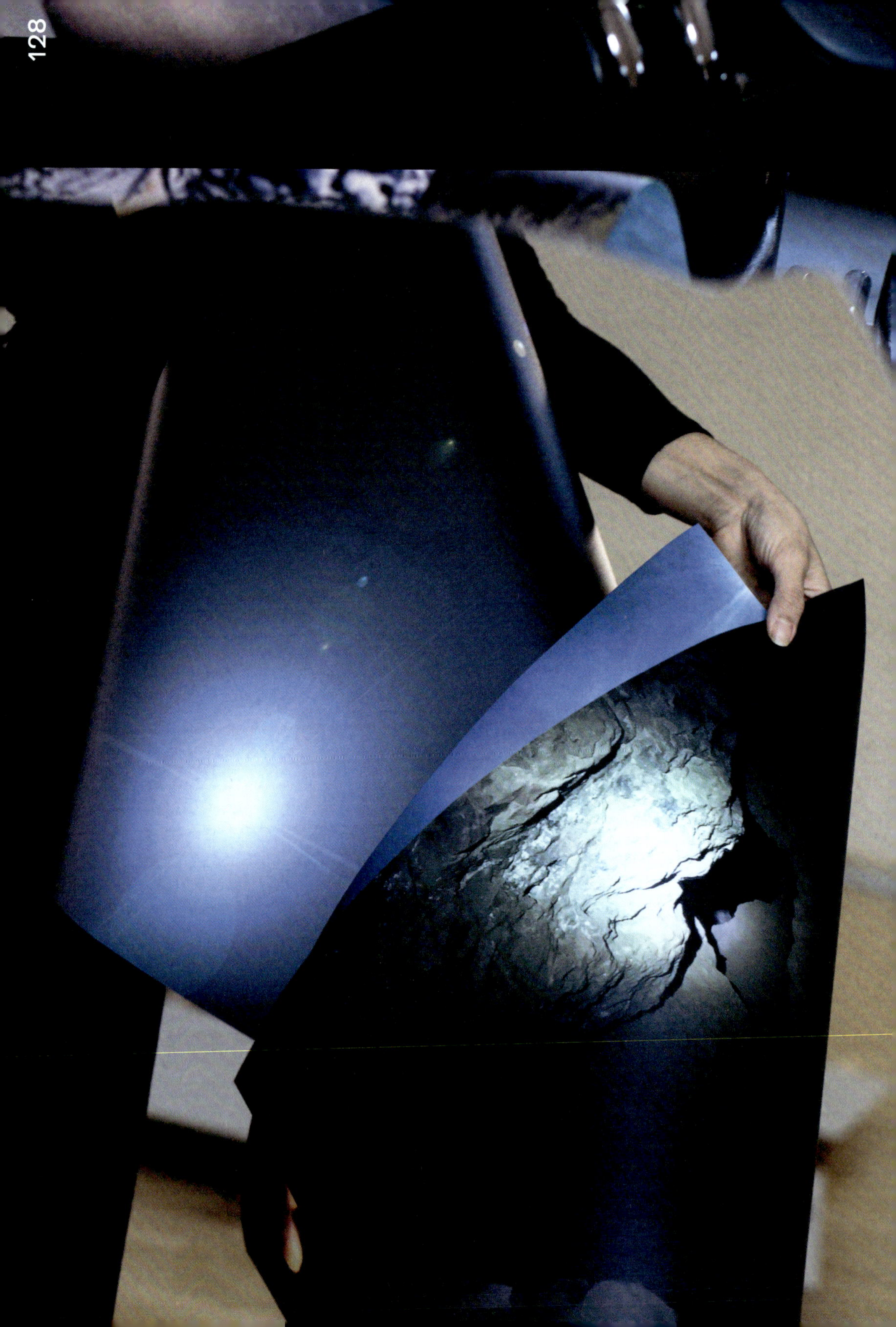

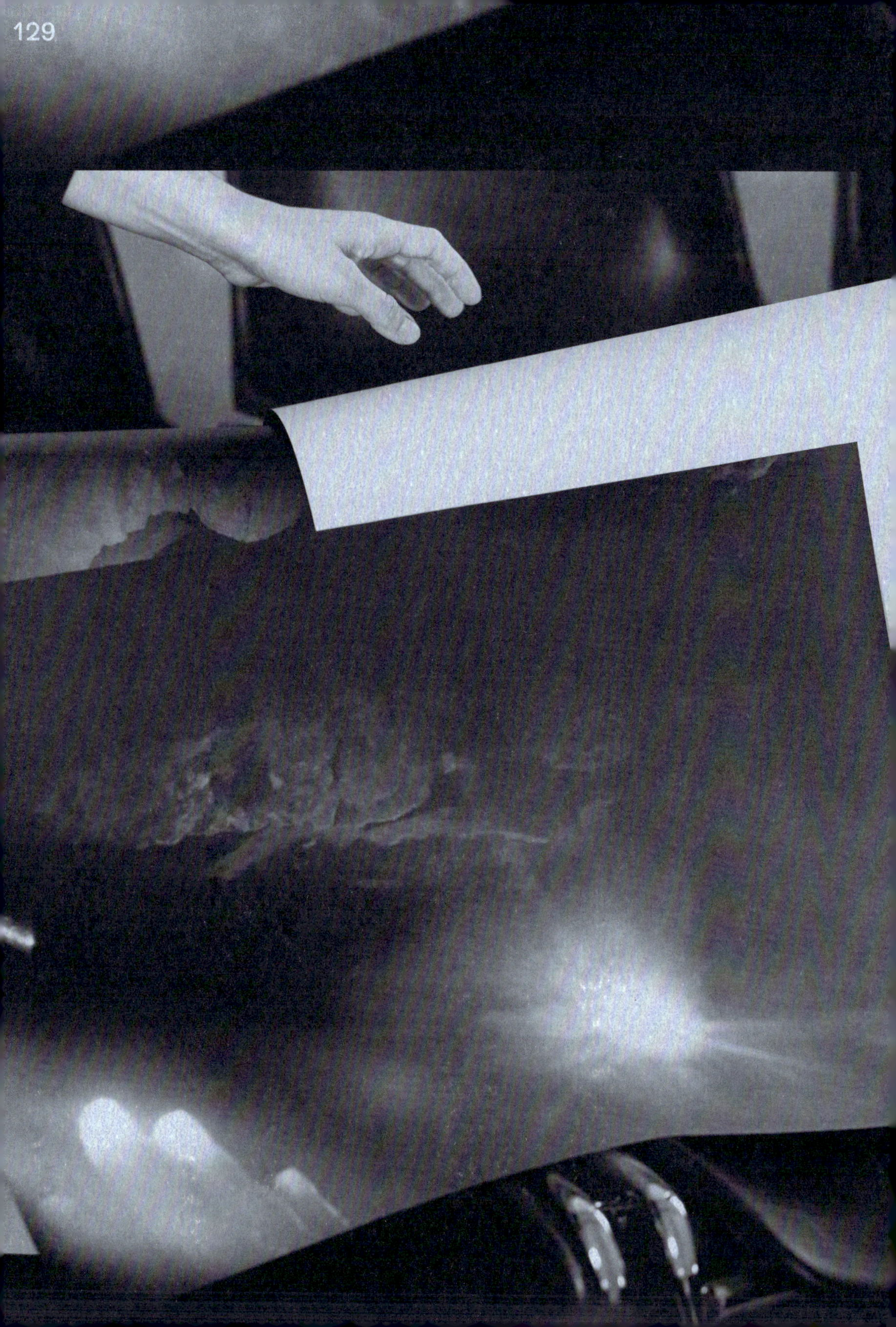

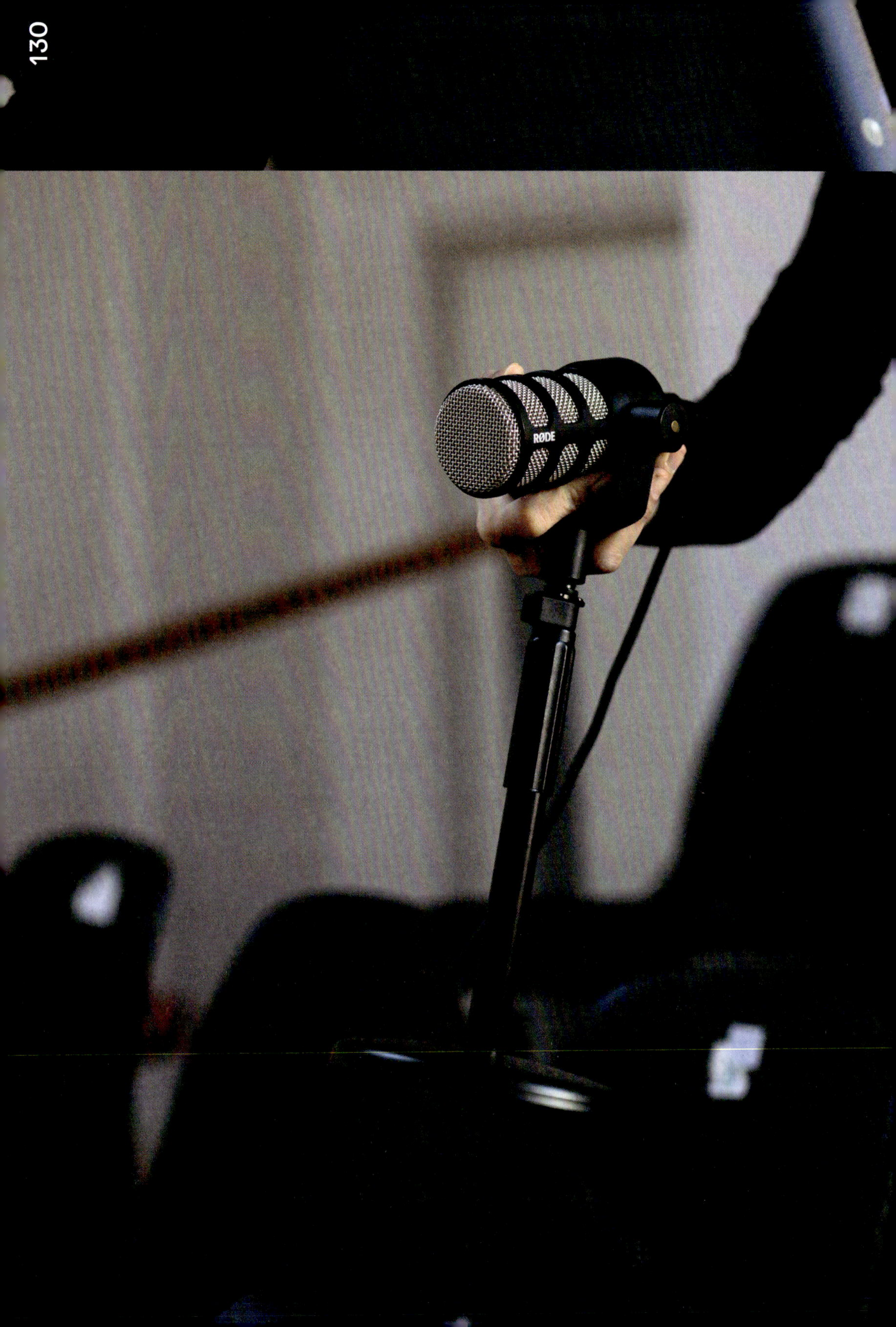
RØDE

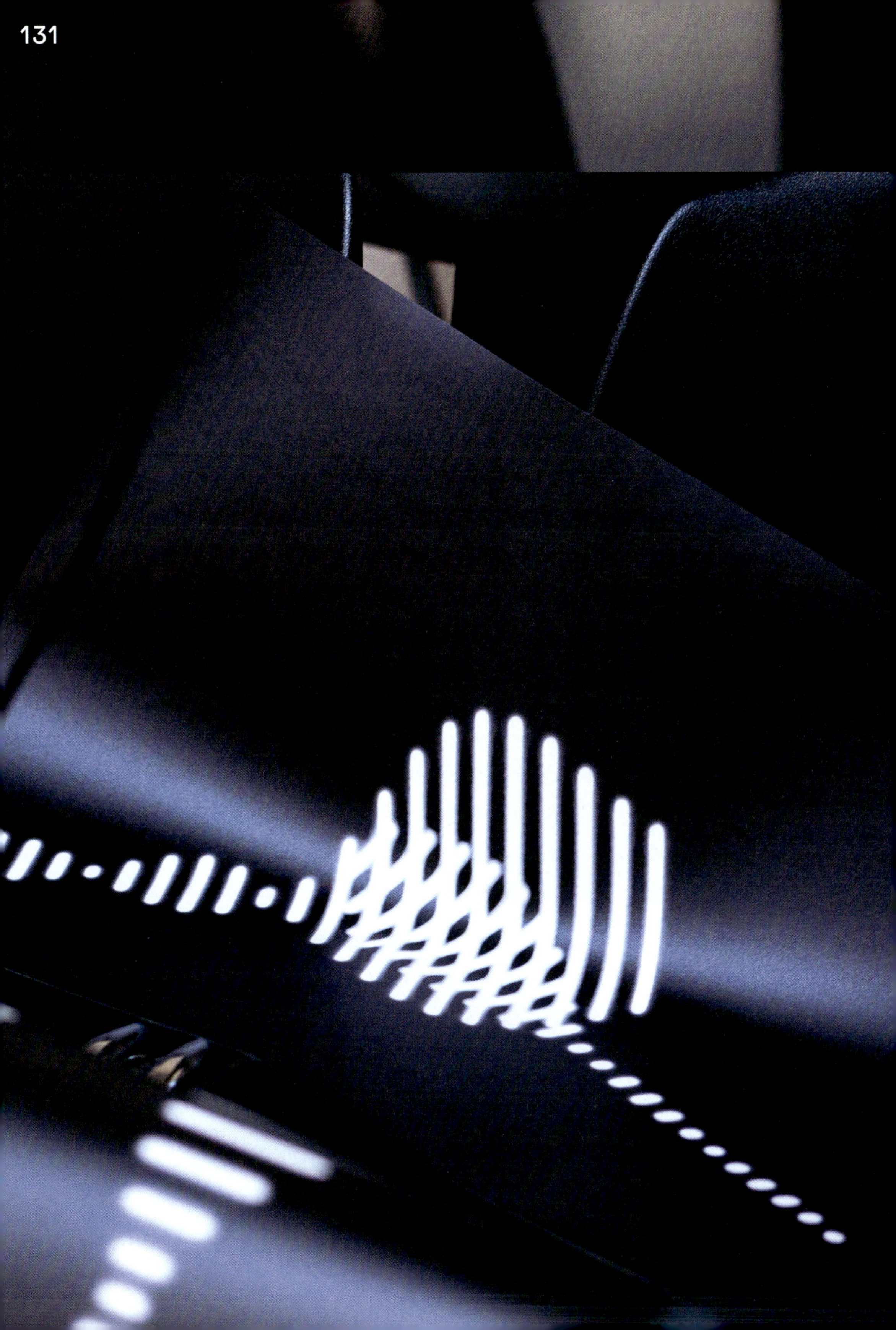

The exhibition *Whispering Dialogues*, curated by Karolina Radenkovic, explores language at the poles of facticity and fiction, plenitude and depletion, examining its purported claim to truth and its performative aspect in reference to speech acts, voice, and physicality. In her presentation, Ricarda Denzer confronts linguistic authority and grand narratives with a display of material and performative fragments, transformed variants, and splinters. Rather than an entire forest, she shows various interpretations or views of the cross-section and stump of a felled tree in *Wald ohne Zentrum* [Wood without a Center] (2018) and *Zentrum* [Center] (2019). The floor-based piece *Wald ohne Zentrum* evokes a comic stylistically and has a hole within it, which the artist realized as a silkscreen print with delicate edging and as a mirror object. Denzer brings together myriad places, bodies, and voices and unfurls a story that seems to have something to show and to reference something absent.

Die von Karolina Radenkovic kuratierte Ausstellung *Whispering Dialogues* thematisiert Sprache in ihrem Spannungsverhältnis von Faktizität und Fiktion, Fülle und Entleerung. Sie verhandelt ihren vermeintlichen Wahrheitsanspruch und untersucht die performative Seite der Sprache – mit Bezug zu Sprechhandlungen, Stimme und Körperlichkeit.

Ricarda Denzer setzt in ihrer Präsentation der sprachlichen Deutungsmacht und den großen Narrativen ein Display mit materiellen und performativen Fragmenten, Abwandlungen und Bruchstücken entgegen: Anstelle des ganzen Waldes zeigt sie mit den Arbeiten *Wald ohne Zentrum* (2018) und *Zentrum* (2019) verschiedene Interpretationen bzw. Ansichten der Schnittstelle eines Baumstamms bzw. -stumpfs. Das Bodenstück *Wald ohne Zentrum* ist comichaft ausgeführt und mit einem Loch versehen, das die Künstlerin wiederum als Siebdruck, mit zarter Umrandung, und als Spiegelobjekt ausführen ließ. Denzer bringt verschiedene Orte, Körper und Stimmen zusammen und breitet eine Geschichte im Raum aus, die gleichzeitig etwas zu zeigen und auf etwas Abwesendes zu verweisen scheint.

Multimedia assemblage for the exhibition *Whispering Dialogues*, Galerie 5020 Salzburg, 2019, curated by Karolina Radenkovic

With work by Ricarda Denzer, FAXEN, Michael Heindl, Andrea Maurer, and Christine Schörkhuber

Multimediale Assemblage im Rahmen der Ausstellung *Whispering Dialogues*, Galerie 5020 Salzburg, 2019 kuratiert von Karolina Radenkovic

Mit Arbeiten von Ricarda Denzer, FAXEN, Michael Heindl, Andrea Maurer und Christine Schörkhuber

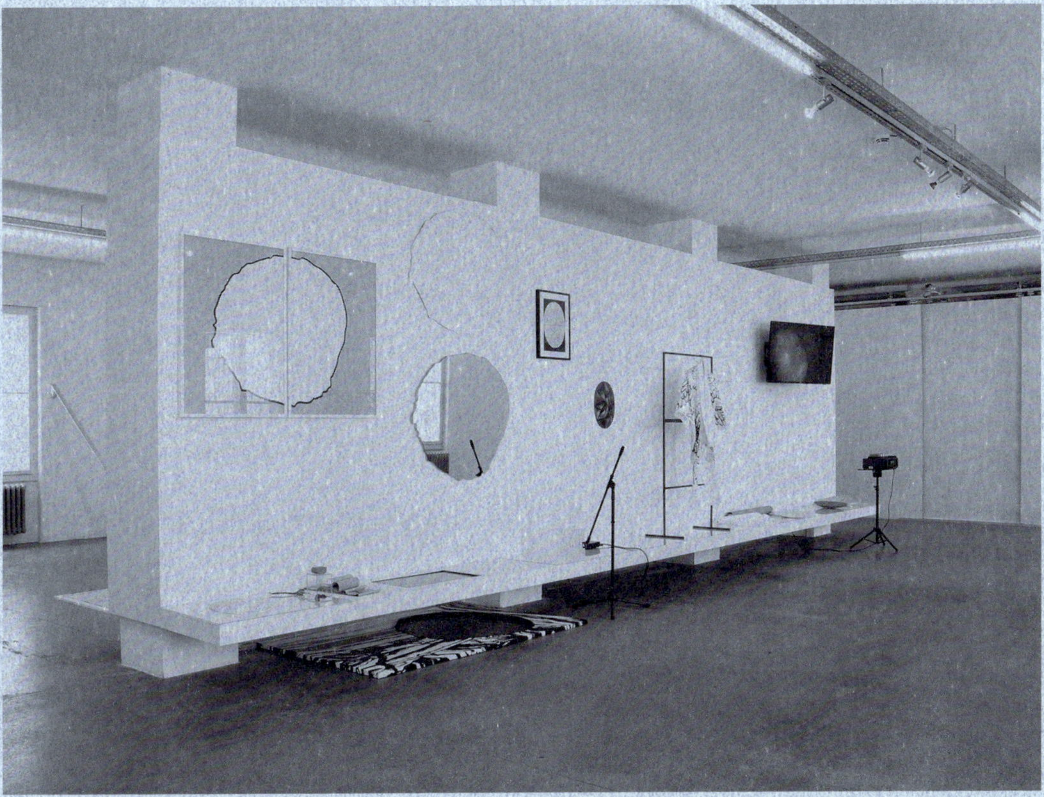

en Exhibition view, *O. T.*, multimedia assemblage for the exhibition *Whispering Dialogues*, Galerie 5020, Salzburg, 2019

de Ausstellungsansicht *O. T.*, Multimediale Assemblage im Rahmen der Ausstellung *Whispering Dialogues*, Galerie 5020, Salzburg, 2019

176–177 ←

en *Zentrum* [Center], primed canvas, 2018

de *Zentrum*, Leinwand grundiert, 2018

174 ←

en *Zentrum* [Center], laser print on 70 g paper, 2019

de *Zentrum*, Grafik, Laserdruck auf Papier 70 g, 2019

en *Stern* [Star], wall drawing with neon pigments, 2019

de *Stern*, Wandzeichnung mit Neon-Pigmenten, 2019

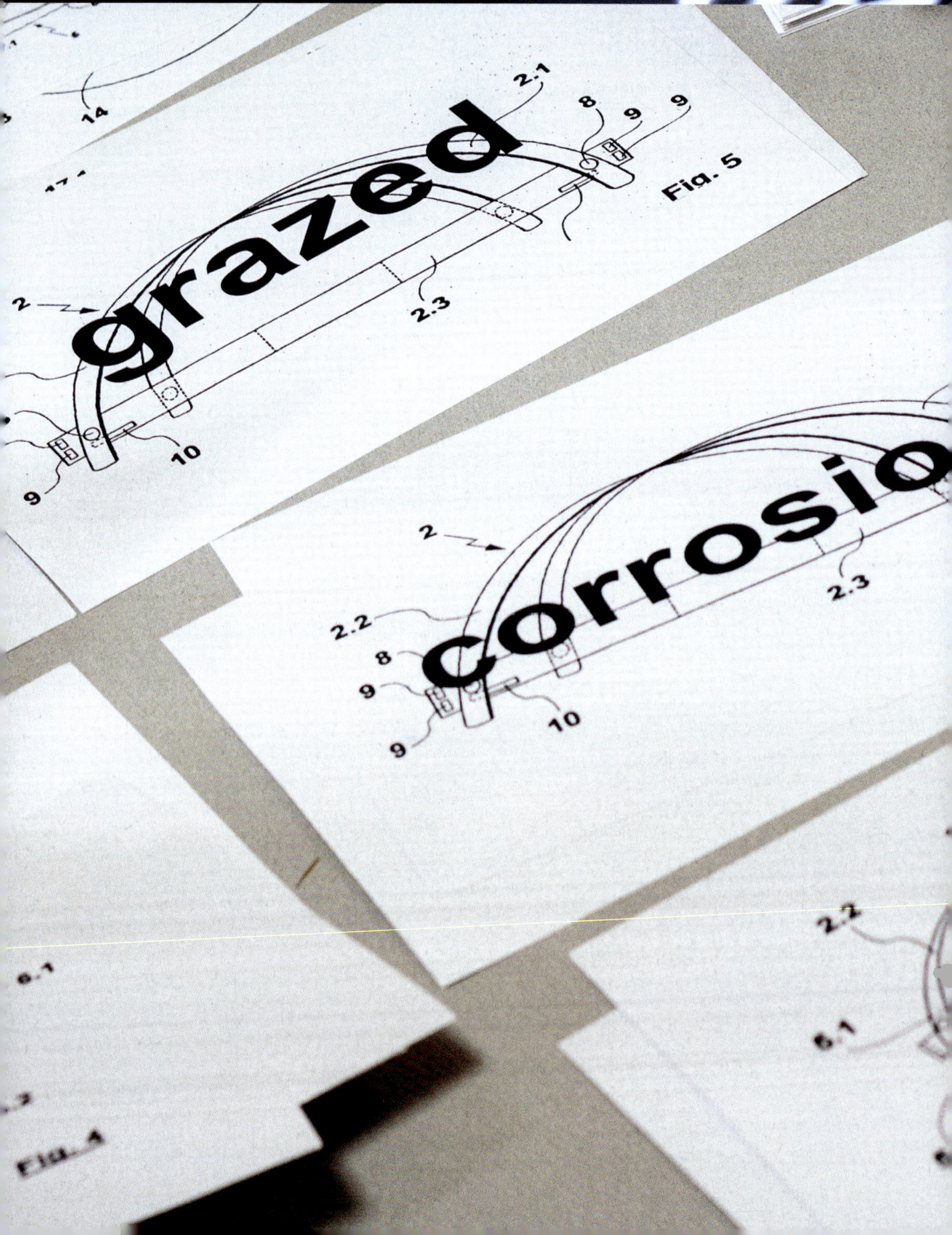
grazed
Fig. 5
2.1
8
9
9
2
2.3
10
9
14
corrosio
2
2.2
8
9
10
9
2.3

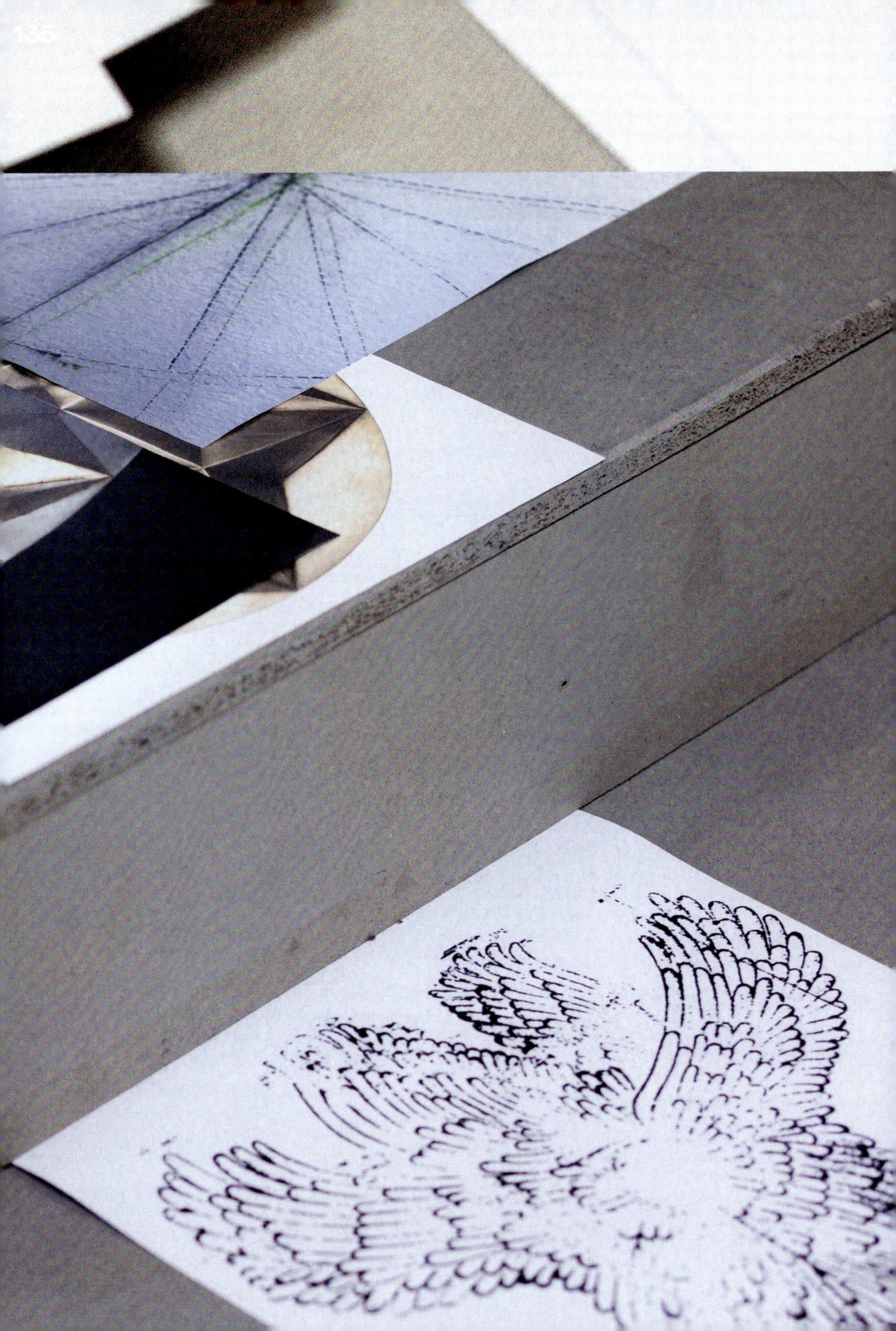

As in her earlier work, Denzer addresses the conversational setting in *To Tell a Story* and examines the media formats that can be used to record it by staging on-the-spot live conversations or artistic audiovisual pieces. The exhibition's title comes from a conversation between British author and art critic John Berger and his American colleague Susan Sontag, shown in the 1980s by British broadcaster Channel 4 as part of its *Voices* series.

For Denzer one central aspect of this dialogue is an exploration of how Berger's storytelling grows out of real-world circumstances and how he sees images while writing, whereas Sontag understands writing as something detached from such events and hears voices while writing.

Denzer synchronizes the television format's filming style and visual idiom and those selected for the site-specific video in *To Tell a Story*. In the light of the found objects and artworks in the exhibition space, she thus examines the significance of hearing and seeing, and of the documentary and fictional aspects involved in storytelling within her work.

Denzer also refers to the Berger–Sontag dialogue from 1983 with an abstract sound diagram in the exhibition space, visible yet silent. Alongside it, the precisely positioned Kunstraum Lakeside furniture can be seen—two armchairs, partition screens, a table, shelving, and so on. Blueprints, traces of which remain visible on the gallery wall, are shown under glass. Neon-yellow potato prints hang on a partition screen, while black half-tone prints can be seen on the glass front.

Reproduction through media transformation is a central theme here, although meaning always shifts too. One of the artworks, for example, consists only of printing remnants in a reference to narrative imperfections and gaps. This is also expressed in the exhibition space by found biographical material like the video projection *Das Fenster von Gegenüber* [The Window Opposite] (1994) and the type-written poem "Tapetenwechsel" [Change of Scene] (1983), which ends with the words "Endlich wieder etwas Neues" ("at last something new").

Wie schon in früheren Arbeiten beschäftigt sich Denzer auch in *To Tell A Story* mit dem Setting von Gesprächssituationen und deren medialer Aufzeichnung, indem sie inszenierte Gesprächsformate live oder auch als audiovisuelle künstlerische Arbeiten umsetzt. Den Titel der Ausstellung entlehnt Denzer einem Gespräch zwischen dem britischen Essayisten, Kunstkritiker und Schriftsteller John Berger und seiner US-amerikanischen Kollegin Susan Sontag, das die britische TV-Anstalt Channel 4 in den 1980er-Jahren im Rahmen ihrer Serie *Voices* ausgestrahlt hat.

Ein für Denzer zentraler Moment in diesem Dialog ist die Verhandlung der Frage, wie sich das Erzählen von Geschichten bei Berger aus wahren Begebenheiten ergibt und wie er beim Schreiben Bilder sieht, während Sontag das Schreiben als von wahren Begebenheiten losgelöste Kunstform versteht und beim Schreiben Stimmen hört.

Denzer übernimmt für die in *To Tell A Story* enthaltene ortsspezifische Videoarbeit – zeitlich synchronisiert – die Bildregie des Fernsehformats. Mit Blick auf die im Ausstellungsraum vorgefundenen und geschaffenen Objekte thematisiert sie so die Bedeutung von Hören und Sehen, von dokumentarischen und fiktionalen Eigenschaften beim Erzählen von Geschichten innerhalb ihrer Arbeit.

Auf den 1983 von Berger und Sontag geführten Dialog verweist Denzer auch mit einem abstrakten, tonlosen Sounddiagramm im Ausstellungsraum. Daneben ist das präzise positionierte Mobiliar des Kunstraums Lakeside – zwei Sessel, Stellwände, Tisch, Regal etc. – zu sehen. Hinter Glas sind Blaupausen ausgestellt, deren Abrieb auf der Galeriewand zu sehen ist. Neongelbe Kartoffeldrucke hängen über einer Stellwand, man sieht zudem schwarze Rasterdrucke an der Glasfront.

Die Vervielfachung durch mediale Abwandlung ist hier ein zentrales Motiv, wobei es immer auch Bedeutungsverschiebungen gibt: So sieht man auf einem der Blätter nur noch Reste der Drucke, was auf Fehlstellen und Lücken beim Erzählen verweist. Zum Ausdruck kommt das im Ausstellungsraum auch über biografische Fundstücke wie die Videoprojektion *Das Fenster von Gegenüber* von 1994 sowie mit dem mit Schreibmaschine auf Papier geschriebenen Gedicht *Tapetenwechsel* mit dem Schlusssatz „Endlich wieder etwas Neues" aus dem Jahr 1983.

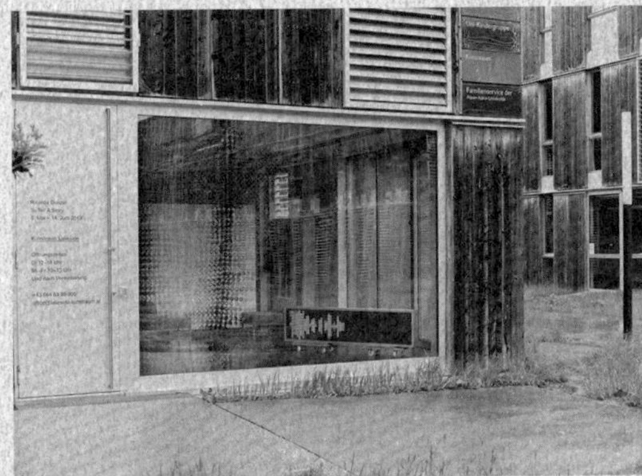

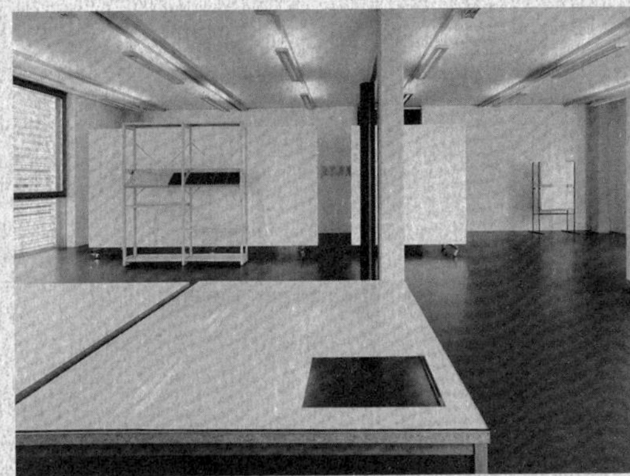

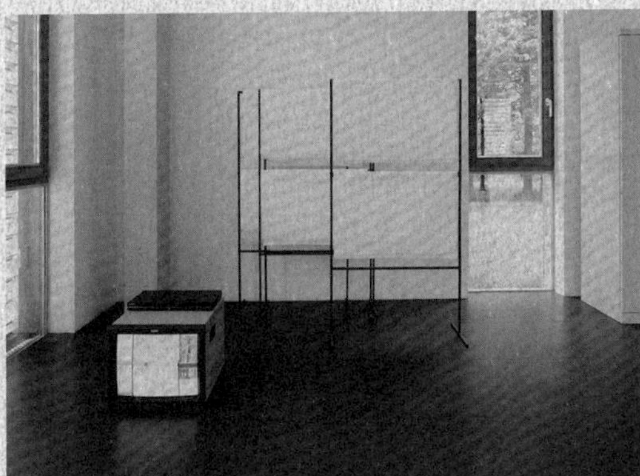

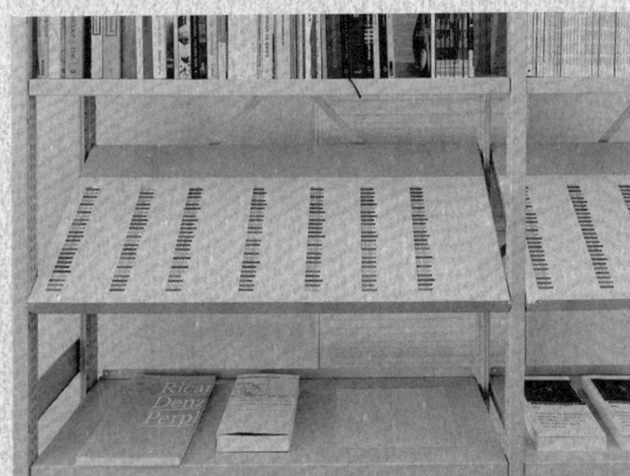

ɸ⊂ Exhibition view, *To Tell A Story*, solo exhibition, Kunstraum Lakeside, Klagenfurt, 2019

ʊɸ Ausstellungsansicht, *To Tell A Story*, Einzelausstellung, Kunstraum Lakeside, Klagenfurt, 2019

89, 125, 167 ←

ɸ⊂ *Das Fenster von Gegenüber* [The Window Opposite], video loop, 1994

ʊɸ *Das Fenster von Gegenüber*, Videoloop, 1994

116–117, 120–121 ←

ɸ⊂ *Tapetenwechsel* [Change of Scene], text, typewriter on paper, 1983

ʊɸ *Tapetenwechsel*, Text, Schreibmaschine auf Papier, 1983

ɸ⊂ *O. T.* [Untitled], blueprint of the gallery wall under glass, 2019

ʊɸ *O. T.*, Blaupausen der Galeriewand hinter Glas, 2019

ɸ⊂ Video loop on 2 monitors, directorial notes with color system for camera settings (close-up, long shot, medium shot) for *To Tell a Story* ([soundless] dialogue: Susan Sontag & John Berger, 1983)

ʊɸ Videoloop auf 2 Monitoren, Regieanweisung mit Farbsystem für Kameraeinstellungen (Close-up, Totale, Halbtotale) von *To Tell a Story* ([tonloser] Dialog: Susan Sontag & John Berger 1983)

ɸ⊂ Potato prints on window pane

ʊɸ Kartoffeldrucke auf Fensterscheibe

ɸ⊂ Curtain, upholstered chairs, tables; panes of glass, shelving and partition screens from the Kunstraum

ʊɸ Vorhang, Sessel, Tische; Glasscheiben und Regale sowie Stellwände des Kunstraums

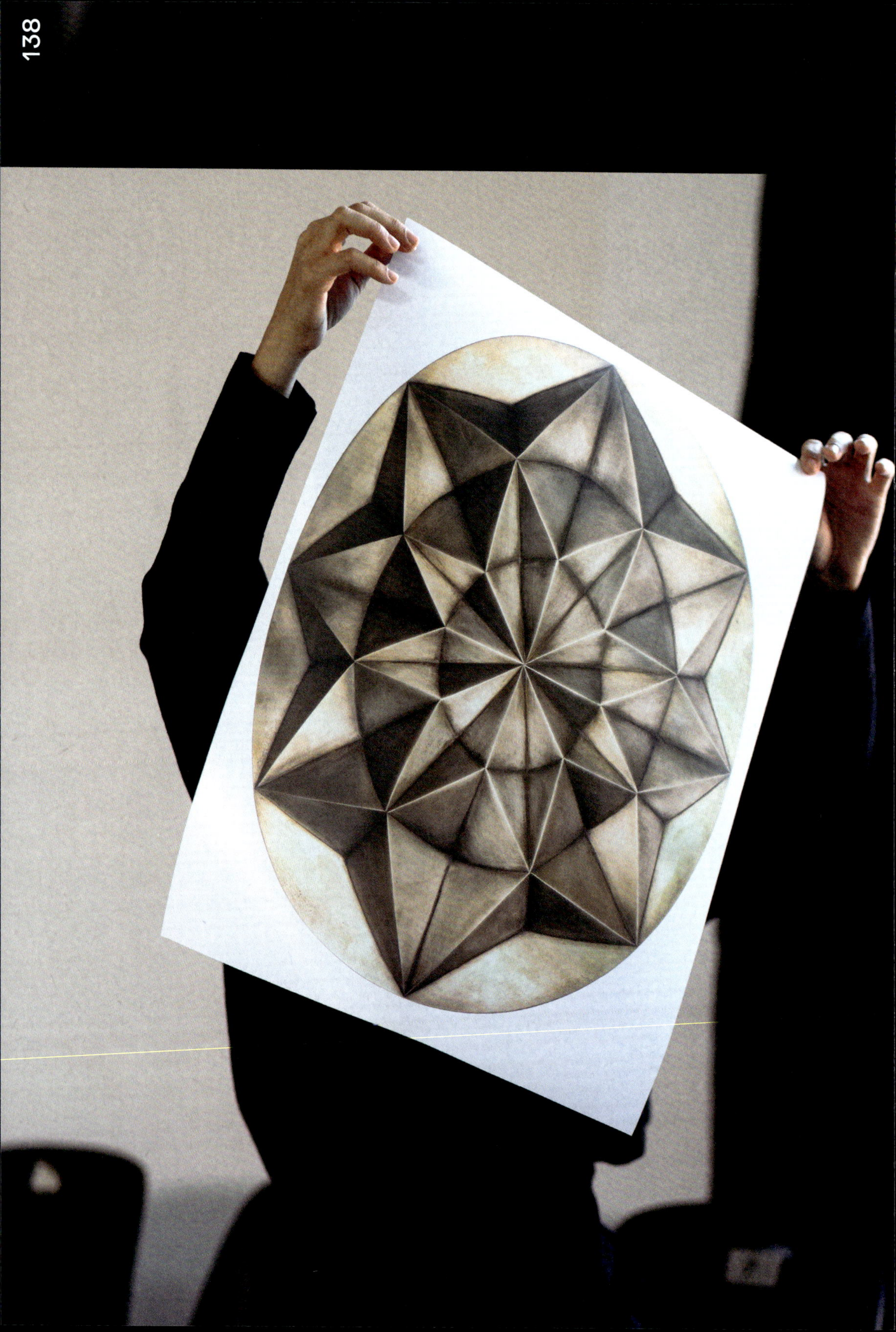

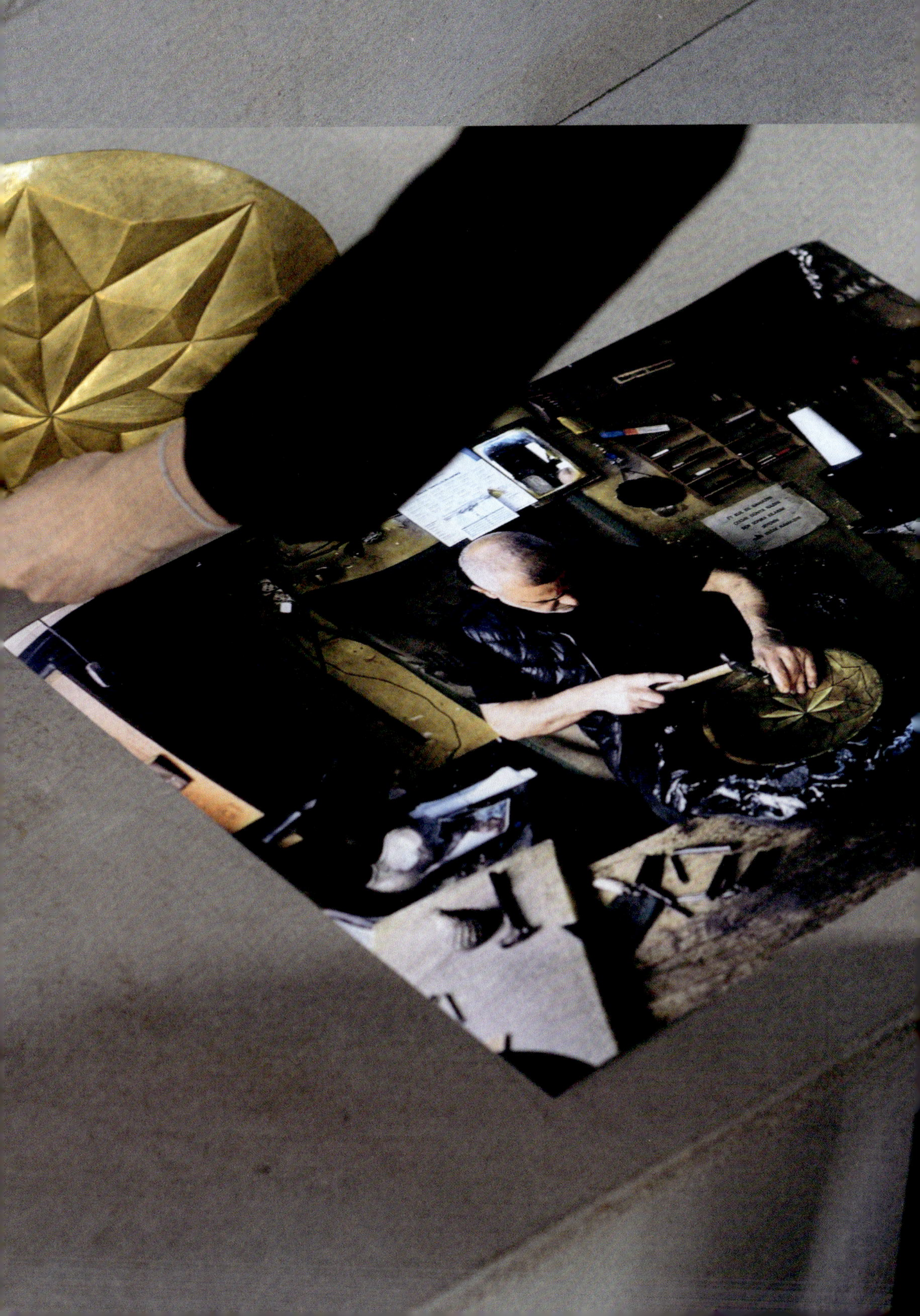

Untitled (Prussian Bitch)
O. T. (Saupreissin)

2020

In a display window with a view of her former school in Kufstein, Denzer projects a mask-shaped oval beam of light onto a poem from her days as a pupil there. This biographical found object is part of the exhibition *Augenhöhe* [Eye Level], dedicated to the former art teacher at the school, Luise Clay. In *Tapetenwechsel* [Change of Scene] (1983) Denzer, who grew up in Kufstein, gives the exact coordinates for every bloodstain on the patterned wallpaper in her room that was made by swatting mosquitos and recounts “brutal small-town boredom” (Franz Ellinger). The color print *Audio Trouble* links this to an examination of sound and image and potentially faulty dubbing. The title quotes the video *Boomerang* (1974), produced by Richard Serra and Nancy Holt, in which the image is replaced for several minutes by the intertitle “Audio Trouble,” as if in a transmission failure.

In the context of this exhibition the work is a reference to Denzer’s interest in acoustic expressions and questing searches, also reflected in the installation’s title, *O. T. (Saupreissin)* [Untitled (Prussian Bitch)]. A further component of the installation is a packing case full of padding—a possible reference to Denzer only being temporarily in that Tyrolean small town.

In einem Schaufenster mit Blick auf ihre ehemalige Schule in Kufstein projiziert Denzer einen maskenförmigen, ovalen Lichtkegel auf ein Gedicht aus ihrer Schulzeit. Das biografische Fundstück ist Teil der Ausstellung *Augenhöhe*, die der ehemaligen Kunsterzieherin Luise Clay am dortigen Gymnasium gewidmet war. Als Teenager, in Kufstein aufgewachsen, lokalisiert Denzer unter dem Titel *Tapetenwechsel* (1983) mit Zahlen- und Reihenangaben ganz exakt jene Kästchen auf der gemusterten Tapete ihres Zimmers, wo erschlagene Gelsen Blutflecken hinterlassen haben, und erzählt von der „brutalen Fadesse in der Kleinstadt“ (Franz Ellinger). Mit dem Farbdruck *Audio Trouble* schließt Denzer an eine Auseinandersetzung mit Bild und Ton sowie potenzielle Fehlsynchronisationen an. Der Titel verweist auf das von Richard Serra gemeinsam mit Nancy Holt produzierte Video *Boomerang* (1974), in dem das Bild wie während eines Senderausfalls für einige Minuten durch den Zwischentitel „Audio Trouble“ ersetzt ist.

Im Rahmen der Ausstellung ist die Arbeit ein Hinweis auf Denzers Interesse an akustischen Ausdrucksformen und Suchbewegungen, worauf nicht zuletzt auch der Titel der Installation *O. T. (Saupreissin)* verweist. Weiterer Bestandteil der Installation ist ein Karton voller Verpackungsreste – möglicherweise ein Hinweis darauf, dass ihre Anwesenheit in der Tiroler Kleinstadt nur temporär war.

Display-window installation, Kufstein
Part of the exhibition *Augenhöhe* [Eye Level]

With work by Luise Clay and her fromer pupils Ricarda Denzer, Norbert Steiner, Bernhard Lochmann, James Clay, Nikolaus Schletterer, Werner Richter, Christiane Erharter, Gerlinde Richter-Lichtblau, Maria Vill, Margareta Langer, Stephan Obergemeiner, and Kurt Härting

Schaufenster-Installation im Rahmen der Ausstellung *Augenhöhe*, Kufstein

Mit Arbeiten von Luise Clay und ihren ehemaligen Schüler*innen Ricarda Denzer, Norbert Steiner, Bernhard Lochmann, James Clay, Nikolaus Schletterer, Werner Richter, Christiane Erharter, Gerlinde Richter-Lichtblau, Maria Vill, Margareta Langer, Stephan Obergemeiner und Kurt Härting

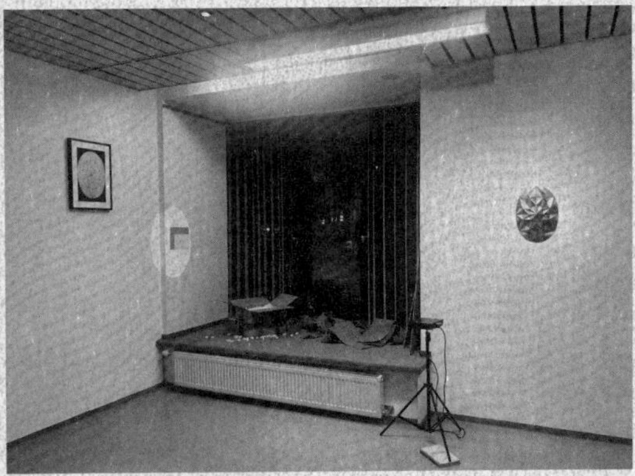

Exhibition view, *O. T. (Saupreissin)*, display-window installation, in the exhibition *Augenhöhe* Kufstein, 2020

Ausstellungsansicht, *O. T. (Saupreissin)*, Schaufensterinstallation, Ausstellung *Augenhöhe* Kufstein, 2020

Packing case with padding, plaster star and scraps of rug

Umzugskarton mit Verpackungsmaterialien, Gipsstern und Teppichreste

124 ←

Audio Trouble, framed color print, 70 × 100 cm, 2018

Audio Trouble, Color Print gerahmt, 70 × 100 cm, 2018

Oval beam of light, projected onto the poem *Tapetenwechsel* [Change of Scene], typewritten text on paper, 1983, packaging, 2020

Ovaler Lichtkegel, Lichtprojektion auf das Gedicht *Tapetenwechsel*, Schreibmaschine auf Papier, 1983, Kartonverpackung, 2020

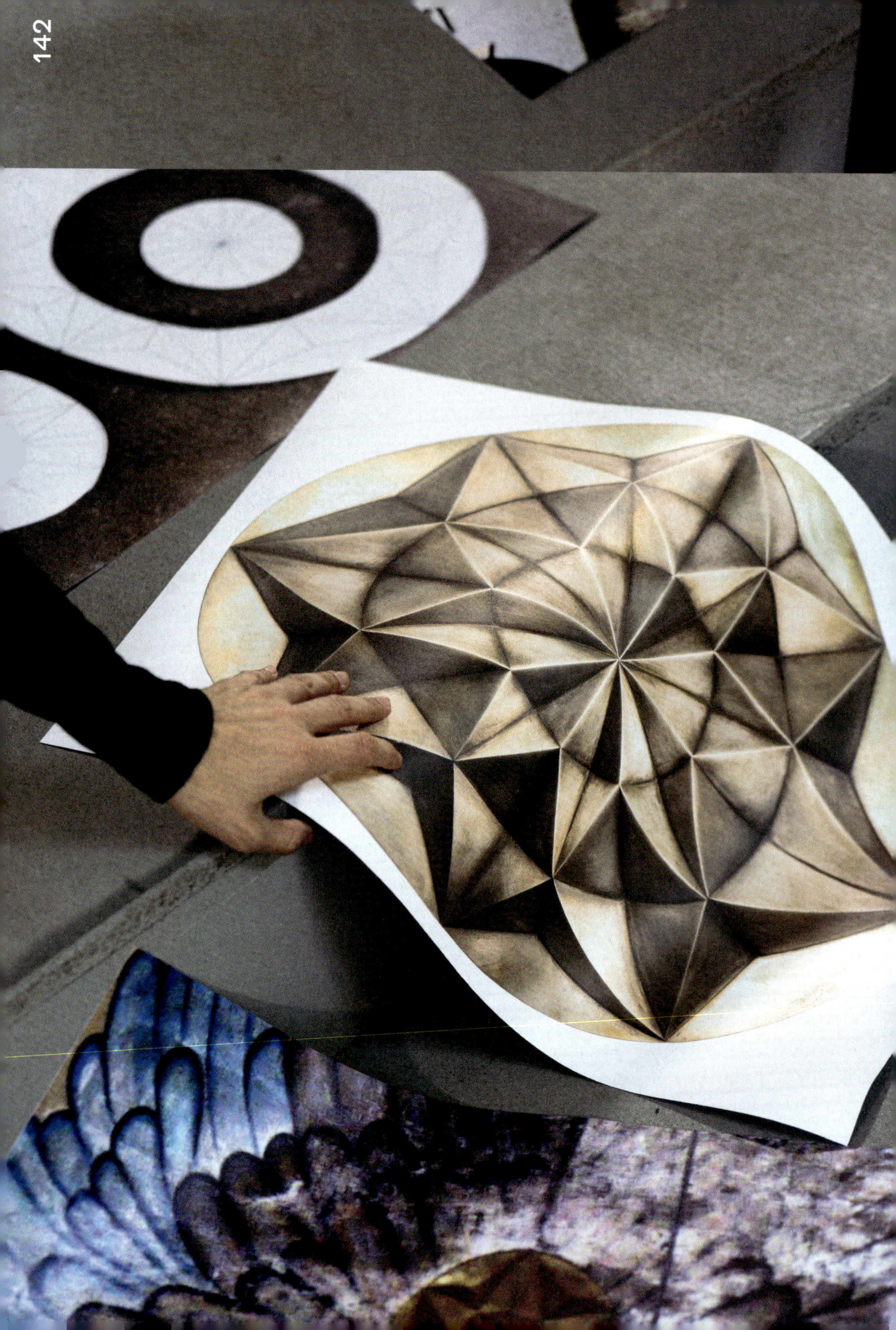

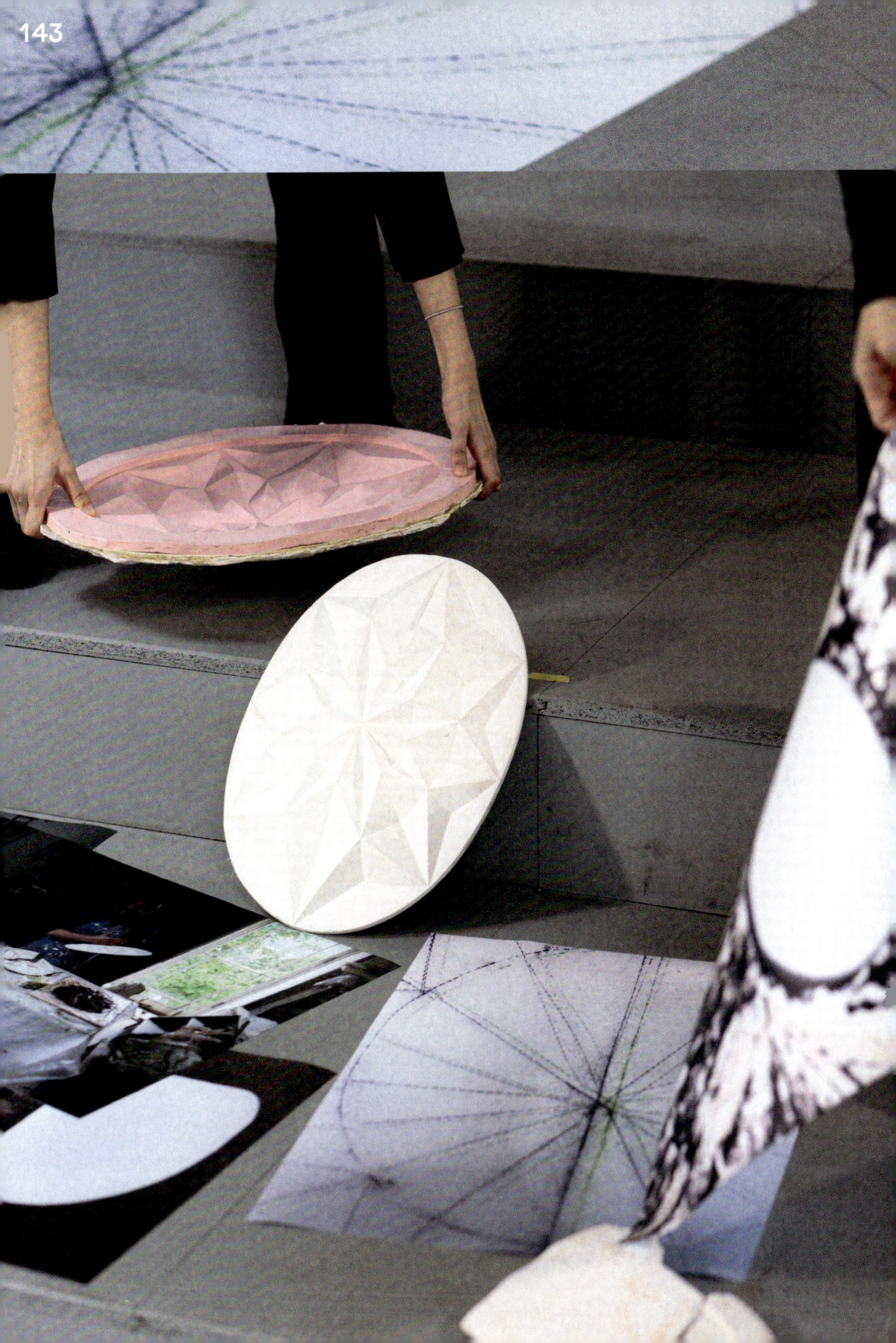

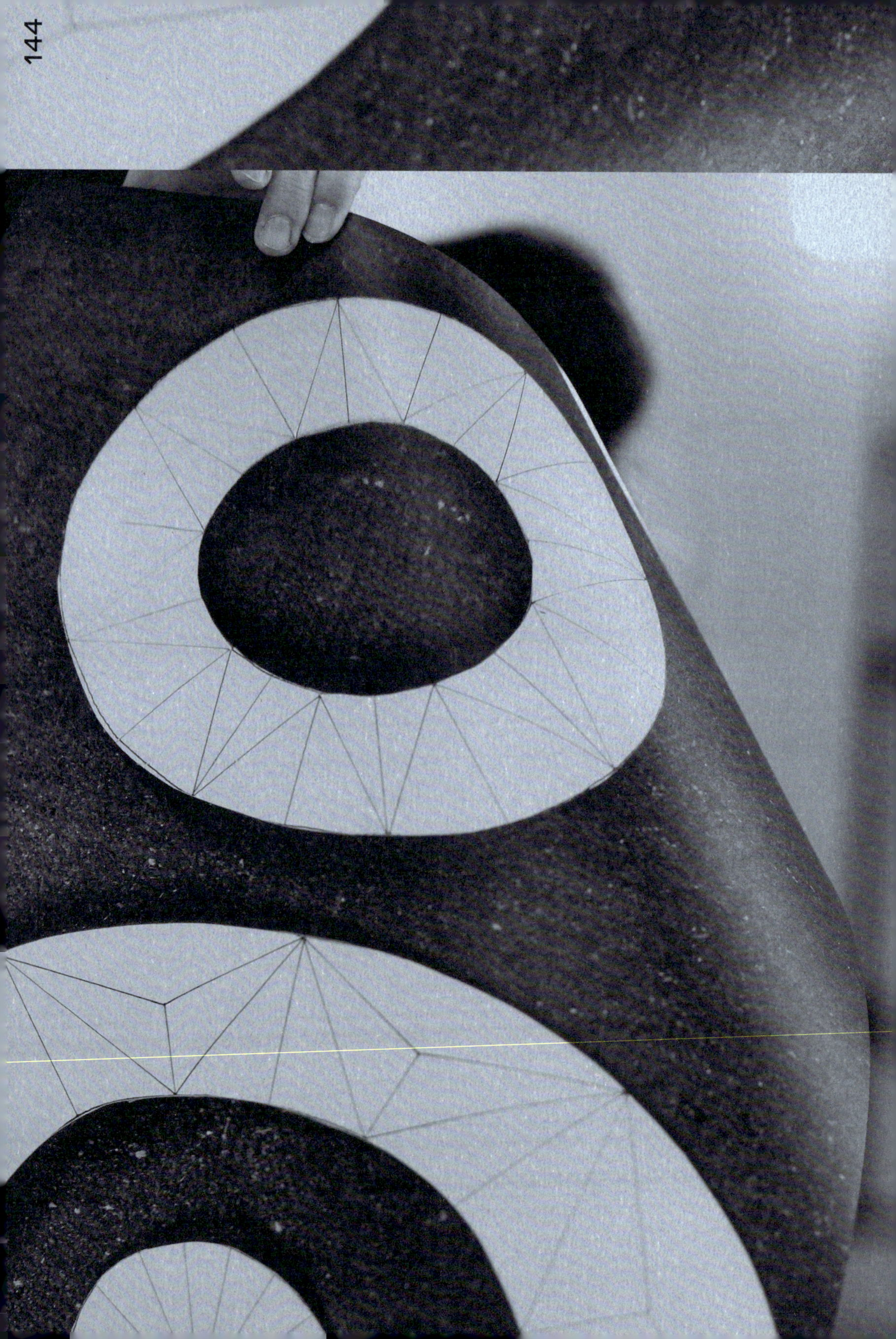

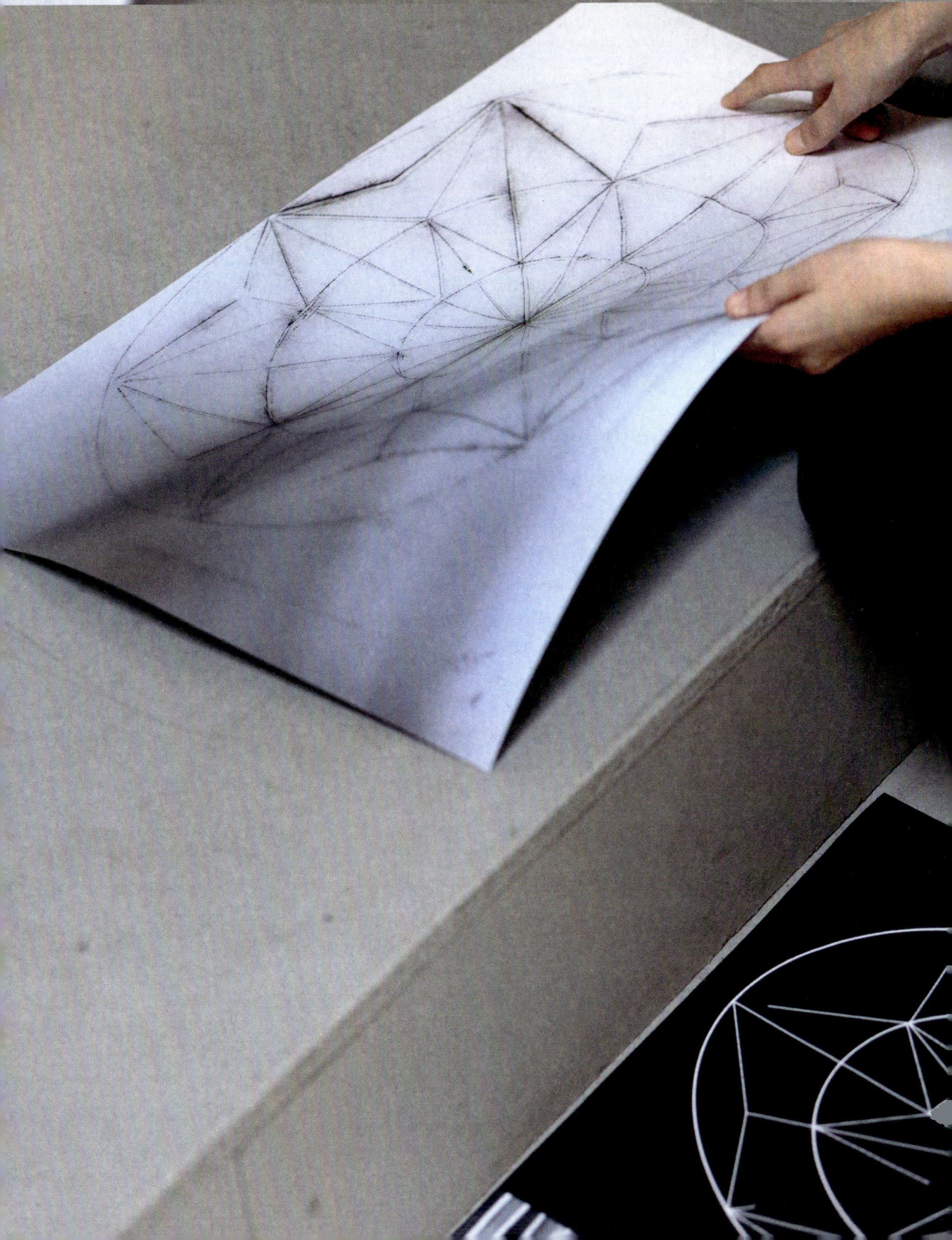

"This oval object drew my attention. Its regular form, the perfection of the star's gleaming brass structure, and the colorful, soft-looking angel feathers evoke a futuristic image," writes Ricarda Denzer about the object she discovered in Hagia Sophia in Istanbul. When the Byzantine church was converted into a mosque, the faces of the Christian seraphim were covered by brass star-shaped masks in accordance with Muslim belief, which forbids figurative religious portrayal.

On the audio track to the work, Denzer comments: "In one of Alexander Kluge's interviews with cultural historian Hans Belting, I hear that the Arab mathematician Alhazen talks about how images, figurative illustrations only exist in the mind. So there are images in the Muslim philosophy of science, but they are internal images. A fine example of a misunderstanding in cultural transfer. According to Belting, cultural understanding takes the place of reception here."

The object is central to the exhibition *Was uns wichtig ist!* [What's Important to Us!] to the extent that it refers to the continuing rewriting and overwriting of cultural heritage that has been going on for centuries (in this case an ornament in Hagia Sophia conceived to conceal Christian iconography). Denzer's artistic practice of an "acoustic questing search" can be experienced in an accompanying video-text audio piece that proceeds from this object. This practice never emerges from a pre-determined idea, but through montage gives rise to ideas, forms, and possibilities that resonate with other disciplines and contexts.

„Dieses ovale Objekt zog meine Aufmerksamkeit auf sich. Die Regelmäßigkeit der Form, die Perfektion der glänzenden Messingstruktur des Sterns auf den bunten, weich wirkenden Engelsfedern evoziert ein futuristisches Bild", schreibt Ricarda Denzer über das Objekt, das sie in der Hagia Sophia in Istanbul entdeckte. Als die byzantinische Kirche in eine Moschee umgewandelt wurde, wurden die Gesichter der christlichen Seraphim-Engel in Übereinstimmung mit dem muslimischen Glauben, der gegenständliche religiöse Darstellungen nicht erlaubt, durch eine Maske aus Messing mit Sternprägung bedeckt.

Auf der Audiospur zur Arbeit sagt Denzer: „In einem der Interviews von Alexander Kluge mit dem Kulturhistoriker Hans Belting höre ich, dass der arabische Mathematiker Alhazen darüber spricht, wie Bilder, figurative Abbildungen nur im Kopf existieren. Es gibt also Bilder in der muslimischen Philosophie der Wissenschaft, aber es sind innere Bilder. Ein schönes Beispiel für ein Missverständnis im Kulturtransfer. Nach Belting tritt kulturelles Verständnis hier an die Stelle der Rezeption."

In der Ausstellung *Was uns wichtig ist!* stellte das Objekt insofern ein zentrales Exponat dar, als es auf das laufende, seit Jahrhunderten stattfindende Um- und Überschreiben des kulturellen Erbes (in diesem Fall ein Ornament in der Hagia Sophia, das christliche Ikonografie überdeckt) verweist. Ausgehend von dem Objekt wird in einem begleitenden Video-Text-Hörstück Denzers künstlerische Praxis als „akustische Suchbewegung" erfahrbar, wobei sie nicht von einem vorgefertigten Thema ausgeht, sondern durch Montage Ideen, Formen und Möglichkeiten schafft, die hier ausgehend von unterschiedlichen Disziplinen und Kontexten anklingen.

Bronze object, 2017–2018 and video/audio/text, 21 min, 2022/2023 for the exhibition *Was uns wichtig ist! Künstlerische Perspektiven auf Kulturerbe* [What's Important to Us! Artistic Perspectives on Cultural Legacy], curated by Christa Benzer and Sabine Benzer, Volkskundemuseum Vienna, 2022, Vorarlberg Museum, Bregenz, 2023

With work by Muhammet Ali Baş, Ricarda Denzer, Carola Dertnig, Gregor Eldarb, Vasilena Gankovska, Andrés Ramírez Gaviria, Nilbar Güreş, Anna Jermolaewa, Belinda Kazeem-Kamiński, Aglaia Konrad, Tatiana Lecomte, Toni Schmale, Susanne Schuda, Johannes Schweiger, Viktoria Tremmel, Maja Vukoje, Klemens Wihlidal, Hannes Zebedin

Bronzeobjekt, 2017–2018 und Video-Audio- Textarbeit, 21 min, 2022/2023 im Rahmen der Ausstellung *Was uns wichtig ist! Künstlerische Perspektiven auf Kulturerbe*, kuratiert von Christa Benzer und Sabine Benzer, Volkskundemuseum Wien, 2022, Vorarlberg Museum, Bregenz, 2023

Mit Arbeiten von Muhammet Ali Baş, Ricarda Denzer, Carola Dertnig, Gregor Eldarb, Vasilena Gankovska, Andrés Ramírez Gaviria, Nilbar Güreş, Anna Jermolaewa, Belinda Kazeem-Kamiński, Aglaia Konrad, Tatiana Lecomte, Toni Schmale, Susanne Schuda, Johannes Schweiger, Viktoria Tremmel, Maja Vukoje, Klemens Wihlidal, Hannes Zebedin

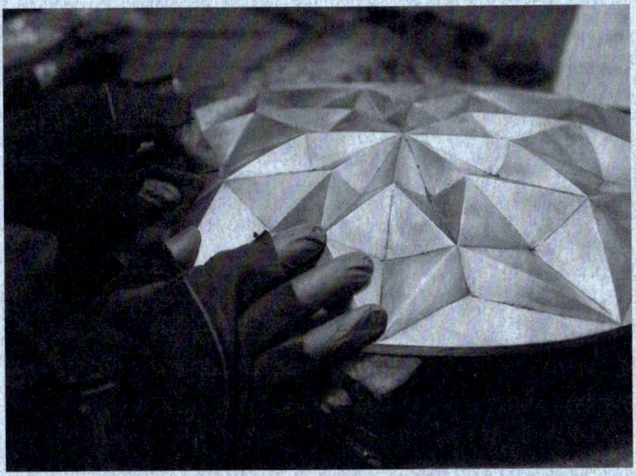

Video still from *Reflections on a Star-Shaped Masque*, video-audio text piece, 21 min, 2022/2023, for the exhibition *Was uns wichtig ist! Künstlerische Perspektiven auf Kulturerbe*, Volkskundemuseum Wien, 2022

Videostill *Reflections on a Star-Shaped Masque*, Video-Audio-Textarbeit, 21 min, 2022/2023 im Rahmen der Ausstellung *Was uns wichtig ist! Künstlerische Perspektiven auf Kulturerbe*, Volkskundemuseum Wien, 2022

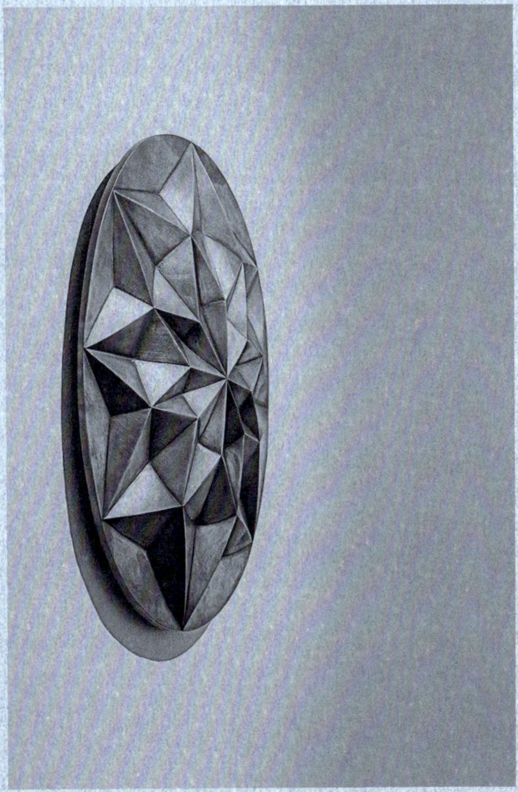

Reflections on a Star-Shaped Masque, bronze object, 2018

Reflections on a Star-Shaped Masque, Bronzeobjekt, 2018

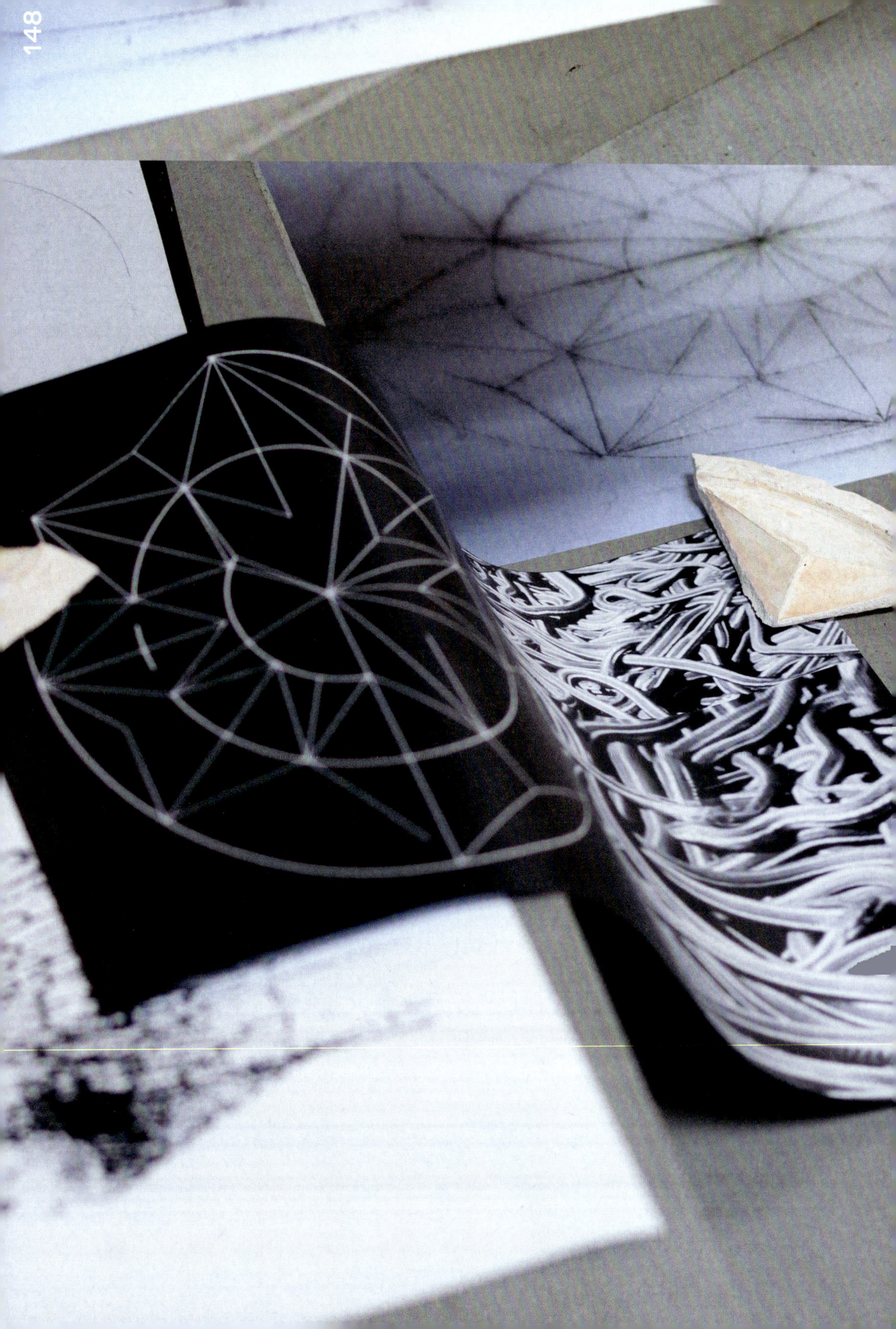

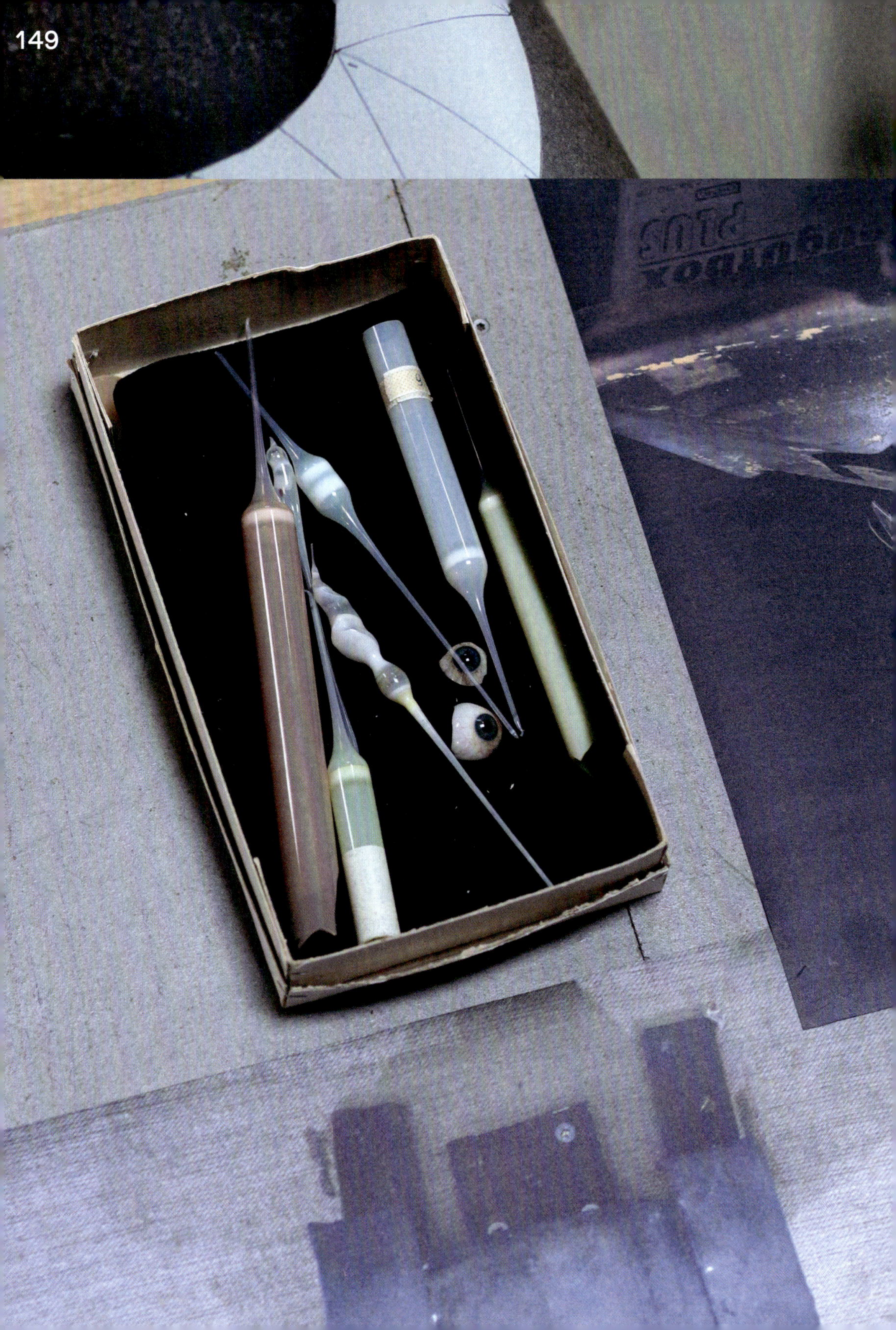

In the audio paper *Para-Listening. Eine Bricolage*, Ricarda Denzer puts the phenomenon of acousmatics to the test. The term describes the presentation of sounds entirely acoustically, without the listeners being able to identify or see their source. In the video we see the artist holding a white sheet of paper between herself and the camera. It functions as a divider between sound—her voice—and source—her mouth, whose "performance" is perceived through the slight vibrations of the paper. Behind this "curtain" Denzer lectures on her artistic interest in perceiving the world via listening and associates herself with a circle of "good" listeners by means of quotations from Pauline Oliveros (founder of the Deep Listening Institute), Roland Barthes, Gertrude Stein, and James Baldwin. Roland Barthes defined hearing as a physiological phenomenon and listening as a psychological one, and suggested a fundamental rethinking of listening—also in order to induce a radical change in language. James Baldwin understood listening as a decidedly political act, making a case for developing a sense of intuition about other people and responding to what *they* hear.

"What does it mean to move through the world listening?" asks Denzer in her sampling, which not only provides specialized theoretical or poetic answers but also involves the listeners in a meditative sound exercise devised by Pauline Oliveros: "Put your feet on the ground. Inhale ... and exhale with sound. Inhale ... and exhale with sound..."

Audio paper, text, video, 9 min, 2021

Presented during the *APL Practice (!) Week* 2021, at the live panel *In_Visibilities in Recent Sound Interventions*, with Ricarda Denzer, Kristina Pia Hofer, and Huda Takriti, in the studio of the Angewandte Performance Lab as part of the *Ambivalente Un_Sichtbarkeiten* annual conference of the Österreichische Gesellschaft für Geschlechterforschung (ÖGGF, Gender Studies Association Austria); *Sounding Research*, audio-paper presentations curated by Ricarda Denzer, Auditorium, University of Applied Arts Vienna, 2022; *Sonic Sensitivity*, an exhibition with performances and panel discussion at AIL, the Angewandte Interdisciplinary Lab, curated by Elisabeth Falkensteiner, 2022; photographic sequence, *springerin* 1/2023

In dem Audio Paper *Para-Listening. Eine Bricolage* stellt Ricarda Denzer das Phänomen der Akusmatik auf die Probe: Der Begriff beschreibt die Präsentation von Klängen allein auf akustische Weise, ohne dass die Zuhörenden die Geräusch- oder Tonquelle identifizieren oder sehen. Im Video sieht man die Künstlerin, die ein weißes Blatt zwischen sich und die Kamera hält. Es fungiert als trennendes Element zwischen Klang, ihrer Stimme und der Klangquelle – ihrem Mund, dessen „Performance" durch ein leichtes Vibrieren des Blattes wahrnehmbar ist. Hinter dem „Vorhang" referiert Denzer über ihr künstlerisches Interesse, die Welt zuhörend wahrzunehmen, und verortet sich mit Zitaten von Pauline Oliveros (Gründerin des Deep Listening Institute), Roland Barthes, Gertrude Stein, James Baldwin in einem Kreis „guter" Zuhörer*innen: Roland Barthes definierte Hören als ein physiologisches und Zuhören als ein psychologisches Phänomen und regte ein grundlegendes Überdenken dieses Zuhörens an, auch um die Sprache radikal verändern zu können. James Baldwin begriff das Zuhören als dezidiert politischen Akt, wenn er dafür plädierte, ein Gespür für die Menschen gegenüber zu entwickeln und darauf zu reagieren, was diese hören.

„What does it mean to move through the world listening?", fragt die Künstler in ihrem Sampling, in dem sie nicht nur theoretisch-fachliche oder poetische Antworten liefert, sondern die Zuseher*innen mit einer meditativen Soundübung von Pauline Oliveros auch körperlich involviert: „Put your feet on the ground. Inhale ... and exhale with sound. Inhale ... and exhale with sound ..."

Audio Paper: Text, Video, Sound, 9 min, 2021

Im Rahmen der „APL Practice (!) Week" 2021, beim Live-Panel „In_Visibilities in Recent Sound Interventions" mit Ricarda Denzer, Kristina Pia Hofer und Huda Takriti im Rahmen der Jahrestagung „Ambivalente Un_Sichtbarkeiten" der Österreichischen Gesellschaft für Geschlechterforschung (ÖGGF); *Sounding Research*, Audio-Paper-Präsentationen, kuratiert von Ricarda Denzer, Auditorium, Universität für angewandte Kunst Wien, 2022; *Sonic Sensitivity*, einer Ausstellung mit Performances und Panel Diskussion im AIL, dem angewandte Interdisciplinary Lab, kuratiert von Elisabeth Falkensteiner, 2022; Bildstrecke *springerin* 1/2023

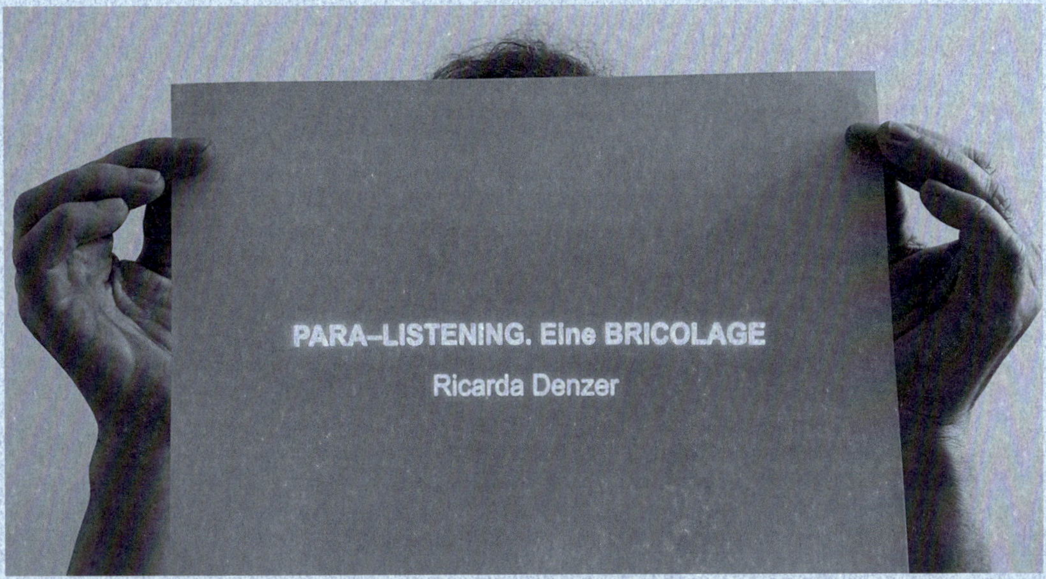

Video still, audio paper
Para-Listening. Eine Bricolage, 19 min, 2021

Videostill, Audio Paper
Para-Listening. Eine Bricolage, 19 min, 2021

Selected Collaborative Projects 2013–2023

Auswahl kollaborativer Projekte 2013–2023

Ronda Zheng, a phantom and cult figure, entered the Viennese art scene in the 1990s. Her biography is closely connected to the artistic careers of Ricarda Denzer and Isa Rosenberger. Zheng's *Ronda Zheng Retrospective 1993–1997* was shown as part of the exhibitions *I am another world: Artistic Authorship between Desubjectivization and Recanonization*, Academy of Fine Arts Vienna, 2014; *With a Name Like Yours, You Might Be Any Shape*, Kunstpavillon, Innsbruck, 2013; UC Irvin University Gallery, Los Angeles, 2012/13. Curated by Georgia Holz, Claudia Slanar.

"There have been various reasons for artists to create alter-egos, personae, doppelgangers and adopt pseudonyms: to blur the boundaries of fact and fiction, of reality and imagination, and to (re-)insert themselves into historic canons."

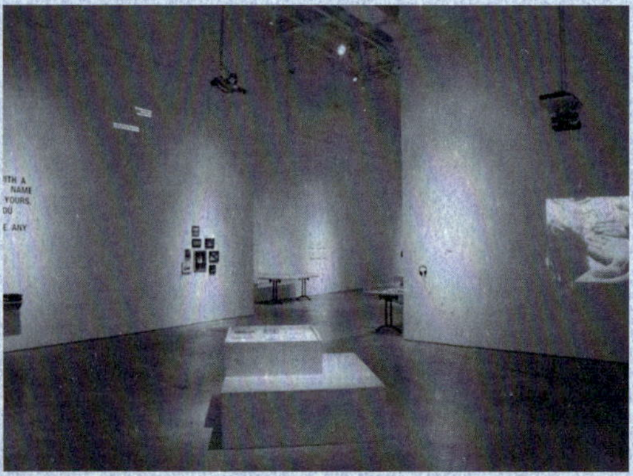

ɵ⊏ Exhibition view, Ronda Zheng, *Neulich bei Frau Novak*, 1995, in the exhibition *With a Name Like Yours, You Might Be Any Shape*, UC Irvin University Gallery, Los Angeles, 2012/2013

ᘓɵ Ausstellungsansicht Ronda Zheng *Neulich bei Frau Novak*, 1995, im Rahmen der Ausstellung *With a Name like Yours, You might be any Shape*, UC Irvin University Gallery, Los Angeles, 2012/2013

Ronda Zheng, Phantom und Kultfigur, betrat die Wiener Kunstszene in den 1990er-Jahren. Ihre Biografie ist eng verknüpft mit jener der beiden Künstlerinnen Ricarda Denzer und Isa Rosenberger. Zheng zeigte ihre Werkschau *Retrospektive Ronda Zheng 1993–1997* im Rahmen der Ausstellungen *Ich bin eine andere Welt. Künstlerische Autor*innenschaft zwischen Desubjektivierung und Rekanonisierung*, xhibit, Akademie der bildenden Künste Wien, 2013; *With a Name Like Yours, You Might Be Any Shape*, Kunstpavillon, Innsbruck, 2014; UC Irvin University Gallery, Los Angeles, 2012. Kuratiert von Georgia Holz und Claudia Slanar.

„Es gibt verschiedene Gründe, warum Künstler*innen Alter-Egos, Personae, Doppelgänger schaffen und Pseudonyme annehmen: um die Grenzen von Fakt und Fiktion, von Realität und Imagination zu verwischen und sich (wieder) in den historischen Kanon einzufügen."

With works by Hina Berau / Judith Fischer, Ursula Bogner, Dagmar Buhr, The Buried Alive Group, Zoe Crosher, Carola Dertnig / Lora Sana, Justine Frank, Mario Garcia Torres, Janez Janša, Janez Janša, Janez Janša, Barbara Kapusta, Matthias Klos, Maxim Komar-Myshkin, Warren Neidich, Roee Rosen, SUPER VÉRO, Mathilde ter Heijne, Unknown Artist, Laura Wollen, Donelle Woolford, Ronda Zheng / Ricarda Denzer / Isa Rosenberger

Mit Arbeiten von Hina Berau / Judith Fischer, Ursula Bogner, Dagmar Buhr, The Buried Alive Group, Zoe Crosher, Carola Dertnig / Lora Sana, Justine Frank, Mario Garcia Torres, Janez Janša, Janez Janša, Janez Janša, Barbara Kapusta, Matthias Klos, Maxim Komar-Myshkin, Warren Neidich, Roee Rosen, SUPER VÉRO, Mathilde ter Heijne, Unknown Artist, Laura Wollen, Donelle Woolford, Ronda Zheng / Ricarda Denzer / Isa Rosenberger

Inspired by the phrase "form is healing," which Denzer heard in a radio interview, the two artists based the form of their artist talk on mirroring, a technique from Imago Therapy, in which couples generate and express their appreciation for each other by repeating as literally as possible what the other person has said.

Ausgehend von dem Satz „Form ist heilsam", den Denzer in einem Radiointerview gehört hat, lehnten die beiden Künstlerinnen die Form ihres performativen Gesprächs an das Spiegeln an, einer Technik aus der Imago-Therapie, bei der Paare ihre Wertschätzung für den/die die andere/n durch möglichst wörtliche Wiederholung des vom Gegenüber Gesagten herbeiführen und ausdrücken.

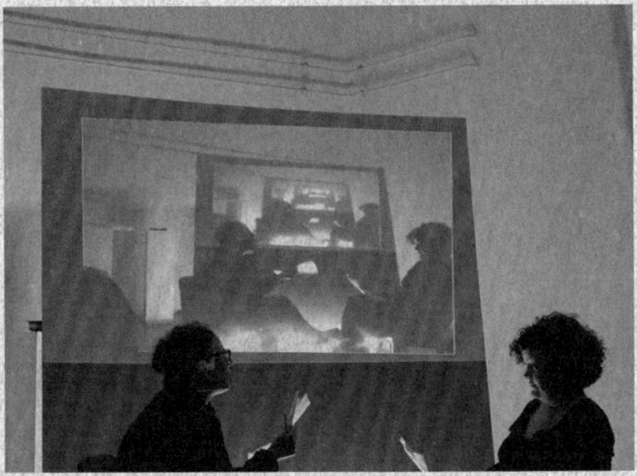

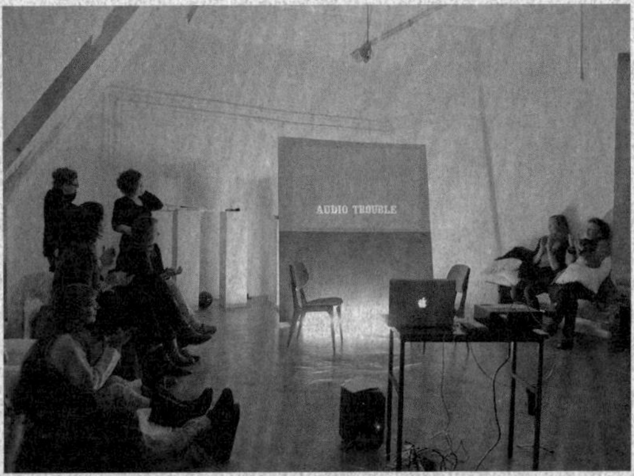

en Speech performance, *Ricarda Denzer calls Susanne Schuda*, VBKÖ – Vereinigung Bildender Künstlerinnen Wien, 2014, part of the project series *There Are Some Things We Need To Talk About*

de Sprachperformance *Ricarda Denzer calls Susanne Schuda*, VBKÖ – Vereinigung Bildender Künstlerinnen Wien, 2014, im Rahmen der Projektreihe *There Are Some Things We Need To Talk About*

Performance in the context of *There Are Some Things We Need To Talk About*, "a series of artist talks about shared necessities, conceived and organized by Katrin Hornek and Johanna Tinzl, who invited artists to create an evening of talks at VBKÖ with a partner of their choice. The starting point of each evening is a sentence proposed by the discussion partners, which manifests the evening textually and at the same time connects the individual events with each other"

en

Eine Performance im Kontext von *There Are Some Things We Need To Talk About*, einer Reihe von Künstlerinnengesprächen „über geteilte Notwendigkeiten, konzipiert und organisiert von Katrin Hornek und Johanna Tinzl, die Künstlerinnen dazu einladen, mit einer Partnerin ihrer Wahl je einen Gesprächsabend in der VBKÖ zu gestalten. Ausgangspunkt jedes Abends ist ein von den Gesprächspartnerinnen vorgeschlagener Satz, der den Abend textlich manifestiert und gleichzeitig die einzelnen Veranstaltungen miteinander verbindet"

de

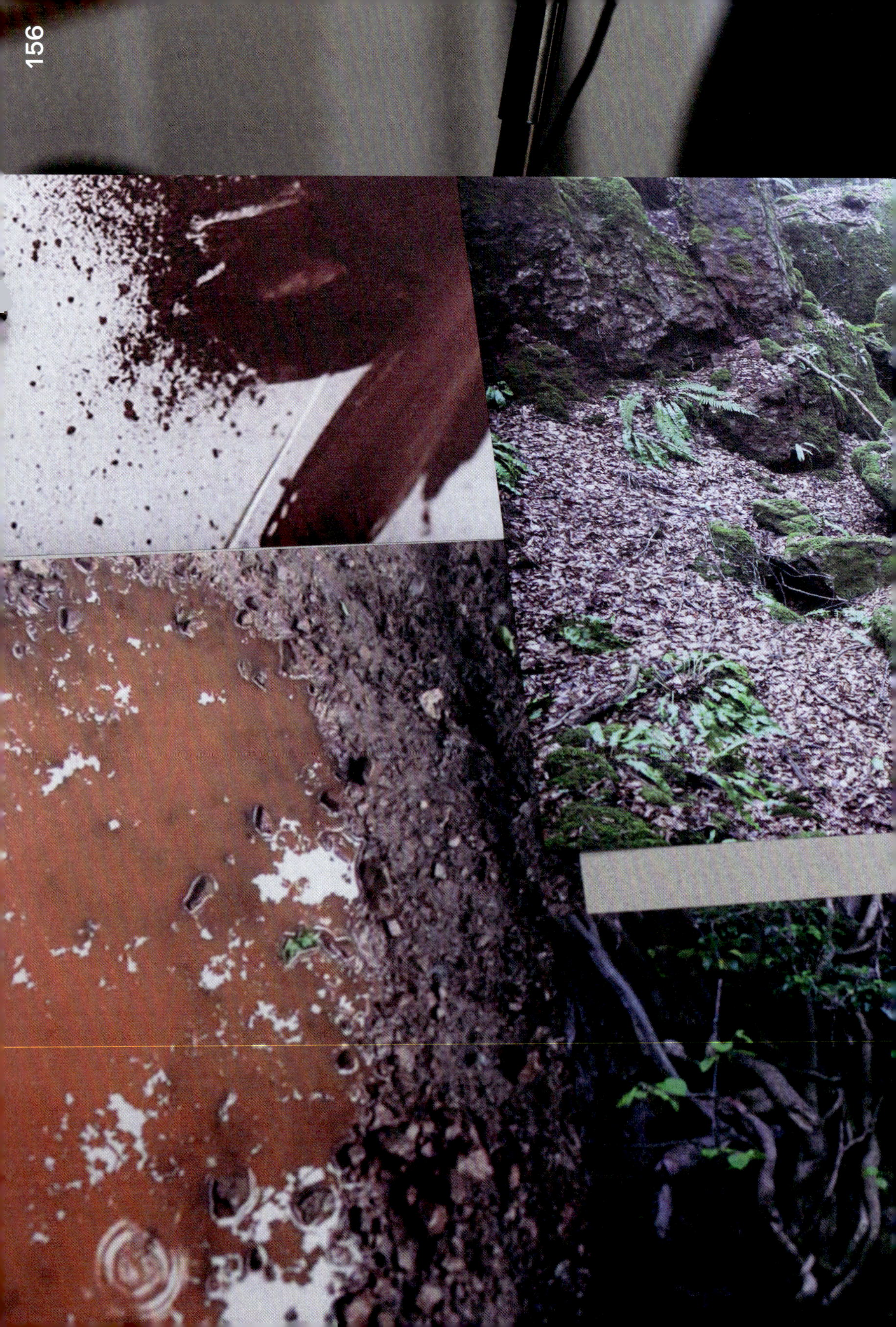

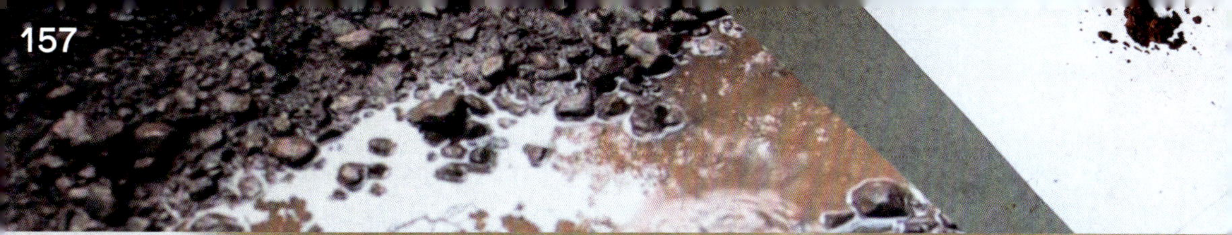

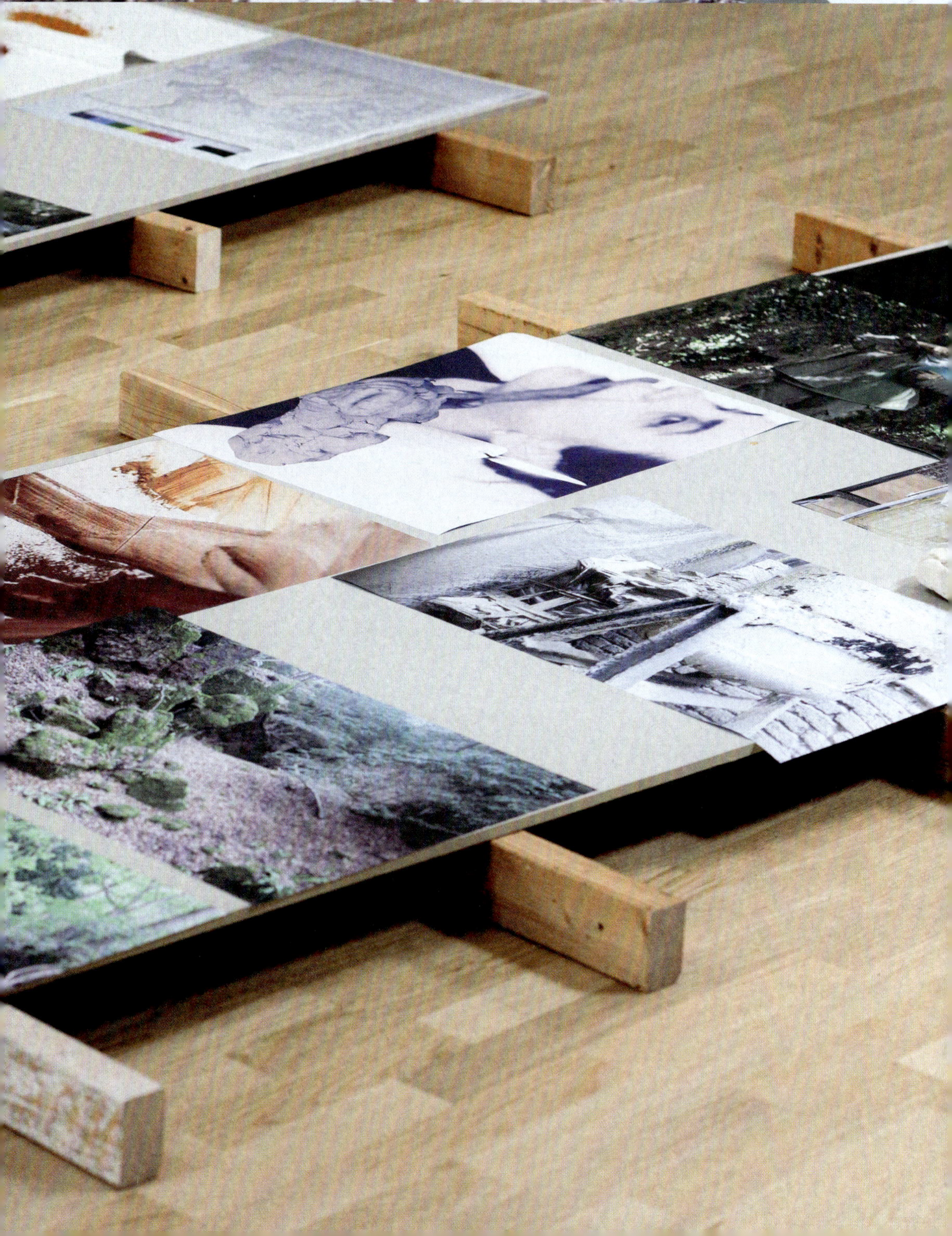

The project series *Hörvergessen* revolves around the question of the extent to which sound is a force that constructs the world around us and whether sound is a medium that produces knowledge about the world we live in. *Hörvergessen* examines the meaning of hearing in art and as a cognitive instrument. The voice as a liminal phenomenon plays a particular role here, as does the question of how the voice is materialized in the various artistic disciplines. How is the particular mediality of the voice constituted? Ultimately, language is not simply a neutral conveyance; rather, the symbolic meaning of words goes hand in hand with the material, physical aspects of the voice, its modulation, breath, rhythm, timbre, hesitations, pauses, and so on. A selection of projects is outlined here: *All You Have is a Voice*, 2014, *Hörzirkel Rusti*, 2017, *The Lost Hour*, 2018, and *Situated Sounds*, 2020.

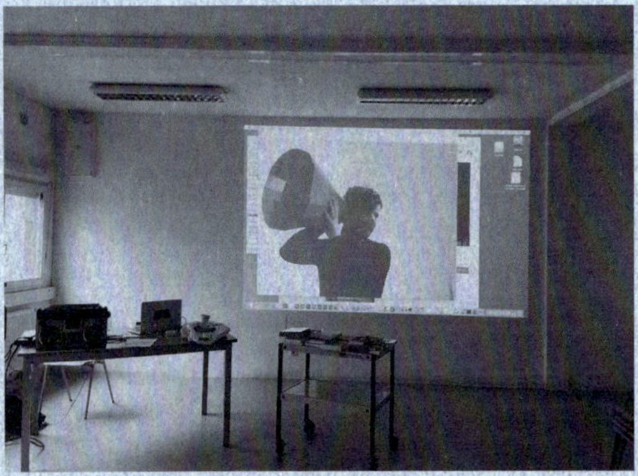

en *Hörvergessen*, TransArts seminar room, container, Rustenschacherallee, Vienna, 2014

de *Hörvergessen*, Seminarraum TransArts, Container, Rustenschacherallee, Wien, 2014

Die Projektreihe *Hörvergessen* dreht sich um die Frage, inwiefern Sound eine Kraft ist, die die Welt um uns herum konstruiert, und inwiefern Sound ein Medium ist, das Wissen über die Welt produziert, in der wir leben. *Hörvergessen* beschäftigt sich mit der Bedeutung des Hörens in der Kunst und mit dem Hören als Instrument der Erkenntnisfähigkeit. Die Stimme als Schwellenphänomen spielt dabei eine besondere Rolle, ebenso wie die Frage, wie sich die Stimme in den verschiedenen künstlerischen Disziplinen materialisiert. Was macht die besondere Medialität der Stimme aus? Schließlich ist Sprache nicht einfach ein neutrales Transportmittel, sondern die symbolische Bedeutung der Worte geht Hand in Hand mit der materiellen, körperlichen Seite der Stimme, der Modulation, dem Atem, dem Rhythmus, der Stimmlage, dem Zögern oder Innehalten usw. Eine Auswahl an Projekten findet sich in *All You Have is a Voice*, 2014, *Hörzirkel Rusti*, 2017, *The Lost Hour*, 2018 und *Situated Sounds*, 2020 skizziert.

On the evening of December 17, 2014, twelve young artists performed a joint work based on graphic scores engaging with the voice at the art space k48. *All You Have is a Voice* was a collective project by students at the University of Applied Arts Vienna and the Academy of Fine Arts Vienna. The participants researched the role of the voice as an artistic medium, as a method of translation, and as an interpretive tool.

Am Abend des 17. Dezember 2014 führten zwölf junge Künstler*innen im Kunstraum k48 eine gemeinsam entwickelte Arbeit auf, die sich anhand von grafischer Notation mit der Stimme beschäftigte. *All You Have is a Voice* ist ein Gemeinschaftsprojekt von Studierenden der Universität für angewandte Kunst Wien und der Akademie der bildenden Künste Wien.
Die Teilnehmer*innen erforschten die Rolle der Stimme als künstlerisches Medium, als Methode der Übersetzung und als Werkzeug der Interpretation.

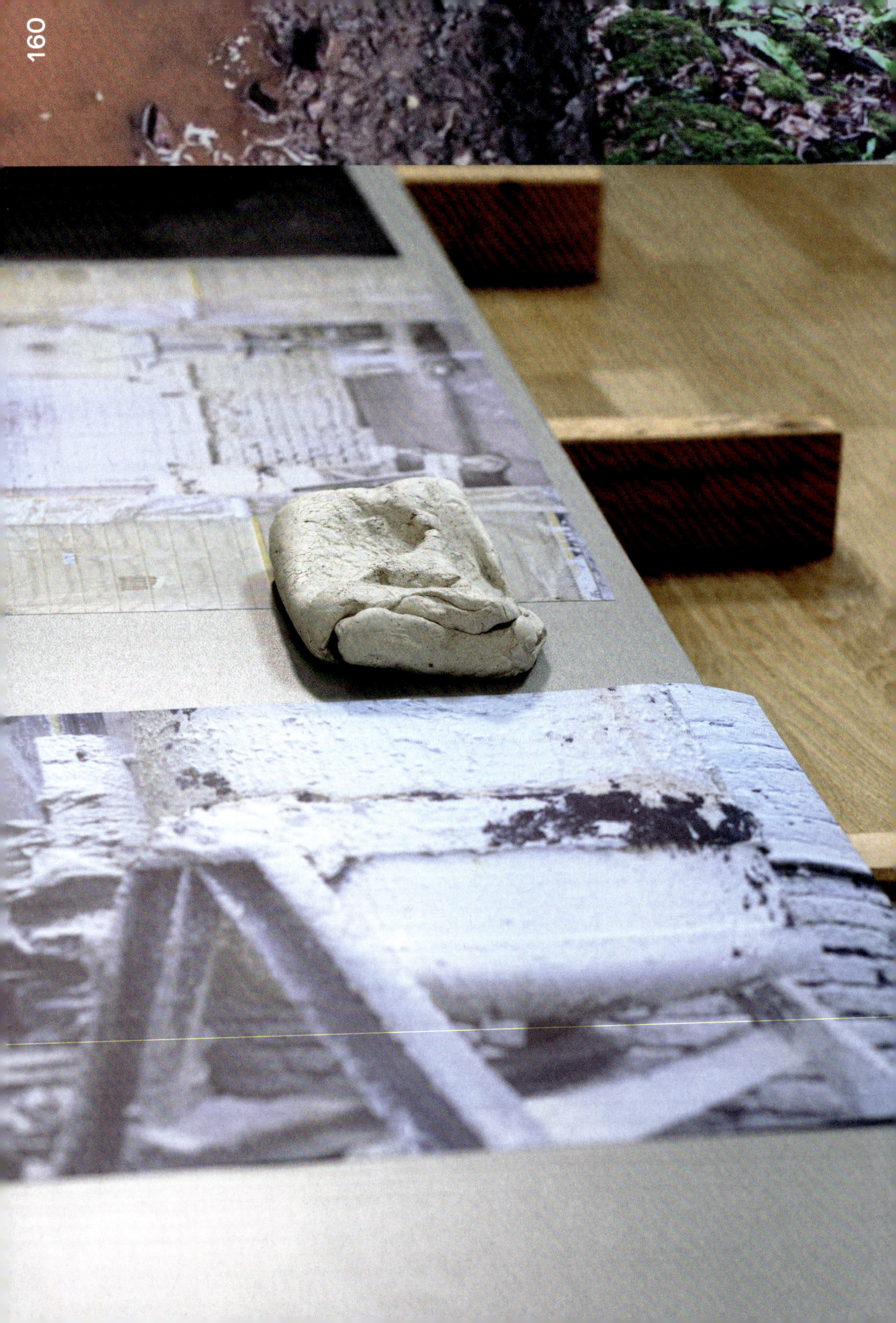

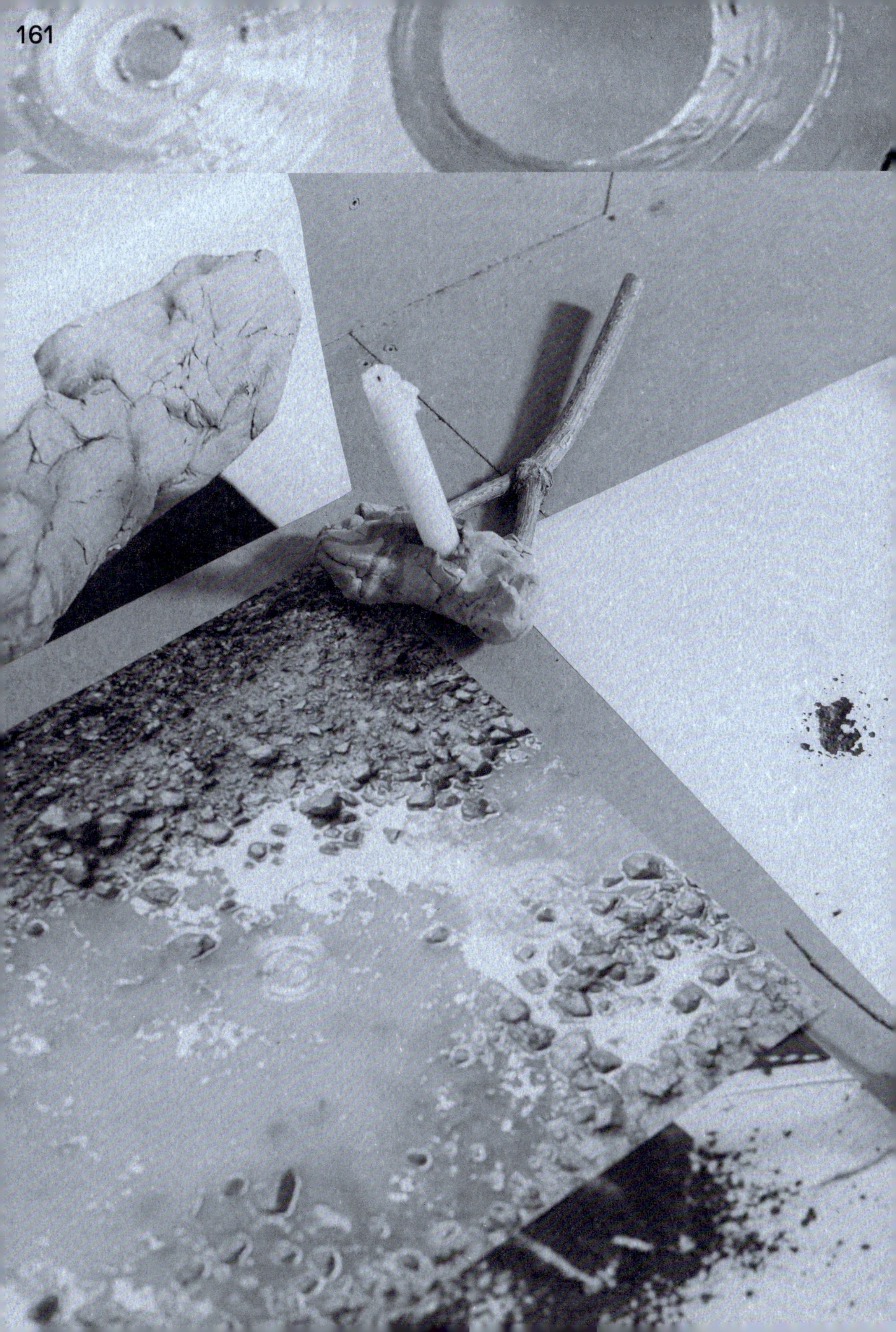

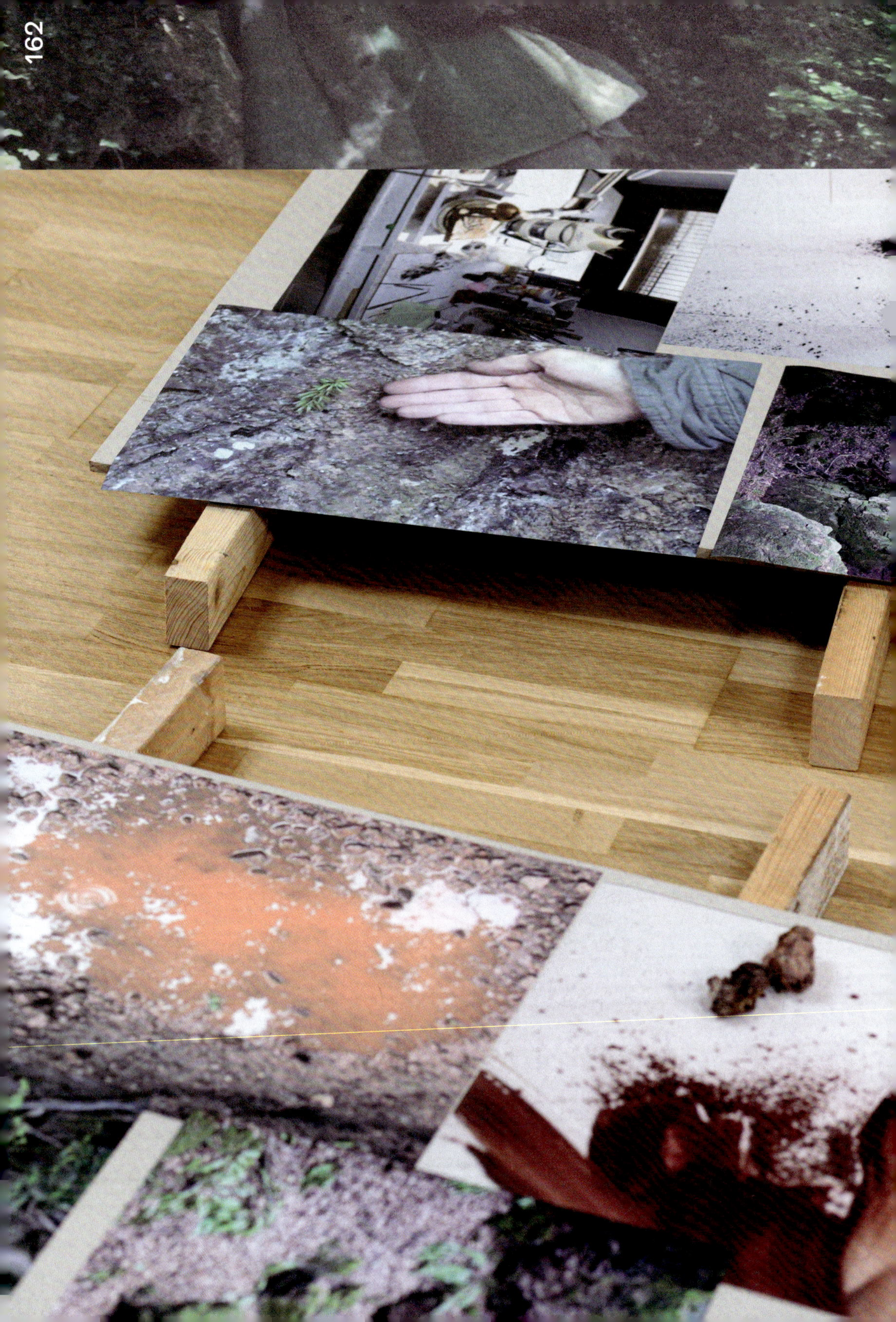

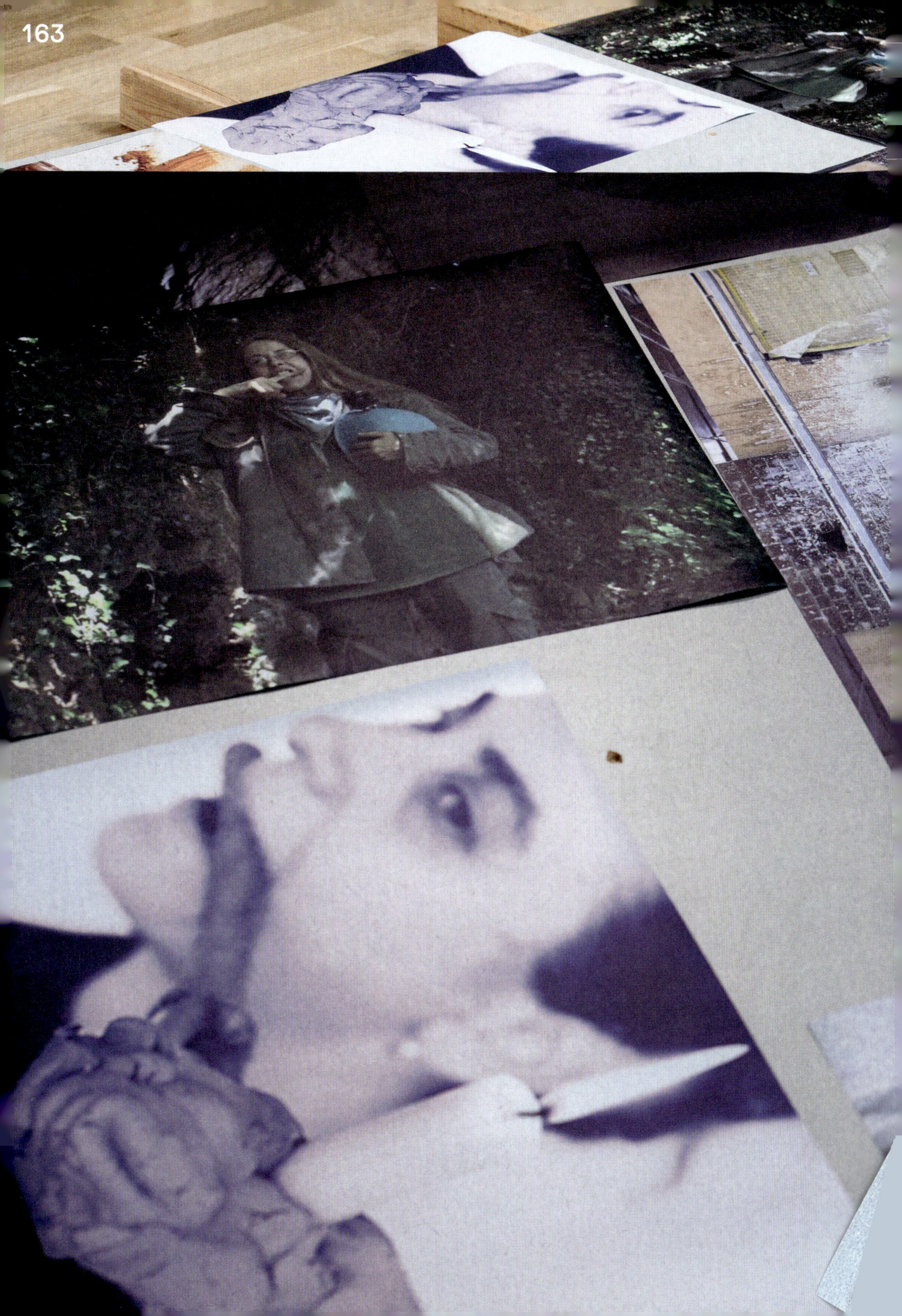

As part of the *Hörvergessen* [Forgetting-listening] series, Ricarda Denzer extended an invitation to the TransArts Department on Rustenschacherallee in Vienna. Along with DJnes and invited artists, students also engaged through language performances with sound pieces produced and performed on vinyl records.

Im Rahmen der Reihe *Hörvergessen* lud Ricarda Denzer zu *Hörzirkel Rusti* in das TransArts-Department in der Wiener Rustenschacherallee. Neben DJnes und eingeladenen Künstler*innen setzten sich auch die Studierenden in Sprach-Performances mit Soundstücken auseinander, die auf Vinyl-Schallplatten produziert und aufgeführt wurden.

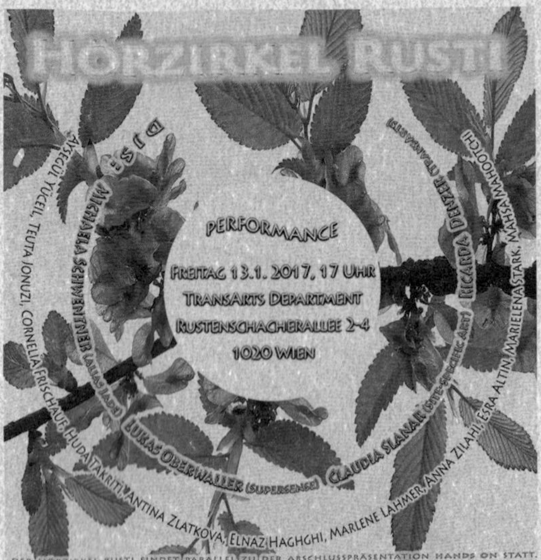

en Flyer, *Hörzirkel Rusti*, design: Esra Altin, 2017

de Flyer, *Hörzirkel Rusti*, Design: Esra Altin, 2017

University of Applied Arts Vienna, TransArts Department

With guest DJnes Michaela Schwentner (alias Jade), Claudia Slanar (Department of Site-Specific Art) and sound pieces by students at the University of Applied Arts Vienna

en

Universität für angewandte Kunst Wien, TransArts Department

Mit Guest DJnes: Michaela Schwentner (alias Jade), Claudia Slanar (Site Specific Art) sowie Soundstücke von Studierenden der Universität für angewandte Kunst Wien

de

The multivocal “auto-ethnographic radio sound piece” *The Lost Hour* was realized by students in the *Hörvergessen* seminar led by Ricarda Denzer with Cornelia Frischauf, Karen Werner, and Radio Orange at the University of Applied Arts Vienna.

Das multivokale „radio-auto-ethnografische Klangstück“ *The Lost Hour* wurde von Studierenden der Universität für angewandte Kunst Wien im Rahmen des Seminars *Hörvergessen* von Ricarda Denzer gemeinsam mit Cornelia Frischauf, Karen Werner und Radio Orange realisiert.

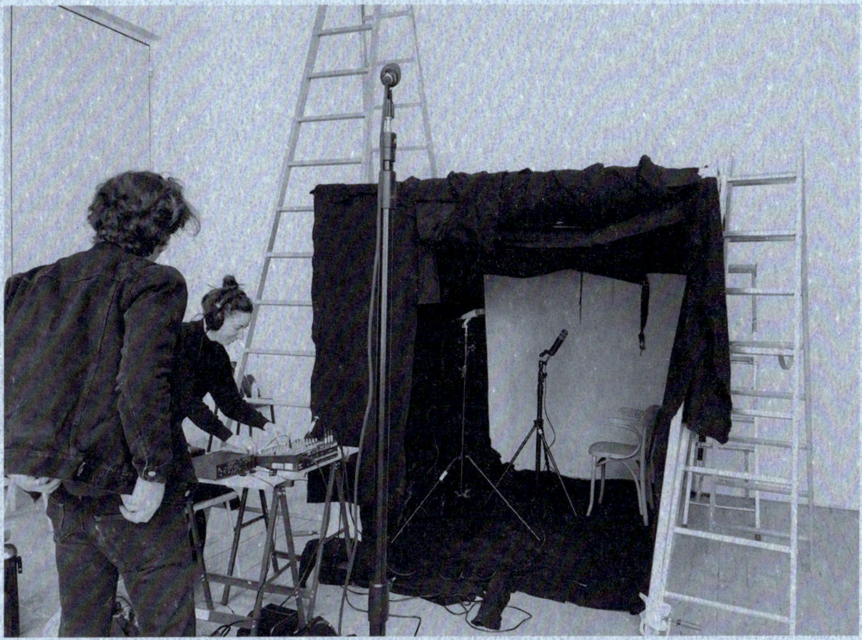

ɐɔ Temporary recording setting fo the radio piece *The Lost Hour*, TransArts, Rustenschacherallee, Vienna, 2018

ʊɑ Temporäres Aufnahmesetting für das Radiostück *The Lost Hour*, TransArts, Rustenschacherallee Wien, 2018

Radio Orange, 2018

With sound pieces by Ahreum Kwag, Aral Cimcim, Ayse-Gül Yüceil, Binta Giallo, Elnaz Haghghi, Hanna Kucera, Hannah Sakai, Hector Schofield, Huda Takriti, Karl Kühn, Katharina Spanlang, Laura Irmer, Laurids Oder, Lea Föger, Liim Jang, Martina Pouchlá, Nazanin Mehraein, Oscar Cueto, Ramiro Wong, and Simeon Jaax

Radio Orange, 2018

Mit Soundpieces von: Ahreum Kwag, Aral Cimcim, Ayse-Gül Yüceil, Binta Giallo, Elnaz Haghghi, Hanna Kucera, Hannah Sakai, Hector Schofield, Huda Takriti, Karl Kühn, Katharina Spanlang, Laura Irmer, Laurids Oder, Lea Föger, Liim Jang, Martina Pouchlá, Nazanin Mehraein, Oscar Cueto, Ramiro Wong und Simeon Jaax

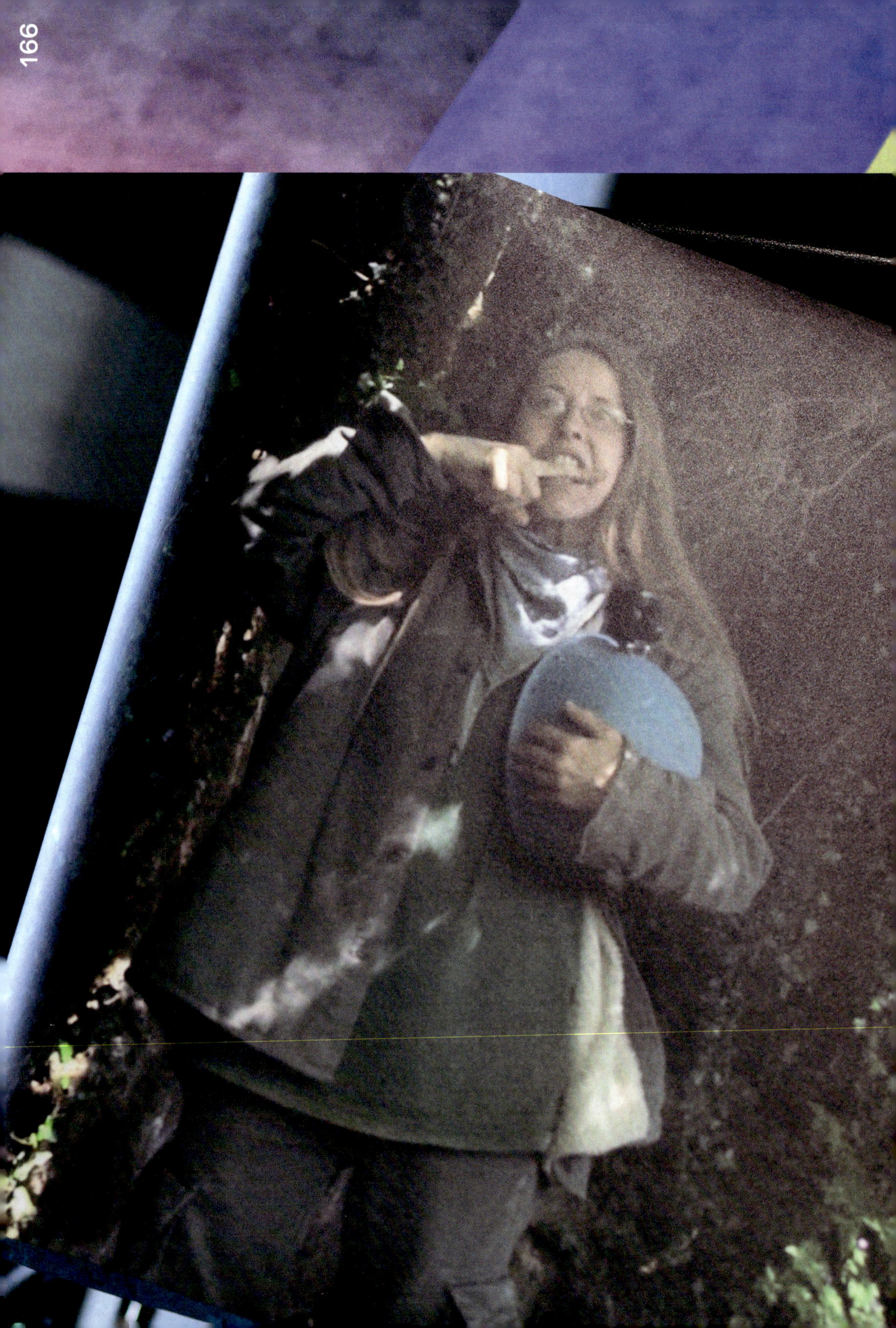

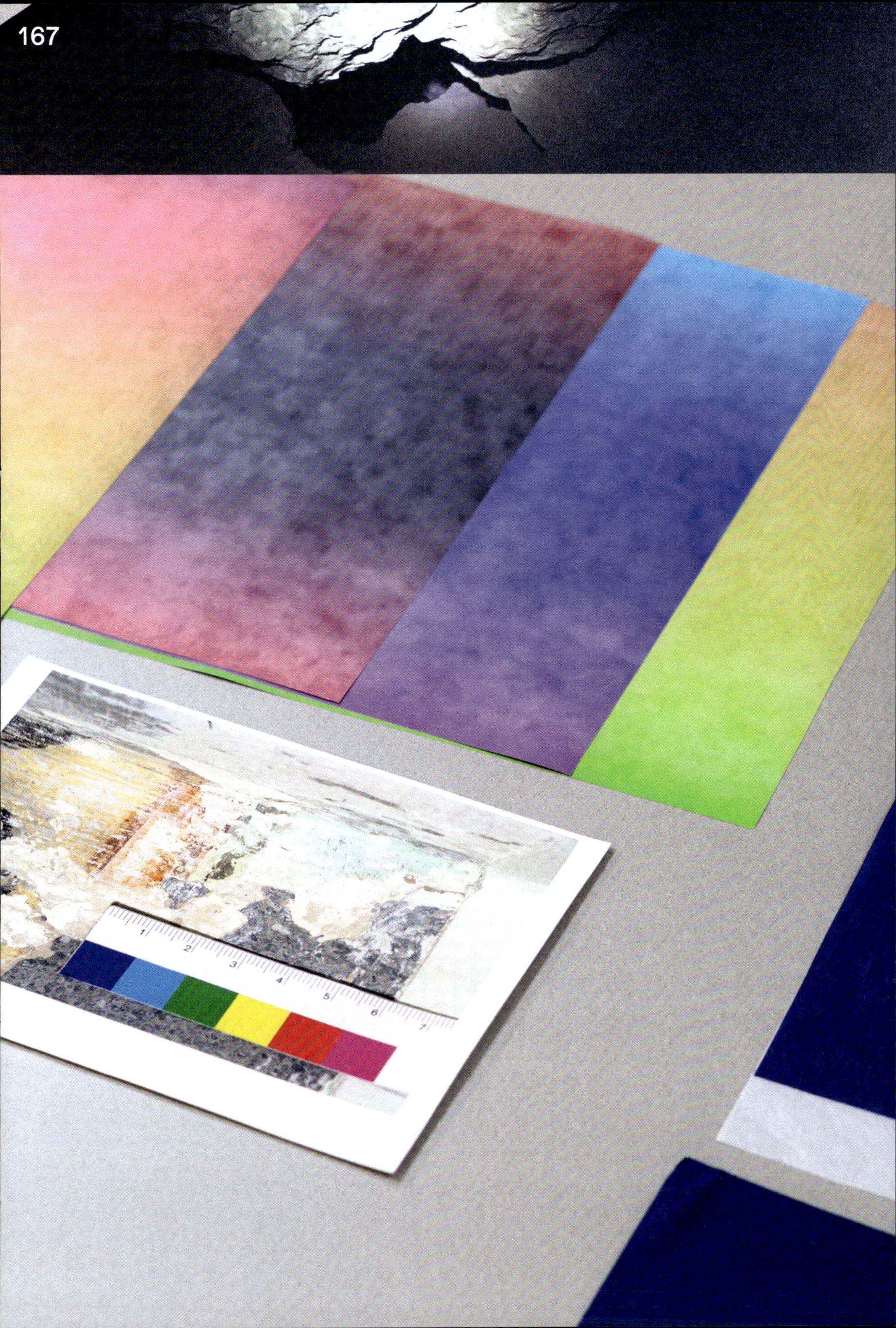

The idea for the *Situated Sounds* project arose during the pandemic lockdown in early 2020. The starting point was the question of how teachers and students could come into contact with one another through listening in a socially distanced situation. What do we hear? And which conditions shape our hearing during this period? While listening to the students' audio pieces, a collective sound poem was created for each piece using the chat function. This poem consisted of the sounds being listened to and participants' sonic environments. This gave rise to a composition in which situated sounds are linked with parts of the auditive artworks.

Die Idee zu dem Projekt *Situated Sounds* entstand zur Zeit des Lockdowns während der Pandemiekrise im Frühjahr 2020. Ausgangspunkt war die Frage, wie die Lehrenden und Studierenden in einer distanzierten Situation durch Zuhören miteinander in Beziehung treten können. Was hören wir? Und was sind die Bedingungen unseres Hörens in diesen Zeiten? Während des Anhörens der von den Studierenden entwickelten Audiostücke wird mit Hilfe der Chatfunktion ein gemeinsames Klanggedicht für jedes dieser Stücke erstellt. Dieses setzt sich aus den gehörten Klängen und den Umgebungsgeräuschen der Teilnehmer*innen zusammen. Das Ergebnis ist eine Komposition, in der sich situierte Klänge mit Teilen der auditiven Kunstwerke verbinden.

An experimental online radio and text format in three chapters, initiated by Ricarda Denzer in collaboration with aka – angewandte kunst audio, Martin Krenn, and students of the Department of Art and Communication Practices at the University of Applied Arts Vienna

Ein experimentelles Online-Radio- und Textformat in drei Kapiteln; initiiert von Ricarda Denzer in Zusammenarbeit mit aka – angewandte kunst audio, Martin Krenn und Studierenden des Fachbereichs Kunst- und Kommunikative Praxis an der Universität für angewandte Kunst Wien (KKP)

Referencing the term "anarchitecture," the *Un_University* platform discussed forms of teaching and learning in and beyond (art) universities. How do academic formats influence how subject matter is communicated? How can these formats be reconsidered from the perspective of artistic work? And which formats and approaches are being developed elsewhere, also outside academic contexts? The underscore in the title marks a movement of critical thought from negation to affirmation and vice versa. Forms of *un_university* thinking, speaking, hearing, and reading were discussed; academic and non-academic contexts and institutions were appraised in terms of the ways in which they enable—or impede— production of socio-critical knowledge.

Bezugnehmend auf den Begriff der „Anarchitektur" diskutierte die Plattform *Un_Universität* Formen der Lehre und des Lernens in und außerhalb von (Kunst-)Universitäten. Wie prägen akademische Formate der Wissensvermittlung die Lehrinhalte? Wie können diese Formate aus der Perspektive künstlerischen Arbeitens neu betrachtet werden? Und welche Formate, welche Sicht- und Herangehensweisen werden anderswo, auch abseits akademischer Kontexte, entwickelt? Der Unterstrich im Titel markiert eine kritische Denkbewegung von der Negation zur Affirmation und vice versa. Diskutiert wurden Formen des *un_universitären* Denkens, Sprechens, Hörens und Lesens; inner- und außeruniversitäre Kontexte beziehungsweise Institutionen wurden nur darauf befragt, welche gesellschaftskritischen Wissensproduktionen sie ermöglichen – oder auch verunmöglichen.

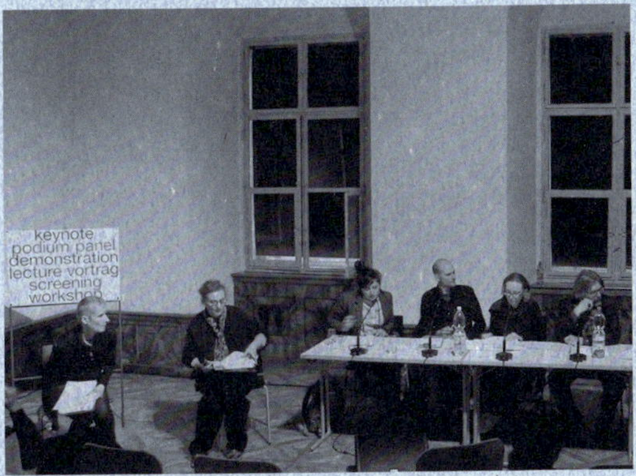

Podium/Panel, part of *Un_University*, Heiligenkreuzerhof, Vienna, 2016

Podium/Panel, im Rahmen von *Un_University*, Heiligenkreuzerhof Wien, 2016

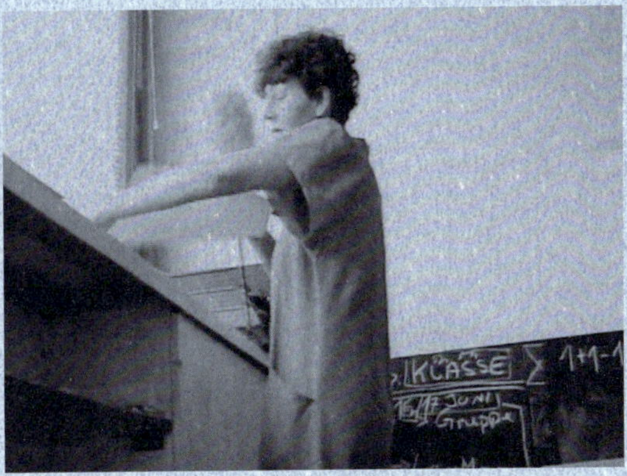

Video still, *Klasse*, Ricarda Denzer, *Video 40 min*, 1992, screening during *Un_University*, Heiligenkreuzerhof, Vienna, 2016

Videostill, *Klasse*, Ricarda Denzer, *Video 40 min*, 1992, Screening im Rahmen von *Un_University*, Heiligenkreuzerhof Wien, 2016

Concept and realization
by Ricarda Denzer and Jo Schmeiser

With text contributions, lectures, workshops, screenings and panels, presented at Heiligenkreuzerhof, University of Applied Arts Vienna, as well as in the e-journal *Art Education Research* #13, Vienna/Zurich

By and with Jamika Ajalon, Fouad Asfour, Sabine Bitter & Helmut Weber, Ricarda Denzer, Sandro Droschl, Eva Egermann, Simon Harder, Agnes Katschner, Elke Krasny, Annette Krauss, Gerald Bast, Brandon LaBelle, Marlene Lahmer, Oellinger/Rainer, Yen Noh, Barbara Putz-Plecko, Jianan Qu, Roee Rosen, Rúbia Salgado, Jo Schmeiser, Nora Sternfeld, Studio Without Master, Universität der Ignorant_innen, Hong-Kai Wang

Konzept und Durchführung
von Ricarda Denzer und Jo Schmeiser

Mit Textbeiträgen, Vorträgen, Workshops, Screenings und Panels, präsentiert im Heiligenkreuzerhof, Universität für angewandte Kunst Wien sowie im e-Journal *Art Education Research* #13, Wien/Zürich

Von und mit Jamika Ajalon, Fouad Asfour, Sabine Bitter & Helmut Weber, Ricarda Denzer, Sandro Droschl, Eva Egermann, Simon Harder, Agnes Katschner, Elke Krasny, Annette Krauss, Gerald Bast, Brandon LaBelle, Marlene Lahmer, Oellinger/Rainer, Yen Noh, Barbara Putz-Plecko, Jianan Qu, Roee Rosen, Rúbia Salgado, Jo Schmeiser, Nora Sternfeld, Studio Without Master, die „Universität der Ignorant*innen", Hong-Kai Wang

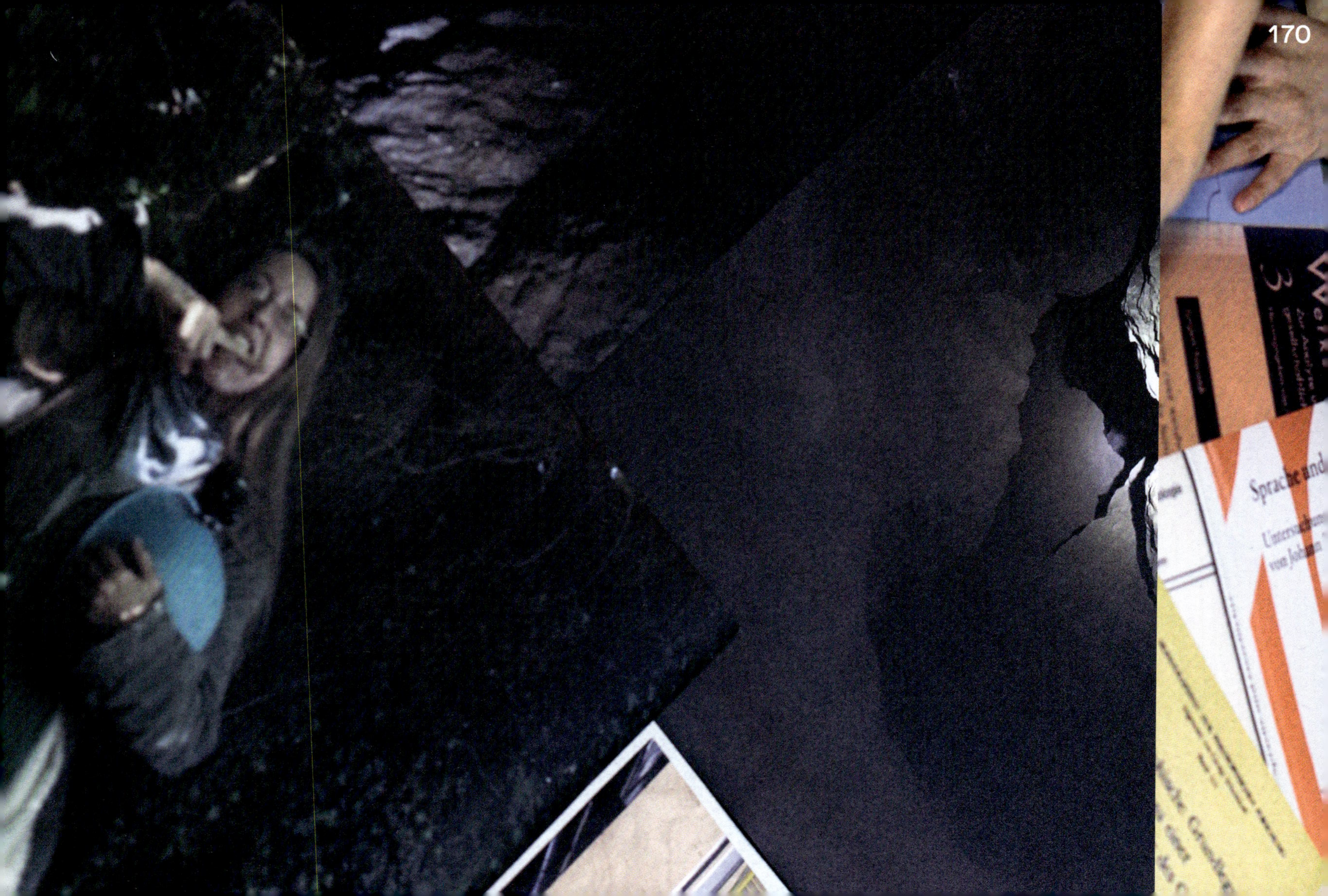

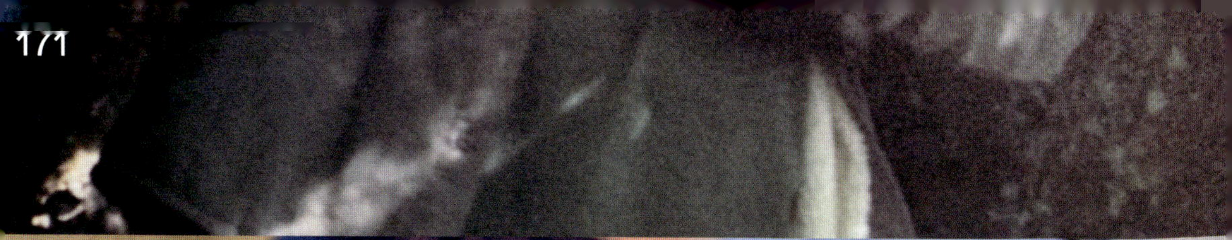

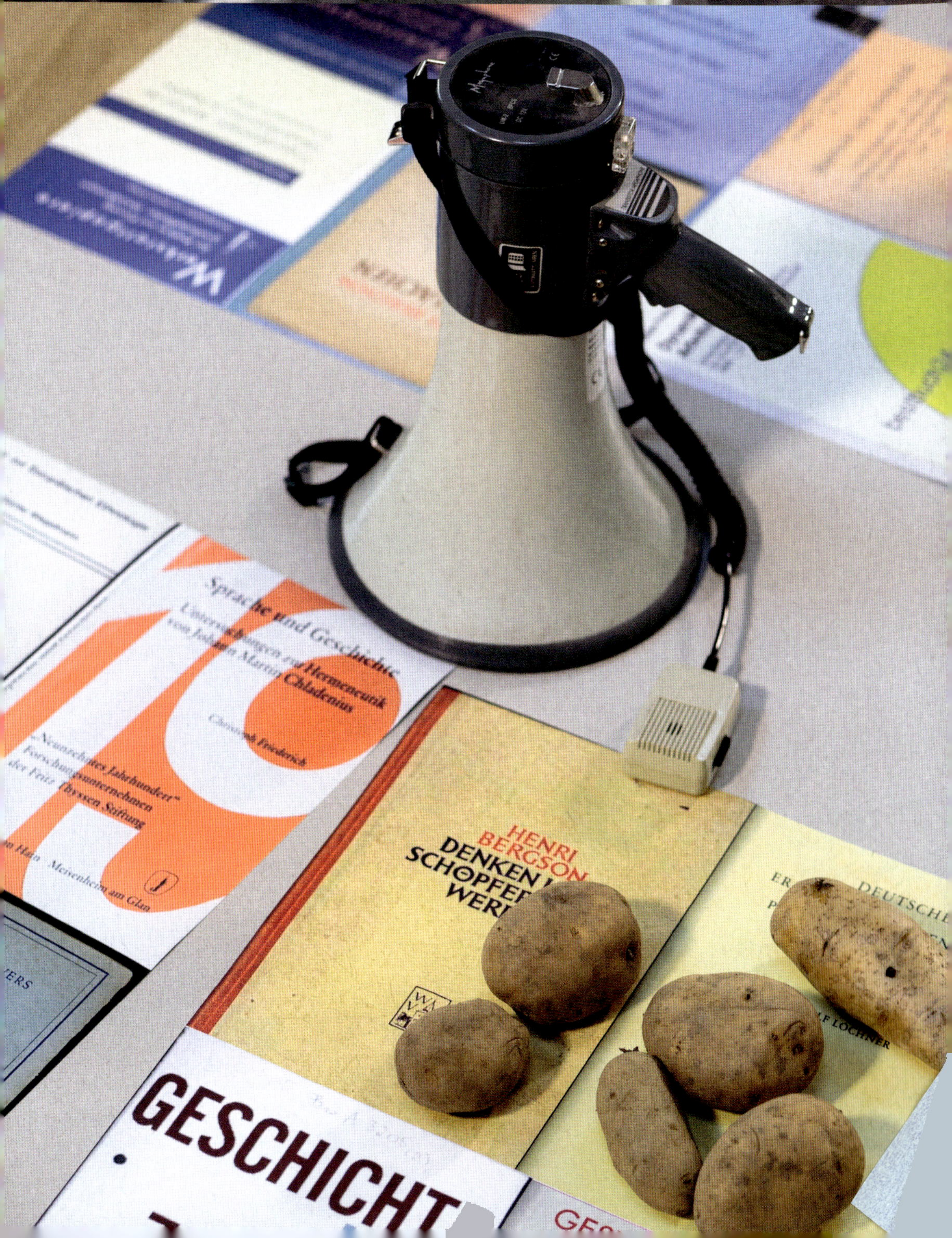
Sprache und Geschichte
Untersuchungen zur Hermeneutik von Johann Martin Chladenius
Christoph Friederich
„Neunzehntes Jahrhundert"
Forschungsunternehmen
der Fritz Thyssen Stiftung
Meisenheim am Glan
HENRI BERGSON
GESCHICHT

A collective piece was developed, drawing on a collaborative process at Studio Šaloun in Prague. The starting point was a found wooden structure—"the box," a remnant of a previous exhibition—which was used as a shared conceptual model. "We considered whether we should keep it or delete it. Do we say yes? Or do we say no? We discussed the box and reflected on various aspects of restoration. We discussed and negotiated, did exercises, wrote on the box, moved it, climbed on it, immersed ourselves in thought, structured those cognitive processes, took measurements, and ultimately converted it all into a display for an exhibition of the work we had created during our time at Studio Šaloun."

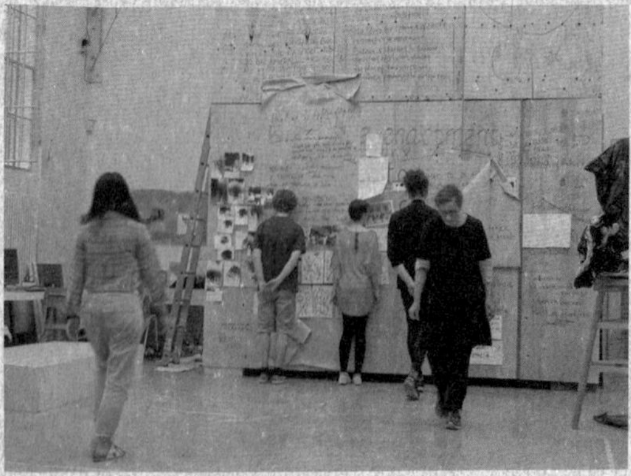

Auf Basis eines kollaborativen Prozesses, der im Studio Šaloun in Prag stattfand, wurde eine gemeinschaftliche Arbeit entwickelt. Ausgangspunkt war ein gefundenes Holzgebäude, „die Kiste", ein Überbleibsel einer früheren Ausstellung, die als gemeinsames Denkmodell verwendet wurde: „Wir haben gefragt: Behalten wir es oder löschen wir es aus? Sagen wir ja? Oder sagen wir nein? Wir besprachen die Box und reflektierten über verschiedene Aspekte der Restaurierung. Wir verhandelten und diskutierten, wir machten Übungen, schrieben auf die Kiste, bewegten sie, kletterten auf sie, tauchten in Denkprozesse ein, strukturierten sie, nahmen Messungen vor und verwandelten sie schließlich in ein Display für eine Ausstellung für die Werke, die wir während unserer Zeit im Atelier Šaloun geschaffen hatten."

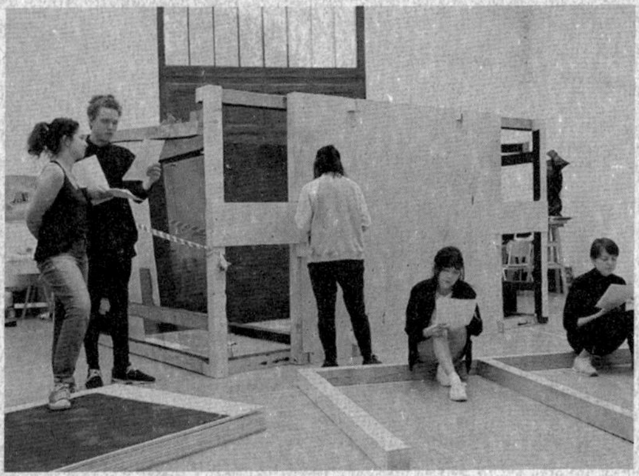

en *Šaloun Studio of Restauration Attempt*, Academy of Fine Arts Prague, 2016

de *Šaloun Studio of Restauration Attempt*, Akademie der Bildenden Künste Prag, 2016

Ricarda Denzer with Tomáš Džadoň and the students at the Academy of Fine Arts Prague: Marky Adamcová, Seiko Hihara, Alexander Martsynyuk, Andrea Sobotková, Gabriela Gažová, Lukáš Kleberc, Ju Yeong Kim, Arum Kim, Markéta Rejmontová

en

Ricarda Denzer gemeinsam mit Tomáš Džadoň und den Studierenden der Akademie der Bildenden Künste Prag, Marky Adamcová, Seiko Hihara, Alexander Martsynyuk, Andrea Sobotková, Gabriela Gažová, Lukáš Kleberc, Ju Yeong Kim, Arum Kim, Markéta Rejmontová

de

The ninth edition of the *Dirty Ear Forum*, conceived by Brandon LaBelle and Ricarda Denzer, aimed to view the acoustic sphere from a political point of view, considering who or what is heard in particular surroundings. The project provided a performative framework for collective experiments with sound material, voice, musical expression, and discourse on urban life and social struggles. The term "liquid acoustics"—a sonic liquidity that adapts to existing conditions to overcome boundaries, bypass obstacles, and seep into cracks and gaps formed an essential strand in the festival's performances, discussions, and workshops.

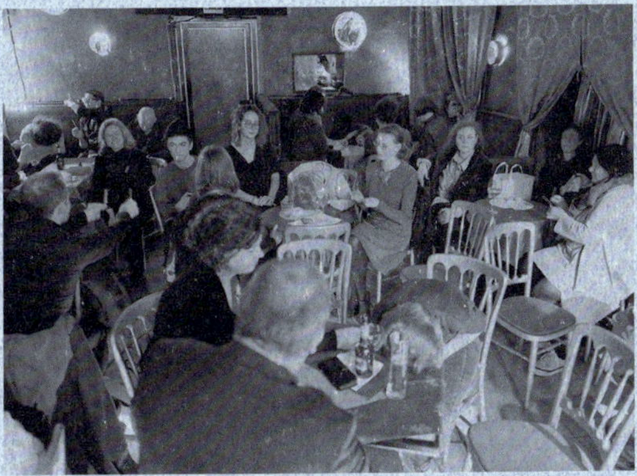

ɸ⊂ Performance by Lissie Rettenwander and her *Weltweit Erstes Stimmgabel Ensemble*, part of the Dirty Ear Forum #9, Arena Bar Vienna, 2019

ʊɸ Performance von Lissie Rettenwander und ihr *Weltweit Erstes Stimmgabel Ensemble*, im Rahmen von dem *Dirty Ear Forum #9*, Arena Bar Wien, 2019

Diese Ausgabe des von Brandon LaBelle und Ricarda Denzer konzipierten *Dirty Ear Forum #9* zielte darauf ab, den Bereich des Akustischen unter politischen Vorzeichen zu betrachten, etwa dahingehend, wer oder was in bestimmten Umgebungen gehört wird. Das Projekt bot einen performativen Rahmen für kollektive Experimente mit klanglicher Materialität, Stimme und musikalischem Ausdruck sowie Diskursen über urbanes Leben und soziale Kämpfe. Maßgeblich für das Aufführungen, Diskussionen und Workshops umfassende Festival war der Begriff der „flüssigen Akustik" – eine klangliche Liquidität, die sich den gegebenen Bedingungen anpasst, um Grenzen zu überschreiten, Hindernisse zu umgehen und in Ritzen und Spalten zu sickern.

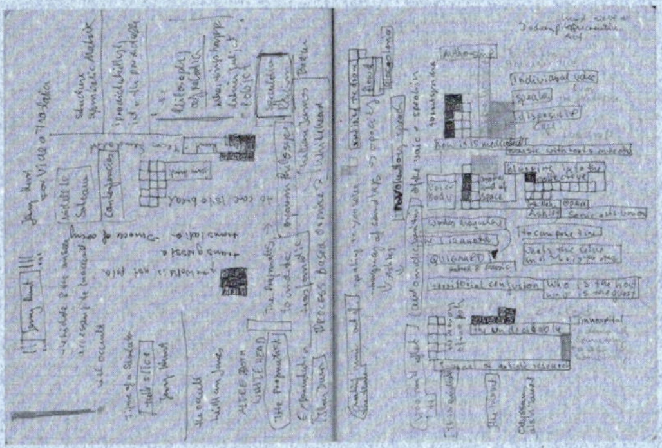

ɸ⊂ Recordings by Ricarda Denzer at the *Dirty Ear Forum #2*, a collective workshop on sound, multiplicity, and radical listening Bergen, Norway, 2014; published in *Dirty Ear Report #2* (Errant Bodies Press), 2016

ʊɸ *Aufzeichnungen* von Ricarda Denzer beim *Dirty Ear Forum #2*, einem kollektiven Workshop über Klang, Multiplizität und radikales Hören in Bergen, Norwegen, 2014. Veröffentlicht in *Dirty Ear Report #2* (Errant Bodies Press), 2016

Arena Bar Vienna and University of Applied Arts Vienna, 2019

Organized and curated by Ricarda Denzer and Brandon LaBelle in collaboration with participating artists, researchers, and students, including Karen Werner, Fouad Asfour, Kristina Pia Hofer, Lissie Rettenwander and her *Weltweit Erstes Stimmgabel Ensemble* [*Worldwide First Tuning Fork Ensemble*], Huda Takriti and aka – angewandte kunst audio, Anamarija Batista and Jelena Petrovic, Lale Rodgarkia-Dara and Nicole Sabella

Additional cooperation with the Department of Art and Communication Practices (KKP) and students at the University of Applied Arts Vienna

ɸ⊂

Arena Bar Wien und Universität für angewandte Kunst Wien, 2019

Organisiert und kuratiert von Ricarda Denzer und Brandon LaBelle in Zusammenarbeit mit teilnehmenden Künstler*innen, Forscher*innen und Studierenden Darunter: Fouad Asfour, Karen Werner, Kristina Pia Hofer, Lissie Rettenwander und ihr Weltweit Erstes Stimmgabel Ensemble, Huda Takriti und aka – angewandte kunst audio, Anamarija Batista und Jelena Petrovic, Lale Rodgarkia-Dara und Nicole Sabella

Zusätzliche Zusammenarbeit mit Kunst- und Kommunikationspraktiken (KKP) und Studierenden der Universität für angewandte Kunst Wien

ʊɸ

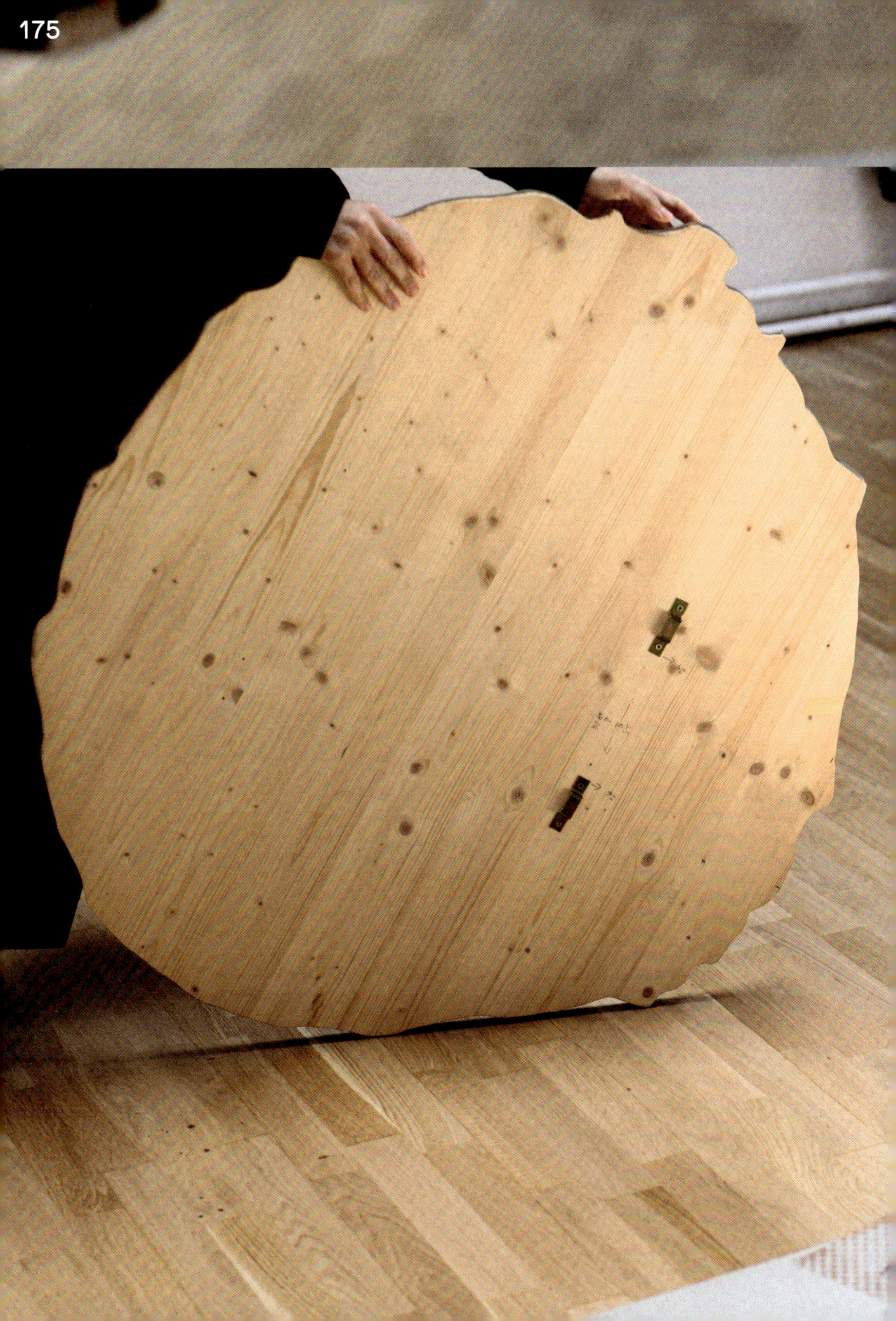

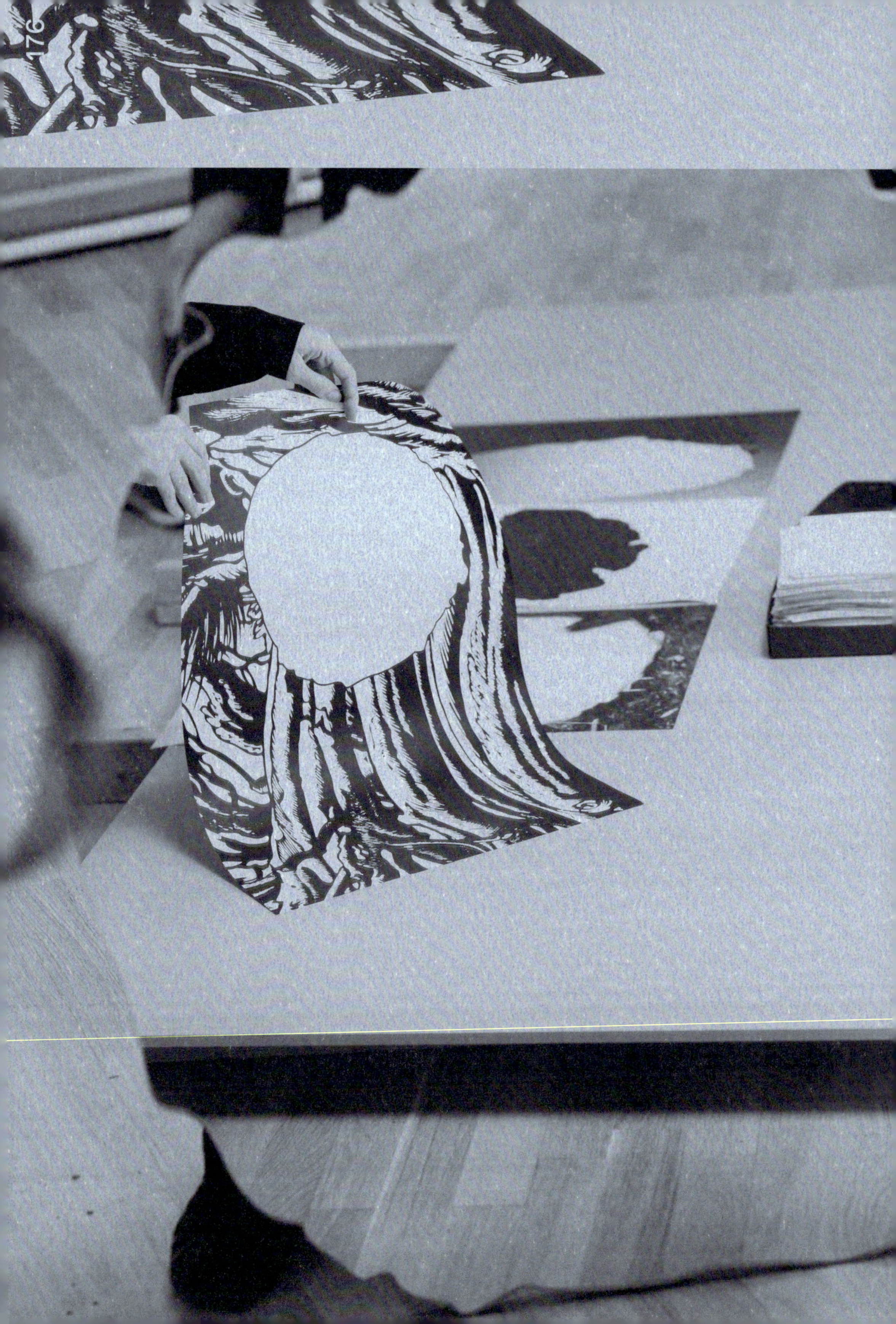

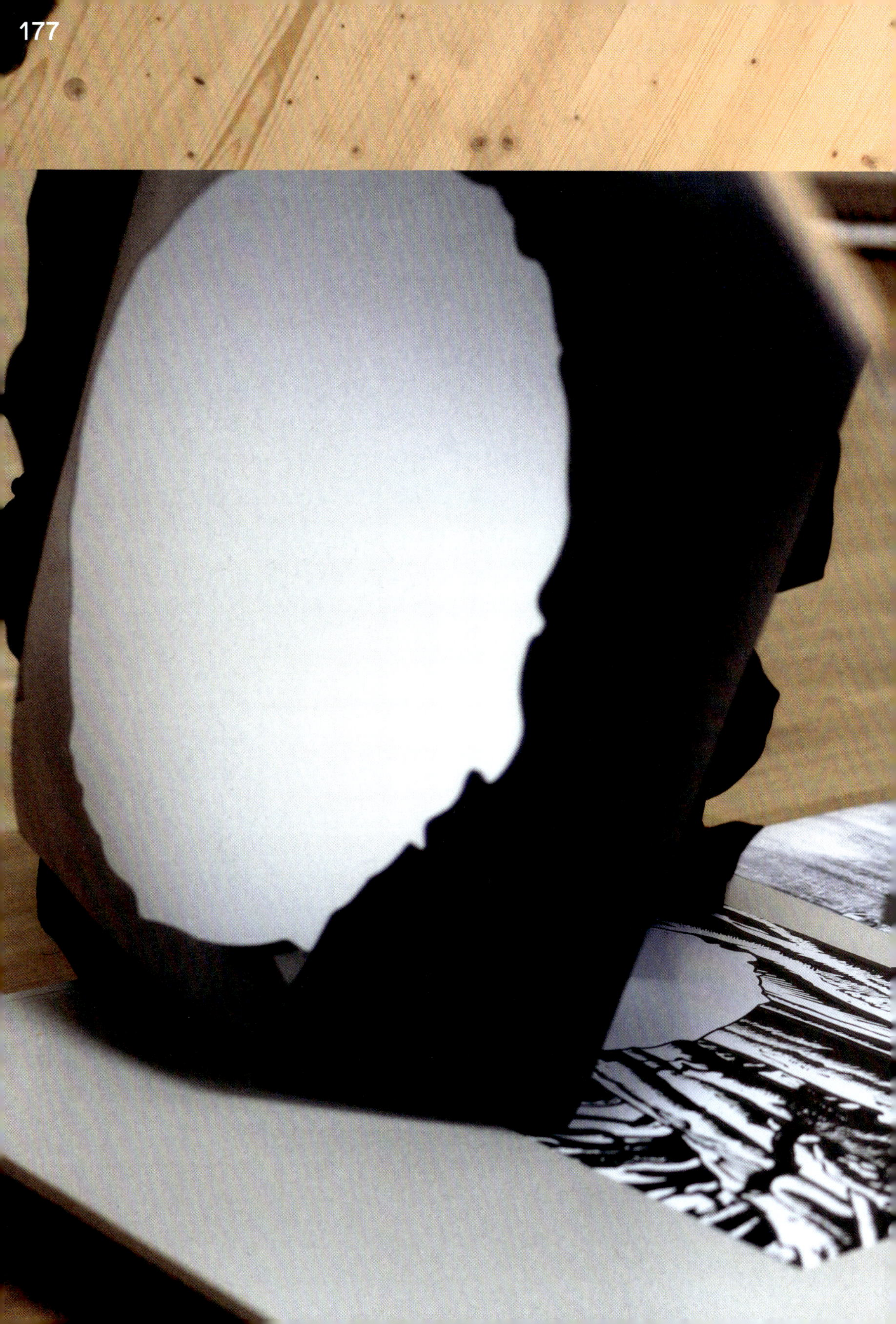

Eleven composers, sound artists, curators, writers, and performers who had been invited to participate switched on their recording devices at the same time for fifteen minutes on March 21, 2021, during the Covid-19 lockdown, in a round-the-world telepathic recording session, in order to connect to one another by documenting their thoughts, habits, or acoustic surroundings. Ricarda Denzer's contribution—inspired by composer Jerry Hunt—records an exactly notated ritual: "With an unexpected flash of insight, I go onto my studio terrace in Vienna at 6 p.m. on March 21, 2021. Overlooking the Vienna Woods I begin a ritual through which I establish a connection with possible sounds elsewhere." This gives rise to a piece that sparks the imagination. *Mental Radio Piece* starts with an atmospheric description of the artist's surroundings and the view of the Vienna Woods, followed by mental prompts numbered "Sound 1" to "Sound 27." These include "think of a friend," "think of nothing," or "a car," "stage illusion," or "comedy."

Heavy breathing can be heard repeatedly between these concepts, a sound Denzer creates by playing an accordion without producing any notes—conveying to the listener with an almost physical immediacy, along with the content, a sense of the mental dimension of self-isolation, loneliness, and the absurdity of the whole situation.

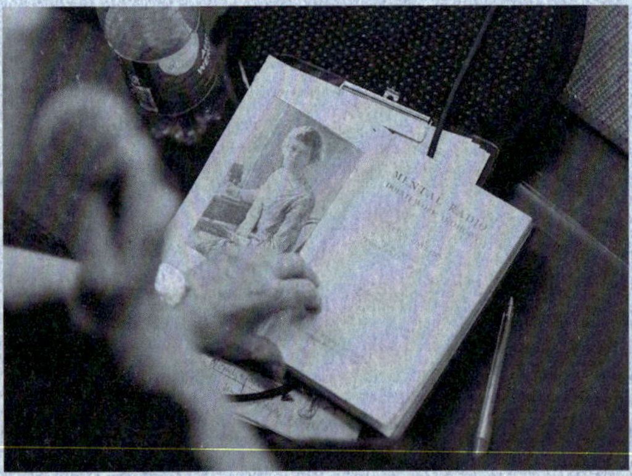

Audio piece for the cassette
The Asocial Telepathic Ensemble, Corvo Records, 2022
Initiated by Alessandra Eramo and Brandon LaBelle, with contributions from Alessandra Eramo, Ambra Pittoni, Brandon LaBelle, Florence Cats, Ines Lechleitner, Israel Martinez, James Webb, Korhan Erel, Lucia Udvardyova, Ricarda Denzer, Thea Farhadian

Am 21. März 2021 schalteten während des Covid-19-Lockdowns in einer weltumspannenden telepathischen Aufnahme-Session elf eingeladene Komponist*innen, Klangkünstler*innen, Kurator*innen, Schriftsteller*innen und Performer*innen gleichzeitig für 15 Minuten ihre Aufnahmegeräte ein, um ihre Gedanken, Gewohnheiten oder ihre akustische Umgebung zu dokumentieren und so miteinander in Verbindung zu treten. Ricarda Denzers Beitrag ist – inspiriert von dem Komponisten Jerry Hunt – die Aufnahme eines von ihr exakt notierten Rituals: „In einer unerwarteten Erkenntnis begebe ich mich am 21. März 2021 um 18 Uhr auf meine Studioterrasse in Wien. Mit Blick auf den Wienerwald beginne ich ein Ritual, durch das ich eine Verbindung zu möglichen Klängen anderswo herstelle." Es entsteht ein Stück für die Vorstellungskraft – das *Mental Radio Piece* beginnt mit einer atmosphärischen Beschreibung ihrer Umgebung und der Aussicht auf den Wienerwald, um dann den als „Sound 1" bis „Sound 27" bezeichneten mentalen Vorgaben zu folgen. Darunter: „an einen Freund denken", „an nichts denken" oder auch „ein Auto", „Bühnenillusion" oder „Komik".

Zwischen den Begriffen ist immer wieder starkes Atmen zu hören, das Denzer durch ein tonloses Akkordeonspiel erzeugt, wodurch sich mit den Inhalten auch das mentale Moment der Selbstisolierung, der Einsamkeit sowie die Absurdität der gesamten Situation beinahe körperlich spürbar auf die Zuhörer*innen überträgt.

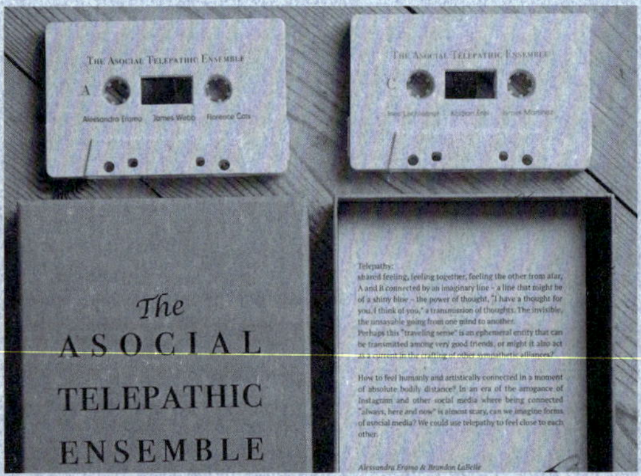

Audio-Stück für eine Kassette
The Asocial Telepathic Ensemble, Corvo Records, 2022
Initiiert von Alessandra Eramo und Brandon LaBelle, mit Beiträgen von Alessandra Eramo, Ambra Pittoni, Brandon LaBelle, Florence Cats, Ines Lechleitner, Israel Martinez, James Webb, Korhan Erel, Lucia Udvardyova, Ricarda Denzer, Thea Farhadian

The point of departure for this live Hörspiel (audio play) *A Line Associated to Other Lines** was a pact between Ricarda Denzer and Karen Werner to each write a "postcard libretto" as a score for a string instrument, two speakers, and "ontological pop songs" (Werner). They shared the librettos with each other on June 26, 2022.

The first performance of two independent interpretations of the same score was on August 13, 2022, at the Bergen Kjøtt cultural center in Norway with the following librettos:

Single string LIVE, ontological pop song 1 LIVE (Karen teaches Ricarda her pop song), ontological pop song 2, ontological pop song 3, slow-reading group LIVE, *Spinne & Fliegenfischen* [Spider & Flying Fish] (video, sound), *Hoacherl* (listening object for an ear, video, sound with some lines), *Krisenlinie* [Crisis Line] (video, string), *Cecilia Vicuña: Word & Thread.

Ausgangspunkt des Live-Hörspiels *A Line Associated to Other Lines** war die Abmachung zwischen Ricarda Denzer und Karen Werner, jeweils ein „Postkartenlibretto" als Partitur mit einem Streicher, zwei Lautsprecher und „Ontologischen Popsongs" (Werner) zu schreiben, die am 26. Juni 2022 miteinander geteilt wurden.

Die Erstaufführung zweier unabhängiger Interpretationen derselben Partitur fand am 13. August 2022 im Kulturhaus Bergen Kjøtt (Norwegen) mit folgenden Librettos statt: Einzelsaite (LIVE) Ontologischer Popsong 1 LIVE (Karen bringt Ricarda ihren Popsong bei), Ontologischer Popsong 2, Ontologischer Popsong 3, langsame Lesegruppe LIVE, *Spinne & Fliegenfischen* (Video, Ton), *Hoacherl* (Hörobjekt für ein Ohr, Video, Ton mit einigen Zeilen), *Krisenlinie* (Video, Saite), *Cecilia Vicuña: Word & Thread

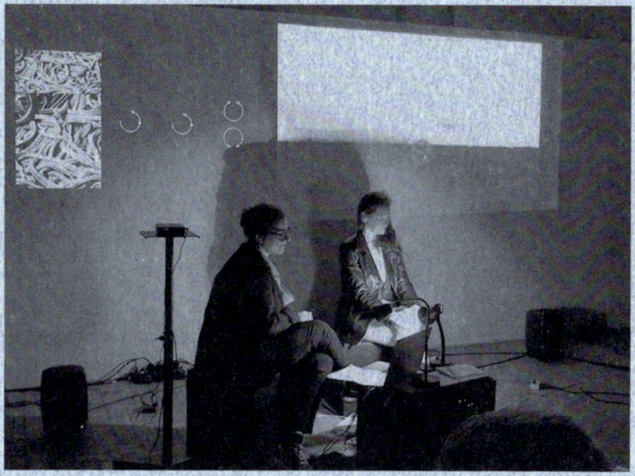

en Live Hörspiel (audio play) *A Line Associated to Other Lines*, by Ricarda Denzer and Karen Werner, for *Social Acoustics*, Bergen Kjøtt (Norway), 2022

de Live-Hörspiel *A Line Associated to Other Lines* von Ricarda Denzer und Karen Werner im Rahmen von *Social Acoustics*, Bergen Kjøtt (Norwegen), 2022

A live audio piece by Ricarda Denzer and Karen Werner, performed during the *Social Acoustics* project

Ein Live-Hörspiel von Ricarda Denzer und Karen Werner, aufgeführt im Rahmen des Projekts *Social Acoustics*

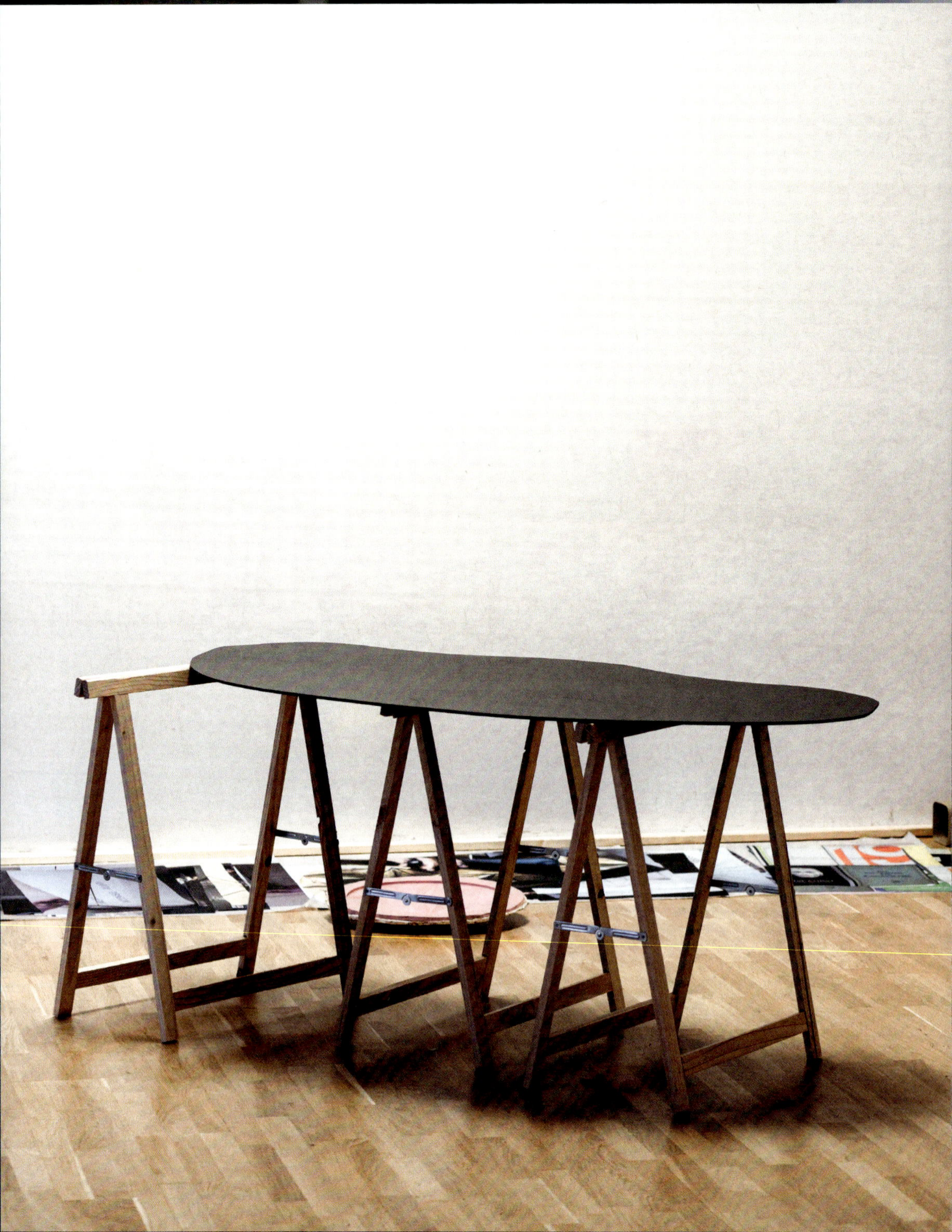

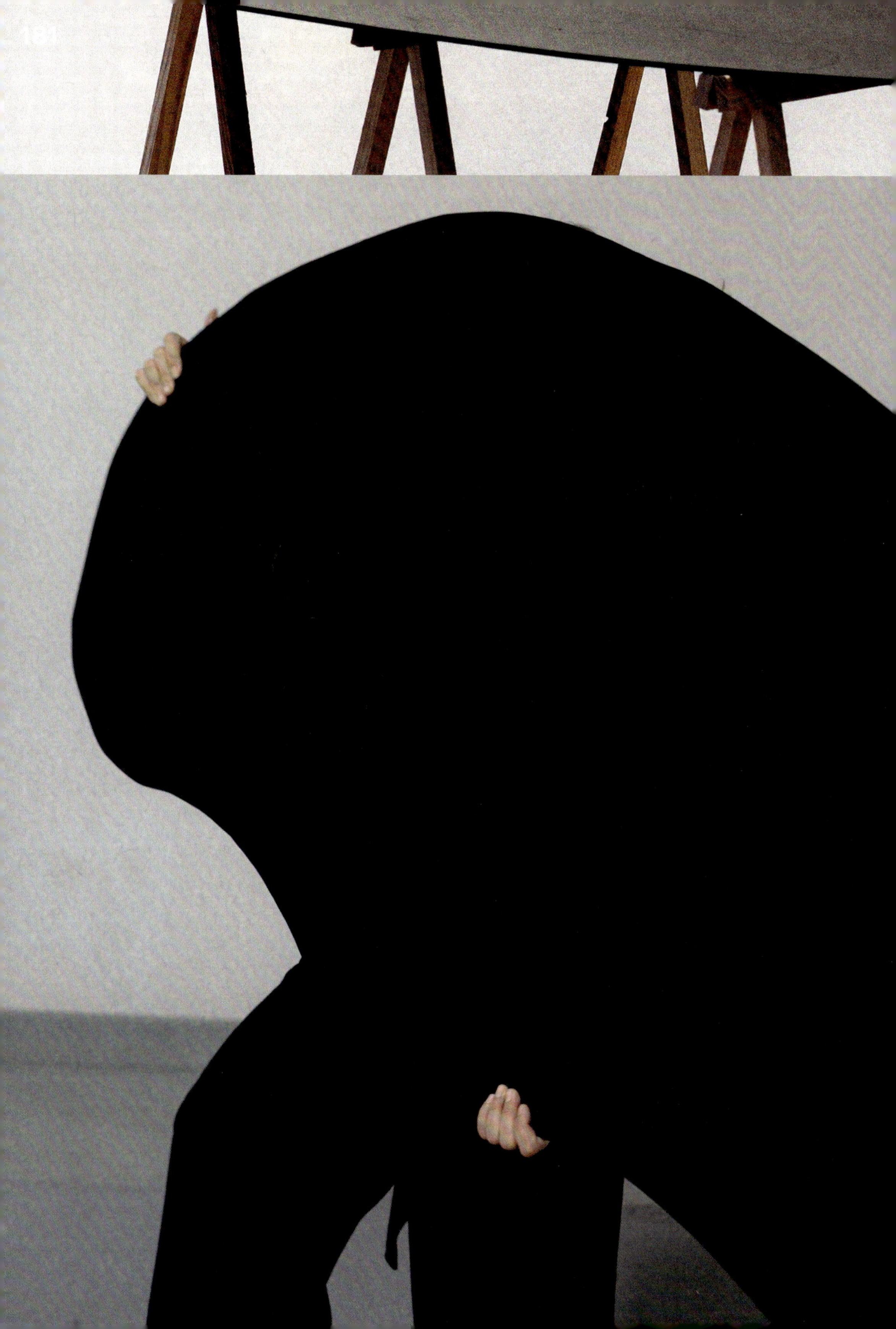

In the *Sounding Research* project Ricarda Denzer pursued the question of the degree to which acoustic access to the world can lead to a variety of social experiences. She sought to find answers by focusing in an initial "Listening Session" on a special interdisciplinary format, the audio paper, seeking to investigate its potential for critical and care-oriented empowerment and alternative narration. This type of form-finding was intended to analyze and deepen the practice of listening, both textually and spatially, in relation to the concept of collectivity. "By pursuing a practice-oriented approach as the methodology for artistic research in relation to situated listening, I engage with art education as a sonic act through experimentation and design, using audio 'papers' for a broader research framework. The material manifestation of the acoustic questing search as performative research forms part of a work process that is composed of several elements. One of those is making tuition as a listening art practice accessible to students."

Mit dem Forschungsprojekt *Sounding Research* geht Ricarda Denzer der Frage nach, inwieweit der akustische Zugang zur Welt zu einer Vielzahl von sozialen Erfahrungen führen kann. Um Antworten zu finden, wurde bei einer ersten „Listening Session" mit dem Audio Paper ein spezielles, die Disziplinen verbindendes Format ins Zentrum gerückt, dessen Potenziale im Hinblick auf eine kritische und fürsorgliche Handlungsfähigkeit sowie alternative Erzählweisen untersucht werden sollten. Die Praxis des Zuhörens sollte durch diese Formfindung analysiert und vertieft werden – sowohl textlich als auch räumlich im Zusammenhang mit dem Konzept der Kollektivität: „Indem ich einen handlungsorientierten Ansatz für die Methode der künstlerischen Forschung in Bezug auf das situierte Zuhören verfolge, beschäftige ich mich mit der Lehre in der Kunst als klanglichem Akt durch Experiment und Design, indem ich Audio-‚Papiere' für einen breiteren Forschungsrahmen verwende. Die materielle Manifestation der akustischen Suchbewegung als performative Forschung ist Teil eines Arbeitsprozesses, der aus mehreren Elementen besteht. Eines davon ist, Unterrichten als hörende Praxis der Kunst für Studierende zugänglich zu machen."

Audio paper presentations, panel discussion, and workshops

An artistic research project by Ricarda Denzer, in the context of the Applied Program for Inter- and Transdisciplinary Projects in Art and Research (INTRA), University of Applied Arts Vienna

With audio papers by Fouad Asfour, Ricarda Denzer, Christina Goestl, Brandon LaBelle, Seth Weiner / Sadie Siegel, Karen Werner, and Hui Ye; https://www.soundingresearch.net

Audio-Paper-Präsentationen, Panel Talk und Workshops

Ein künstlerisches Forschungsprojekt von Ricarda Denzer, im Rahmen von INTRA, dem Angewandte Programm für inter- und transdisziplinäre Projekte in Kunst und Forschung, Universität für angewandte Kunst Wien

Mit Audio Papers von Fouad Asfour, Ricarda Denzer, Christina Goestl, Brandon LaBelle, Seth Weiner/Sadie Siegel, Karen Werner and Hui Ye; https://www.soundingresearch.net

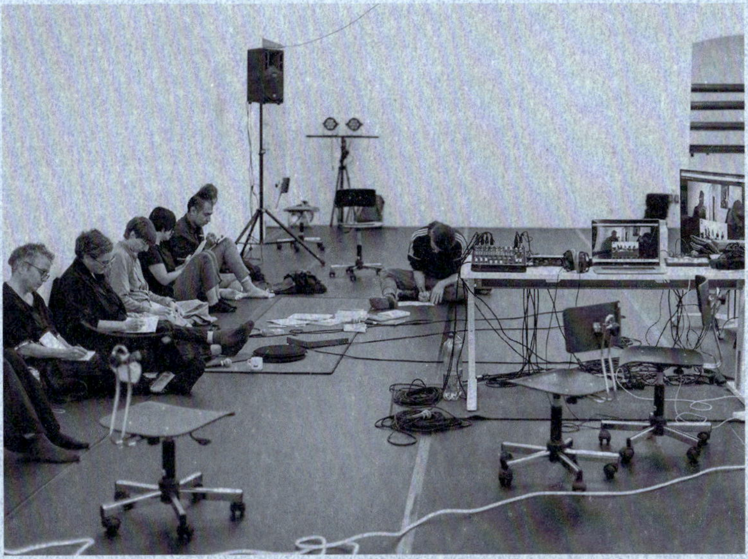

EN *Para-Listening: How to Perform Remotely*, workshop by Ricarda Denzer in *Sounding Research*, for the APL Practice(!)Week, in the studio of the Angewandte Performance Lab, Vienna, 2021

DE *Para-Listening: How to Perform Remotely*, Workshop von Ricarda Denzer im Rahmen von *Sounding Research* für die APL Practice(!)Week, im Studio des Angewandte Performance Labs Wien, 2021

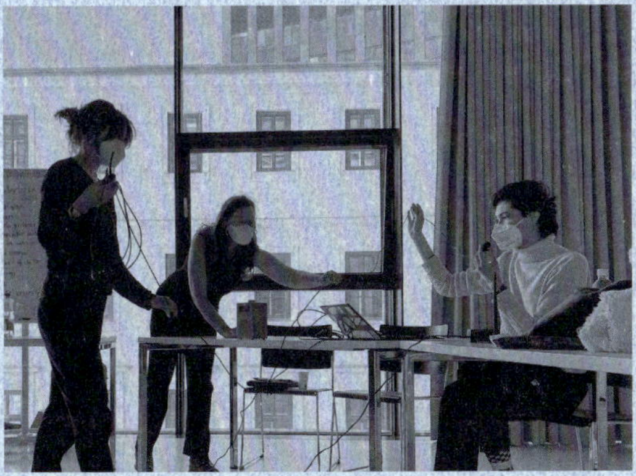

EN *Signals & Connections*, workshop by Karen Werner during *Sounding Research*, March 2022

DE *Signals & Connections*, Workshop von Karen Werner im Rahmen von *Sounding Research*, März, 2022

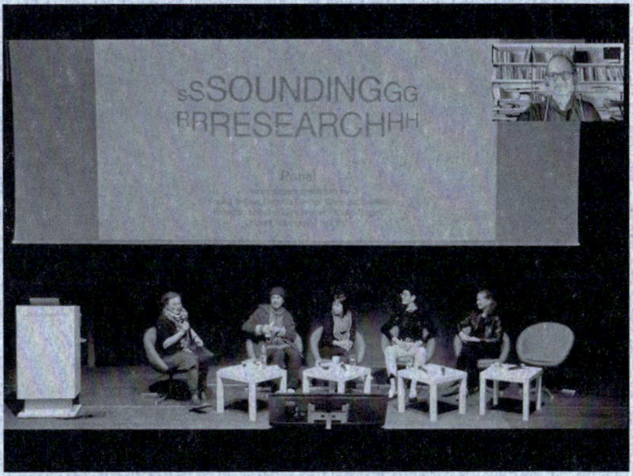

EN *Sounding Research*, audio-paper presentations and panel talk, Auditorium, University of Applied Arts Vienna, March 2022

DE *Sounding Research* Audio Paper Presentation und Panel Talk, Auditorium Universität für angewandte Kunst Wien, März 2022

Biographies
Biografien

Fouad Asfour

Fouad Asfour is a writer and researcher who works in collaborative frameworks of publications, exhibitions, and performance and research projects. He has contributed to numerous contemporary art and research projects and has published widely. He holds an MA in linguistics from University of Vienna, Austria, and an MA in creative writing from Rhodes University, Makhanda, South Africa. He founded the Pole Pole Press publishing project in 2011, and is part of the art research projects *Art on our Mind* and *African Feminisms Conferences* (Afems). In 2008 he received a working grant in the framework of the Igor Zabel Award for Culture and Theory.

Fouad Asfour ist ein im Rahmen von kooperativen Publikations- und Ausstellungsformaten sowie Performance- und Forschungsprojekten arbeitender Schriftsteller und Researcher. Er hat zu zahlreichen zeitgenössischen Kunst- und Forschungsprojekten beigetragen und umfassend publiziert. An der Universität Wien schloss er ein Studium der Sprachwissenschaften (MA) ab, außerdem hat er einen MA in Creavtive Writing von der Rhodes University in Makhanda, Südafrika. 2011 gründete er das Verlagsprojekt Pole Pole Press, und er gehört dem Forschungsprojekt *Art on our Mind* und *African Feminisms Conferences* (Afems) an. 2008 erhielt er im Rahmen des *Igor Zabel Award for Culture* and *Theory* ein Arbeitsstipendium.

Christa Benzer

Christa Benzer is on the editorial staff of the art journal *springerin*. She writes for the newspaper *Der Standard*, magazines, and art catalogues. Co-editor of the publication *Continuing Dialogues – A Tribute to Igor Zabel*, curator of the performance series *13 Lessons in Performance Art* (Top Kino, 2009), and the exhibition *I've left* (Off Space, Vienna 2019). Recently co-curator and editor of the group exhibition and publication *Was uns wichtig ist. Künstlerische Perspektiven auf Kulturerbe* at the Austrian Museum of Folk Life and Folk Art and the vorarlberg museum (Bregenz 2022/2023). She lives in Vienna.

Christa Benzer ist Redaktionsmitglied der Kunstzeitschrift *springerin*. Sie schreibt für *Der Standard*, Magazine und Künstler*innenkataloge. Sie ist Mitherausgeberin der Publikation *Continuing Dialogues – A Tribute to Igor Zabel*. Kuratorin der Performancereihe *13 Lessons in Performance Art*, Top Kino, 2009, und der Ausstellung *I've left*, Off Space (Wien 2019). Zuletzt Co-Kuratorin der Gruppenausstellung und Herausgabe der Publikation *Was uns wichtig ist. Künstlerische Perspektiven auf Kulturerbe* im Volkskundemuseum Wien und im Vorarlberg Museum (Bregenz 2022/2023). Sie lebt in Wien.

Ricarda Denzer

Ricarda Denzer is an artist and has taught since 2013 at the University of Applied Arts Vienna.

Her practice combines collaborative, audiovisual, performative, and curatorial work, frequently around oral narration and listening as a method of situated research and finding form. She was chairwoman of the IG Bildende Kunst, on the advisory committee of the VBKÖ, and is currently on the board of the Vienna Secession and a member of the Angewandte Performance Lab.

She recently initiated the artistic (research) platform Sounding Research (2021–), co-edited the ZHdK Zurich ejournal #13 (*Un_Univerity*, with Jo Schmeiser, 2017), the books *Perplexities* (2013) and *Silence Turned Into Objects* (2014), and curated *About the House – W. H. Auden* in Kirchstetten and other art projects.

Ricarda Denzer ist Künstlerin und lehrt seit 2013 an der Universität für angewandte Kunst Wien.

Ihre Praxis kombiniert kollaborative, audiovisuelle, performative und kuratorische Arbeit, die sich häufig um mündliche Erzählung und Hören als Methode der situierten Forschung und Formfindung dreht. Sie war Vorsitzende der IG Bildende Kunst, im Beirat der VBKÖ, ist derzeit im Vorstand der Wiener Secession und Mitglied des Angewandte Performance Lab.

Zuletzt initiierte sie die künstlerische (Forschungs-) Platform „Sounding Research" (seit 2021), gab das eJournal #13 der ZHdK Zürich (*Un_Univerity* mit Jo Schmeiser, 2017), die Bücher *Perplexities* (2013) und *Silence Turned Into Objects* (2014) mit heraus und kuratierte u. a. das Kunstprojekt *About the House – W. H. Auden* in Kirchstetten.

Christiane Erharter

Christiane Erharter studied painting and graphic arts under Gunter Damisch at the Academy of Fine Arts Vienna and postgraduate critical studies at the Malmö Art Academy, Lund University. She was appointed curator for community outreach and public program at the Belvedere in 2018. She focuses on pop music and sound in relation to feminism and queer theory.

Publications include *Public Matters. Contemporary Art in the Belvedere Garden* (2023); *Pink Labor on Golden Streets: Queer Art Practices* (2015); Re-Punk Electronic Music! (HUB Sonic Landscapes, 3rd Berlin Biennial 2004); XX01 (*First Story – Women Building/New Narratives for the 21st Century*, Porto 2002); *Beiß die Hand, die Dich füttert! Gespräche mit Menschen aus Kufstein* (1997/2020).

Christiane Erharter studierte Malerei und Grafik bei Gunter Damisch an der Akademie der bildenden Künste Wien und postgradual Critical Studies an der Malmö Kunstakademie, Universität Lund. Seit 2018 ist sie Kuratorin für Community Outreach und Public Program im Belvedere. Beschäftigung mit Popmusik und Sound im Verhältnis zu Feminismus und Queer Theory.

Publikationen (Auswahl): *Public Matters. Zeitgenössische Kunst im Belvedere-Garten* (2023); *Pink Labor on Golden Streets: Queer Art Practices* (2015); Re-Punk Electronic Music! (HUB Sonische Landschaften, 3. Berlin Biennale 2004); XX01 (*First Story – Women Building / New Narratives for the 21st Century*, Porto 2002); *Beiß die Hand, die Dich füttert! Gespräche mit Menschen aus Kufstein* (1997/2020).

Michael Giefing

Formerly graduating in biomedical analytics, Michael Giefing still works in an analytical way, constantly questioning his surroundings—now using camera and tripod instead of pipette and microscope. As an artist and photographer he is based in Vienna, and is currently studying applied photography at the University of Applied Arts Vienna.

Als Absolvent der biomedizinischen Analytik hat sich Michael Giefing seine analytische Arbeitsweise bewahrt und stellt seine Umgebung ständig in Frage – mittlerweile mit Kamera und Stativ anstelle von Pipette und Mikroskop. Er lebt als Künstler und Fotograf in Wien und studiert angewandte Fotografie an der Universität für angewandte Kunst Wien.

Christina Goestl

Christina Goestl is an artist. She works in the fields of audiovisual live performance and digital video, utilizing series, sequences, modulations and loops, superpositions, cut-ups and electronic impulses. Central aspects of her artistic work are rhythm, dynamics, movement and temporality, communicative interfaces and semiotic systems. Goestl has accumulated an extensive dossier of projects at the intersections of art/tech/science, many of them linked to a comprehensive reflection of sexualities and gender. On the person side she is a genderfuck, lives in the EU, and holds an MA. Pronouns: as you wish. www.cccggg.net

Christina Goestl ist Künstlerin. Sie arbeitet in den Bereichen audiovisuelle Live-Performance und Digitalvideo und setzt dabei Serien, Sequenzen, Modulationen und Loops, Superpositionen, Cut-ups und elektronische Impulse ein. Im Zentrum ihrer künstlerischen Arbeit stehen Rhythmik, Dynamik, Bewegung und Temporalität, kommunikative Interfaces und semiotische Systeme. Goestl verfügt über ein umfangreiches Dossier an Projekten an den Schnittstellen von Kunst/Tech/Wissenschaft, die in vielen Fällen an Reflexionen über Sexualitäten und Gender geknüpft sind. Sie bezeichnet sich als genderfuck, lebt in der EU und hat einen MA. Pronouns: as you wish. www.cccggg.net

Christian Höller

Christian Höller is co-editor of the journal *springerin – Hefte für Gegenwartskunst*; author, translator and lecturer in the field of art and cultural theory; curator of several film shows at the International Short Film Festival Oberhausen and at the mumok cinema Vienna. Latest book publications (as co-editor): *Kontakt. The Art Collection of Erste Group and ERSTE Foundation* (Cologne 2017); *after youtube: Conversations, Portraits, Texts on Music Video after the Internet* (Cologne 2018); *Stano Filko, Miloš Laky, Ján Zavarský – White Space in White Space, 1973–1982* (Vienna 2021).

DE Christian Höller ist Redakteur und Mitherausgeber der Zeitschrift *springerin – Hefte für Gegenwartskunst*; Autor, Übersetzer und Lehrbeauftragter im Bereich Kunst- und Kulturtheorie; Kurator mehrerer Filmschauen bei den Internationalen Kurzfilmtagen Oberhausen und im mumok Kino Wien. Letzte Buchveröffentlichungen (als Mitherausgeber): *Kontakt. The Art Collection of Erste Group and ERSTE Foundation* (Köln 2017); *after youtube: Gespräche, Portraits, Texte zum Musikvideo nach dem Internet* (Köln 2018); *Stano Filko, Miloš Laky, Ján Zavarský – White Space in White Space, 1973–1982* (Wien 2021).

Brandon LaBelle

EN Brandon LaBelle is an artist, writer, and theorist. His work focuses on questions of agency, community, pirate culture, and poetics, which results in a range of collaborative and extra-institutional initiatives, such as the *Listening Biennial* (2021–), *Communities in Movement* (2019–), *The Living School* (2014–16), *Oficina de Autonomia* (2017), *the Imaginary Republic* (2014–19). In 1995 he founded Errant Bodies Press, a publishing house based in Berlin. His publications include *Acoustic Justice, The Other Citizen, Sonic Agency, Lexicon of the Mouth, Diary of an Imaginary Egyptian*, among others.

DE Brandon LaBelle ist Künstler, Schriftsteller und Theoretiker. Der Schwerpunkt seiner Arbeit liegt auf den Themen Agency, Community, Piratenkultur und Poetik, aus denen eine Reihe von kooperativen und außerinstitutionellen Initiativen entstanden sind, u. a. die *Listening Biennial* (2021-), *Communities in Movement* (2019-), *The Living School* (2014–2016), *Oficina de Autonomia* (2017) und der *Imaginary Republic* (2014–2019). 1995 gründete er den Verlag Errant Bodies Press mit Sitz in Berlin. Zu seinen Publikationen gehören u. a. *Acoustic Justice, The Other Citizen, Sonic Agency, Lexicon of the Mouth, Diary of an Imaginary Egyptian.*

Nazanin Mehraein

EN Nazanin Mehraein, born in 1989 in Tehran, is a multidisciplinary artist with a background in theater, currently based in Vienna. She explores storytelling through various media, including film-making painting, video, video-mapping, sound, sculpture, installation, and performance. She often draws from her own autobiographical stories, which relate to her current environment in both historical and political contexts. Her current focus is primarily on personal narratives and reflections as she visually maps urban spaces, and experimental videos.

DE Nazanin Mehraein, 1989 in Teheran geboren, ist eine multidisziplinäre, ursprünglich vom Theater kommende Künstlerin, die derzeit in Wien lebt. Ihr Thema ist das Geschichtenerzählen, das sie unter Einsatz diverser Medien wie Film, Malerei, Video, Video-Mapping, Sound, Bildhauerei, Installation und Performance erforscht. Oft stützt sie sich dabei auf ihre eigenen autobiografischen Erzählungen, die in historischen wie auch politischen Kontexten einen Bezug zu ihrem gegenwärtigen Umfeld herstellen. Momentan liegt ihr Fokus vor allem auf persönlichen Narrativen und Reflexionen und deren visueller Umsetzung in Form von Karten urbaner Räume und experimentellen Videos.

Jaimini Patel

EN Jaimini Patel is a London-based artist whose work investigates the agency of matter through a negotiation of boundaries, systems, and performative actions. Recent projects include *Bring into Being*, Chiswick House, London, 2021; *hmn edition 19*, Village Club, Barrow Housing Estate, London; *Fragile State*, Museum of Odessa Modern Art, Odessa, 2019; *Every Object is a Thing but not everything is an object*, Hollybush Gardens, London, 2018; *An Inventory of Small Acts*, Archiv der Zeitgenossen, Krems, 2017; *Measure*, Centrum, Berlin, 2016; and *Remainder 10/14-09/15*, blank, Turin, 2015.

DE Jaimini Patel ist eine in London lebende Künstlerin, deren Arbeiten sich über die Verhandlung von Grenzen, Systemen und performativen Aktionen mit der Agency der Materie auseinandersetzen. Zu ihren jüngsten Projekten zählen *Bring into Being*, Chiswick House, London, 2021; *hmn edition 19*, Village Club, Barrow Housing Estate, London; *Fragile State*, Museum of Odessa Modern Art, Odessa, 2019; *Every Object is a Thing but not everything is an object*, Hollybush Gardens, London, 2018; *An Inventory of Small Acts*, Archiv der Zeitgenossen, Krems, 2017; *Measure*, Centrum, Berlin, 2016 und *Remainder 10/14-09/15*, blank, Turin, 2015.

Hannah Sakai

Hannah Sakai (*1994, Sapporo, Japan) is a graphic designer based in Vienna, where she grew up from the age of four. Between cultures and languages, she developed an interest in typography, design, and space. Her practice revolves around book and exhibition design. She graduated from the Werkplaats Typografie (MA), Arnhem (NL).

Hannah Sakai (1994 in Sapporo, Japan, geboren) ist eine Grafikdesignerin, die seit ihrem vierten Lebensjahr in Wien lebt. Aufgewachsen zwischen Kulturen und Sprachen, entwickelte sie ein Interesse für Typografie, Design und Raum. Ihre Arbeiten drehen sich um die Gestaltung von Büchern und Ausstellungen. Sie ist Absolventin (MA) des Werkplaats Typografie in Arnhem (NL).

Seth Weiner

Seth Weiner (& Sadie Siegel)
Often both performance and proposal, Weiner's work employs a wide range of media and explores the gaps between architectural fiction and social convention to create both actual and imagined spatial environments. In 2008 Weiner began the music project *Sadie Siegel*, using his great-grandmother's name to collaborate with himself and explore sound as an architectural act. The two of them currently live and work together in a basement in the 2nd district of Vienna.

Seth Weiner (& Sadie Siegel) Weiner setzt bei seiner Arbeit, die oft Performance und Anregung zugleich ist, eine Vielfalt an Medien ein und erforscht die Leerstellen zwischen architektonischer Fiktion und gesellschaftlicher Konvention, um sowohl gegenwärtige wie auch imaginierte Raumumgebungen zu schaffen. 2008 begann Weiner das Musikprojekt *Sadie Siegel*, bei dem er unter Verwendung des Namens seiner Urgroßmutter mit sich selbst zusammenarbeitet und Sound als architektonische Handlung erforscht. Die beiden leben und arbeiten in einem Keller im 2. Wiener Gemeindebezirk.

Karen Werner

Karen Werner is an artist and sociologist who makes experimental radio stories and live performances for broadcast and narrowcast. She creates conceptual radio stations of various scales and forms including SkottegatenFM, Radio Multe 93.8FM and an unnamed shadow / jamming station. Karen lives in Bergen, Norway, where she is an artistic research fellow at the Faculty of Art, Music and Design, University of Bergen.

Karen Werner ist Künstlerin und Soziologin und gestaltet experimentelle Radiogeschichten und Live-Performances für Rundfunk und Kabelradio. Sie kreiert konzeptuelle Radiosender unterschiedlicher Reichweiten und Formate, darunter SkottegatenFM, Radio Multe 93.8 FM und einen namenlosen Schatten-/Jamming-Sender. Karen lebt in Bergen, Norwegen, und ist künstlerische Forschungsmitarbeiterin an der Fakultät für Kunst, Musik und Design der Universität Bergen.

Hui Ye

Hui Ye (born in Guangzhou, CN) is an artist and composer based in Vienna. She works with different media, including experimental documentary, video, and audio installation, and often addresses the socio-political aspect of the act of listening to examine the fluidity of the individual's social identity and its reflection in technology and sonic culture. In her most recent projects the subject matter of (digitized) voice is essential to her research. Ye's works were exhibited internationally at the Kunsthalle Wien (AT), the Jim Thompson Art Center (TH), the Times Museum (CN), and elsewhere.

Hui Ye (geboren in Guangzhou, China) lebt als Künstlerin und Komponistin in Wien. Sie arbeitet mit unterschiedlichen Medien, so auch mit experimenteller Dokumentation, Video und Audio-Installation, und greift oft den soziopolitischen Aspekt des Zuhörens auf, um die Fluidität der individuellen sozialen Identität und ihre Spiegelung in Technologie und akustischer Kultur zu ergründen. Bei ihren jüngsten Projekten spielt im Rahmen ihrer Forschung die (digitalisierte) Stimme eine wesentliche Rolle. Yes Arbeiten wurden in der Kunsthalle Wien, im Jim Thompson Art Center (TH), dem Times Museum (China) und anderswo auf der Welt gezeigt.

Acknowledgments
Dank

Special thanks to Bruce Stinson and Can Denzer for their multilayered support and our lively discussions over the years. Many thanks to all the authors and all people who have contributed to the realization of this book or who have accompanied the works, projects and cooperations discussed in this book: Helga Aichmaier and the Zentrum Fokus Forschung, Bruce and Novvy Allen, Fouad Asfour, Fatih Aydoğdu, Katharina Blaas, Jacquelin Czuss, Anna Daučíková and Tomáš Džadoň, Christiane Erharter, Richard Ferkl, Katharina Holas, Georgia Holz, Brandon LaBelle, Nazanin Mehraein, Elaine Morman, Lissy Rettenwander, Ammar Khadour, Karen Werner, Jaimini Patel, Franz Thalmair, the colleagues of the TransArts department, the colleagues of the Art and Communication Practices department and the APL, Karolina Radenkovic, Dorota Rapacz, Cornelia Reinisch-Hoffmann, Hannah Sakai, Thomas Sandri, Anja Seipenbusch-Hufschmied, Jo Schmeiser, Stefanie Seibold, Başak Şenova, Claudia Slanar, all participating students, Nik Thoenen, Barbara Wimmer, Hui Ye.

Special thanks to Gerald Bast, President of the University of Applied Arts Vienna, and Barbara Putz-Plecko, Vice-President for Research in Arts and Science, University of Applied Arts Vienna.

Our thanks also go to those who might not have been mentioned in this list.

Photo Credits
Fotonachweis

Performative Fotoarbeit *Listening to Objects* und Poster, Ricarda Denzer, 2023
Fotos: Michael Giefing
Performative photograpgic work *Listening to Objects* and poster, Ricarda Denzer 2023
Photographs: Michael Giefing

86, 87:
Wolfgang Wössner

101, 105, 133, 141, 173:
Bruce Stinson

127:
Daniel Jarosch

137:
Johannes Puch

147:
Kollektiv Fischka /
Kramar © Volkskundemuseum Wien

154:
Claire Trevor School of the Arts

155:
VBKÖ

183:
Suchart Wannaset

Alle sonstigen Fotos oder Videostills:
Ricarda Denzer

1 Colophon
Impressum

Editors:
Ricarda Denzer, Christian Höller, A-Vienna

Project Management "Edition Angewandte" on behalf of the University of Applied Arts Vienna:
Anja Seipenbusch-Hufschmied / Barbara Wimmer, A-Vienna

Content and Production Editor on behalf of the Publisher:
Katharina Holas, A-Vienna

Translations:
Fouad Asfour, Jacquelin Czuss, A-Vienna

Proofreading:
Helen Ferguson, Verena Moritz, A-Vienna

Copyediting:
Ricarda Denzer, Christian Höller, A-Vienna

Layout, cover design, and typography:
Hannah Sakai, A-Vienna

Image editing (black-and-white images):
Pascal Petignat, A-Vienna

Printing:
Holzhausen, the book-printing brand of Gerin Druck GmbH, A-Wolkersdorf

Paper:
Blue back paper 115 gsm, Remake Sand 250 gsm

Typeface:
Formale Grotesque (binnenland.ch)

Library of Congress Control Number:
2023943512

Bibliographic information published by the German National Library
The German National Library lists this publication in the Deutsche Nationalbibliografie; detailed bibliographic data are available on the Internet at http://dnb.dnb.de.

ISSN 1866-248X
ISBN 978-3-11-134216-0
e-ISBN (PDF) 978-3-11-134223-8

www.degruyter.com

Printed with financial support of

Bundesministerium
Kunst, Kultur,
öffentlicher Dienst und Sport